Sarah Corse's analysis of nearly two hundred American and Canadian novels offers a new theory of national literatures. Demonstrating that national canon formation occurs in tandem with nation-building, and that canonical novels play a symbolic role in this, Sarah Corse accounts for cross-national literary differences, addresses issues of mediation and representation in theories of "reflection," and illuminates the historically constructed nature of the relationship between literature and the nation-state. In this way, she also shows that there is no "natural" pattern of national literary difference across literary types, and, specifically, that high-culture national literatures are selected to appear different from other novels. By contrast, popular-culture bestsellers are best understood as mass market commodities for the largest and least differentiated audience.

D1430263

Nationalism and literature

Cambridge Cultural Social Studies

Cambridge Cultural Social Studies is a forum for the most original and thoughtful work in cultural social studies. This includes theoretical works focusing on conceptual strategies, empirical studies covering specific topics such as gender, sexuality, politics, economics, social movements, and crime, and studies that address broad themes such as the culture of modernity. While the perspectives of the individual studies will vary, they will all share the same innovative reach and scholarly quality.

Nationalism and literature

The politics of culture in Canada and the United States

Sarah M. Corse
University of Virginia

CAMBRIDGE
UNIVERSITY PRESS

PUBLISHED BY THE PRESS SYNDICATE OF THE UNIVERSITY OF CAMBRIDGE
The Pitt Building, Trumpington Street, Cambridge, United Kingdom

CAMBRIDGE UNIVERSITY PRESS
The Edinburgh Building, Cambridge CB2 2RU, UK
40 West 20th Street, New York, NY 10011–4211, USA
477 Williamstown Road, Port Melbourne, VIC 3207, Australia
Ruiz de Alarcón 13, 28014 Madrid, Spain
Dock House, The Waterfront, Cape Town 8001, South Africa

http://www.cambridge.org

First published 1997
Reprinted 2001

Printed in the United Kingdom at the University Press, Cambridge

A catalogue record for this book is available from the British Library

A catalogue record for this book is available from the Library of Congress

ISBN 0 521 57002 6 hardback
ISBN 0 521 57912 0 paperback

SE

This book is dedicated to
the loving memory of my godfather
Jan K. Sterling
and to my parents
Nathalie Bird Corse and John Murray Corse II

Contents

Tables

x

Acknowledgments

This book would not have been written without the support of many people. During my Yale days, Paul DiMaggio, Woody Powell, Carl Milofsky, and Eleanor Westney opened my eyes to the world of sociology. Ann Swidler, Marty Lipset, Dick Scott, and Wendy Griswold provided the intellectual and financial support at Stanford that cemented my commitment to sociology.

My Virginia colleagues have been more than generous with their time, advice, and encouragement. James Davison Hunter, Gianfranco Poggi, Murray Milner, Steve Nock, Daphne Spain, Paul Kingston, Mark Lupher, and Richard Handler read some or all of the manuscript. The book is richer for their comments and poorer, no doubt, for the times I ignored their advice. Special thanks are due to Sharon Hays, a true colleague and friend.

Many Canadian colleagues have been kind enough to share their knowledge with me. I wish to thank Robert Lecker, Rod Nelson, Michael Peterman, Gerald Kenyon, Alec Lucas, W. J. Keith, and George Hildebrand for their time and interest in my work.

I was fortunate in spending my year as a Sesquicentennial Fellow visiting at the University of Pennsylvania. Special thanks to Phil Morgan, Sam Preston, the Sociology Department, and Mike Useem, and to Steve Kobrin and the Management Department at Wharton for their arrangements on my behalf. Mabel Berezin, Harold Bershady, Eli Anderson, Jerry Jacobs, and Sam Kaplan were intellectually stimulating colleagues who shared generously of their time during 1993–4.

A variety of colleagues have been important during the writing of this book. Ann Swidler, Wendy Griswold, Paul DiMaggio, Michèle Lamont, Steve Seidman, Janet Wolff, Pete Peterson, Yasemin Soysal, JoEllen Shively, Frank Dobbin, Victoria Alexander, and Connie McNeely have all spent time reading or discussing my analysis of national literatures. Their combined intellect and good will are deeply appreciated.

I received much appreciated financial support from the Association of American University Women, who made possible my final dissertation year; the Canadian Embassy who generously provided research travel money and library help; and the Center for Advanced Studies at Virginia whose Sesquicentennial Fellowship provided for the final year of work on the book.

I am grateful to friends and family for their support and encouragement. The Corses, Donaldsons, Harders, and Parkers have provided both patience and comfort. I especially wish to thank Emily, David, Grace, and Zoë. Many thanks to Blaire French who has frequently shared both her time and formidable writing skills. Finally, and above all, I wish to thank Joseph W. Harder for his interest, intelligence, and love.

1

Introduction: cultural fields and literary use

National literatures are an assumption of modern cultural landscapes. In countries around the world schoolchildren in state-mandated courses read the "Great Works" of their nation. Universities offer literature courses in a smorgasbord of national units: course catalogues list classes such as "Russian Masterpieces," "The Brazilian Novel," and "Major American Authors." The style, themes, and narratives of each nation's literary canon, the pantheon of most valorized and legitimated texts, are analyzed and debated both in the scholarly literature and in more general social commentaries. Educated people are simply assumed to be conversant with their national canons. In the United States "everyone" is familiar with – even if one hasn't actually read – *The Scarlet Letter* and *Moby Dick*. National literatures are the cornerstones of national cultures.

National literature and national character

National literatures have traditionally been understood as reflections of the unique character and experiences of the nation. That is, it is felt that the unique experience of national life generates a national, collective consciousness, or in some formulations a "collective unconscious" marked by a distinctive set of values, tensions, myths, and psychological foci, that produces in turn a certain readily identifiable national character – the American cowboy or the French sophisticate, for example. This character, and the values, tensions, and myths from which it springs, is then discernible in indigenous cultural products. Thus the distinctiveness of a national literature is seen as the *natural embodiment* of the distinctive national character (e.g., Wolfenstein and Leites 1950; Goldmann 1964, 1970).

This reflection perspective is so deeply entrenched in our view of national literatures that it is rarely explicitly taught. Rather, as schoolchildren read their national canon reflection is simply assumed as the appropriate way to understand how the literature they read is "American" or "Canadian" or otherwise nationally distinct. Thus, the American canon, as we learn in high school, is deeply rooted in and reflective of the hallmark of the American national character – individualism. The great American mythic figures are singular individuals; the core attribute of the national character is a self-reliant individualism. Discussions of historical American culture describe a tradition of "self-reliance as the cardinal virtue of individuals" in which even the family – the very center of affiliation, connection, and cooperation – is seen as nurturing a belief in the self-reliant individual (Bellah, Madsen, Sullivan, Swidler, and Tipton 1985: 62). This self-reliant individualism is reflected in a literature that critics and literary historians have described as characterized by men fleeing the social world of women and domesticity (often with a dark-skinned companion) to test their strength in the wilderness in a pure meritocracy (Marx 1964; Fiedler 1966; Griswold 1981; Baym 1985). What makes American literature American in this view is its emphasis on autonomous individuals defined *a priori* to society: the recurring story of a lone individual defining himself in the wilderness.

In Canada, on the other hand, the story of the national character and attendant national literature is very different. Instead of the optimistic self-reliance of the American character, Canadian schoolchildren learn that the Canadian character is enmeshed within its social and familial worlds, haunted by an isolating and malevolent Nature, and therefore cooperative with and defined by society. This social reliance and fear of the hostile wilderness are reflected in a literature that critics and literary historians have described as characterized by a struggle for survival within an entrapping family and an environment of violent and intractable wilderness (Frye 1971; Atwood 1972; McGregor 1985). What makes Canadian literature Canadian, then, is almost the opposite of American literature – a literary preoccupation with the embedding of individuals in relationships, the concomitant constraint this exercises on individuals, and, above all, the *social* identity of individuals.

The widespread assumptions of reflection theory encourage all readers of canonical novels, not just schoolchildren, to read these novels in particular ways – to read them through a nationalist lens. This nationalist lens in turn constructs a dominant interpretation of the novels. One of the most representative texts in American literature and therefore most valorized, according to the national character argument, is Mark Twain's *Adventures of Huckleberry Finn*. American readers are positioned to read the text as a story of Huck's flight from his inadequate and ultimately unimportant family and the prissy repressiveness of Aunt Polly's world to light out for the frontier and the limitless opportunity of re-creating one's life – and to value the novel and its "American-ness" for that reason. One representative Canadian story, on the other hand, is Major John Richardson's *Wacousta*, the story of a beleaguered garrison, a mutually dependent and frightened social group isolated in a vast and uncaring wilderness brimming with menace. Canadian readers are positioned to see the "Canadian-ness" of *Wacousta* as its characterization of the isolating wilderness and of the possibilities for the people in the garrison – none of whom consider abandoning the group for the deadly forest and a chance at self-reliance.

While these renditions of what makes *Huck Finn* "American" and of what makes *Wacousta* "Canadian" give us a clear sense of the reflection perspective and make the connection between nation and literature seem obvious, there are actually a number of problems with this traditional argument. Most importantly, the connection between literature and the nation is far more complex than simple reflection and, far from being "natural" or obvious, the pairing of literature and the nation is in fact a social construction that performs powerful and important cultural work. I will return to a more detailed critique of the traditional reflection argument after presenting an alternative model for understanding national literatures and the cultural work that they perform.

A sociological study of national literatures

Despite the prevalence and importance of national literatures, sociologists have largely ignored the development and importance of national literatures and the weakness of our theoretical explanations for them.[1] The study of national literatures has been left to non-sociologists whose traditional research approaches regard the meaning of cultural products as embedded within the product – and who understand the purpose of the research activity as being to uncover this existing and transcendent meaning. Meaning, in these formulations, exists apart from and independently of the conditions under which artistic production, consumption, and evaluation occur. In addition, such work generally ignores issues of representativeness and generalizability in favor of "close textual analysis" of one or several texts. Issues of sampling, if considered at all, are confined to authorial statements that the text or texts under consideration are particularly representative or of singular significance for one reason or another.

This study, however, is positioned within a more recent literature that

---

[1] For a notable exception see Griswold (1981, 1987b, 1992).

attempts to explicate the meaning of textual characteristics within an understanding of the social and economic arrangements surrounding the text, thus marrying a concern for the symbolic meaning of cultural works with an appreciation for the powerful effects of social contexts (cf. Wolff 1992).[2] By redressing the lack of sociological attention to national literatures through the application of recent theoretical and methodological advances in cultural sociology, I hope to develop a deeper understanding of the formation and significance of national literatures.

In the book I explore existing theoretical assumptions about the origin and function of national literatures and propose an alternative, more sociologically informed understanding of national literatures that incorporates arguments about variations in cultural use, the relationship between production context and cultural content, and the identity formation processes of the nation-state. While reflection theory implies that national literatures are grounded in individual-level psychological differences stemming from a dominant national character or a naturally occurring national culture or some form of "collective unconscious," I demonstrate that these arguments are an insufficient explanation for cross-national literary distinctiveness. I focus instead on the social, cultural, and political process of literary *use* and national identity *construction*. I argue that both national literatures and nations themselves are socially constructed under identifiable political and historical circumstances – and that the two processes are deeply interwoven.

Historically, it was the "nationalism" of texts, in the sense of their affinity with the constructed national character, that became the premier criterion for their evaluation. Selection into the national canon, in other words, was predicated on the responsiveness of texts to the national character interpretive framework and their amenability to being read through the lens of national character. National canonical status is thus rooted in national exceptionalism. Literary explorations of the "unique" nation and its "exceptional" experience in turn help construct available images of the nation.

The heart of the book is an analysis of literary production, evaluation, and use in the bipartite fields of high culture and popular culture. That is, I understand how literature is used and what factors determine literary pro-

---

[2] See, for example, Watt (1957); von Hallberg (1984); Radway (1984); Liebes and Katz (1990); Press (1991); Shively (1992); and Binder (1993). See also recent work in the sociology of literature (e.g., P. Clark 1982; Griswold 1986, 1992; Corse 1995), in the "new literary history" (e.g., Tompkins 1985), and in the "social history of art" and the "new art history" (e.g., Orton and Pollock 1980; T. Clark 1982; Parker and Pollock 1981; Wolff 1981; Baxandall 1985, 1988).

duction and consumption by analyzing the broader conditions of its location in either the field of high culture or that of popular culture. The location of novels in the two fields is important because, as Bourdieu (1984, 1985, 1993) demonstrates, it is the relative positions of the persons and institutions which produce, consume, and evaluate cultural objects that determine their status – and therefore the very conditions of their production, evaluation, and consumption.[3]

High-culture literature is thus used differently and produced under different conditions than popular-culture literature because of its location in a field monopolized by elite agents, consumers, and institutions with a particular set of interests pertaining to their socio-structural positions. The essential opposition of the twin fields of high culture and popular culture and the organizing dynamics of each field structure the ways in which each type of literature is understood and used. Thus, for example, the symbolic role and power of high-culture literature is derived in large part from its juxtapositional, and hierarchical, status vis-à-vis popular literature.

Grounding this analysis of literary field and national literatures is my empirical comparison of forty-nine American and Canadian high-culture novels and over one hundred American and Canadian popular-culture novels. I chose Canada and the United States as the countries for my study because of the high degree of similarity between the two countries. Both are highly industrialized, North American nations with British colonial pasts. Both have largely English-speaking populations with similarly high degrees of literacy and higher education. Because of the degree of similarity between Canada and the United States, a comparison of their literatures provides a strong test for the existence of unique national literatures. In addition, one central difference between Canada and the United States makes these countries especially appropriate for this study. Despite their similarities, the process of nation-building in the two countries occurred at significantly different times, thus further providing a strong test of my argument.

---

[3] A competing line of sociological research argues that the high culture/popular culture split, despite its origination in and persistence since the seventeenth century (Bourdieu 1984: 2), is losing its theoretical power (Gans 1974; Blau, Blau, Quets, and Tada 1986; Blau 1988; Crane 1992). Research taking a "cultural convergence" perspective may argue either that the high/popular distinction is blurring (Levine 1988) or that cultural systems are simply becoming more highly differentiated (Gans 1985; DiMaggio 1987; see Shrum 1991 for a cogent review of these perspectives). Nonetheless, I find Bourdieu's explication of the distinction between the fields of restricted and large-scale production fruitful as an *analytic* distinction. See also Anheier, Gerhards, and Romo for a blockmodel analysis of writers in Cologne, Germany which they interpret as showing that "the primary axis . . . does not differentiate between high and light culture, as one would expect from Bourdieu's theory, but between core and periphery. Only the second, and less important, axis differentiates high from low culture" (1995: 891–2).

The empirical comparison of the American and Canadian high- and popular-culture novels demonstrates the symbolic role played by high-culture national literatures and the attendant requirements of cross-national distinctiveness in contradistinction to the economic role of popular-culture literature and attendant requirements for cross-national similarity. In other words, high-culture literature is driven by forces for international differentiation because of its role as a constructor of the unique nation while popular-culture literature is driven by forces for international homogenization because of its role as an economic commodity.

High-culture literature, restricted production, and the national project

The first part of the analysis focuses on high-culture literature, located in what Bourdieu (1985) refers to as the "field of restricted production."[4] For my analysis, the two most important attributes of the field of restricted production are (1) the central role played by agents and institutions of consecration competing for cultural authority and (2) the central importance of the symbolic value of the cultural products within this field and the concomitant reduced importance of their economic value and thus their status as art-as-art.[5] High-culture literary texts are circulated and consumed within a nexus of institutions and agents invested both in (1) the production of cultural objects with certain attributes and consumers with the requisite skills for appropriating those objects, and (2) the establishment of their own claims to cultural authority vis-à-vis those cultural objects and their consumers. It is the second aspect, the use of high-culture texts as sym-

---

[4] In addition to the two points I emphasize, Bourdieu further defines restricted production by the importance of cultural capital accumulation for producers and consumers, by its highly educated audience, and through the relative autonomy of the field to set its own criteria of production and evaluation. Central to Bourdieu's argument is the recognition of the *positional*, not inherent, nature of these attributes. Cultural objects derive their properties from the relative positions held by agents in the field and from the hierarchical juxtaposition and coexistence of the two fields of restricted and large-scale production, not from inherent attributes (1985: 17–22 especially; 1993).

[5] Although my analysis focuses on the symbolic value of high-culture texts as the central explanatory variable for them and on the economic value of popular-culture texts as their single most important aspect, I disagree with Bourdieu's absolutism on this point (e.g., 1985). This may be partially a difference between American and French culture (Lamont 1992), but I find it excessive to say economic considerations have no relevance for high culture. Similarly, even the basest of popular culture may have an important symbolic value – witness the French dismay at the proliferation of McDonald's or American television soaps. As I mentioned in footnote 3, other theorists have questioned the accuracy of such a sharp divide between high culture and popular culture (e.g., Crane 1992), but I believe the *analytic* distinction is justified given the difference in how high-culture and popular-culture genres are evaluated and used. I return to this point in chapter 7.

bolic resources rather than economic commodities, that turns our attention toward the nation-building process.

Traditional theories imply that national literatures exist because nations are naturally different and this difference is naturally reflected in literature. I hope to show in the following chapters however that national literatures exist not because they arise "naturally," but because they are an integral part of the process by which nation-states create themselves and distinguish themselves from other nations. Huxley, among others, remarked on this situation when he wrote: "nations are to a very large extent invented by their poets and novelists" (1959: 50).

This connection between nation and literature, however natural and inevitable it now seems, is nonetheless a relatively recent historical construction. The idea of national literatures originated with late eighteenth-century and early nineteenth-century theorists of nationalism, particularly the German Romantic nationalists who first promulgated the now accepted idea that literature is defined by its national affiliation and should embody the unique characteristics of a nation (MacLulich 1987). The underlying premise of the literary nationalists was that humanity is naturally divided into homogeneous, but distinctive groups marked by a unique set of values and concerns and by a distinctive "national character."[6] This set of nationalist ideas created a vision both of the nation itself and of national literatures as naturally occurring, as arising without action on the part of specifiable individuals. Reflection theories subsume these assumptions, ignoring the fact that national literatures are created by conscious human action, as indeed are nations themselves. Recent theorists of the nation, on the other hand, have amply demonstrated the constructed nature of nations; they are "imagined communities" built as much in the minds of their citizens as in military or cartographic exercises (Anderson 1991; Gellner 1983; Hobsbawm 1992). National literatures, like nations, are created by the cultural work of specific people engaged in an identifiable set of activities.

Just as it is important to recognize that the connection between nations and literature is a relatively recent one, we need to recognize that prior to

---

[6] This also raises an obvious question about the disparity between the early ideology of nationalism and the current reality of many nation-states. While the rationale for national literatures as reflections of the national character is that the national experience is a homogeneous one and the people are "unified by a common language and culture" (MacLulich 1987: 26), nations such as the United States and especially Canada do not fall neatly into this category of "single language and single culture." If the United States and Canada are both heterogeneous nation-states with large immigrant populations and a multiplicity of racial, regional, ethnic, and religious constituencies with salient subgroup identities, then how does a *unitary* national literature "naturally" arise and persist?

the theoretical developments of the nationalists in the late eighteenth century, literature was not evaluated in national categories, but was valued in large part for its ability to transcend such categories – to speak across time and place. At least until the end of the eighteenth century, the basis for a European humanistic education was the "classics" (MacLulich 1987). These classics were seen as texts that transcended such parochial notions as nationality to speak to all people, or more accurately, all Western people. What made these texts superior was their very *failure* to act as embodiments of a distinct culture and people. They were instead the embodiment of the "best of human thought." Indeed, this assumption that the best literature speaks to all people across all periods and embodies universal human truths continues to endure in tandem with more nationalist understandings of literature (e.g., Brooks 1975; Leavis 1948, 1969).

At the core of my argument then is a conception of national literatures as instrumental in the creation of nations with distinct identities. Far from being simple reflections of extant entities, nations themselves are both products of human invention and tools in support of further invention.[7] Despite Romantic nationalist imagery of the homogeneous culture which underlies the polity and unifies the population, most nation-states need be created from disparate groups, from populations with competing allegiances. The difficulties inherent in the forging of some approximation of the "natural" unit bound by "a common culture" and "distinctive traits" (the nationalist model) are attacked in part with a cultural artillery. High-culture literatures allow nations to posit "a transcendent realm of essential identity"; a vision of unity rooted in a common national identity, overarching all subsidiary differences (Lloyd 1987: x). High-culture literature is powerfully implicated in this process of "imagining" the nation (Anderson 1991).

In addition to helping produce a vision of the nation and an identity for internal consumption, national literatures also assist in the international arena. Since one of the "standard marks of nationhood" is "the possession of a national literature" (MacLulich 1987: 24), canonical national literatures also allow nation-states to compete for full status in the international community. In order to lay claim to full nationhood, nascent nation-states need not only military and political independence, but cultural independence as well (Schudson 1994). In the modern world, a unique national

---

[7] As McCrone (1992: 29) has argued about nationalism more generally, national literatures are "not the expression of objective differences, but the mobilisation of those [differences] which the actors believe to be salient." McCrone is discussing Barth's *Ethnic Groups and Boundaries*, specifically his contention that "cultural differences should be seen, not as primary and definitional characteristics, but as the outcome or implication of social struggles" (1992: 29–30).

culture is as much a part of full status as a nation-state as is the formalization of geographic boundaries and the establishment of independent political control (Dominguez 1992). Thus national literatures serve a dual audience in the cultural work they perform.

Because of these pressures for a distinct national literature, the primary selection criteria for national literatures becomes differentiation from other national literatures. In order to proclaim cultural independence, a nation-state must produce and identify a literature that differentiates it from other states, particularly the most relevant others – e.g., "Mother England" for the United States and both England and the United States for Canada. Thus any understanding of the source of distinct national literatures must acknowledge the overwhelming importance of the political need for national differentiation. National literatures are both the product *and* partial creator of the nation and our collective sense of national identity. National literatures are not passive reflections of naturally occurring phenomena, but integral components in the process of national development, consciously constructed pieces of the national culture, and creators of the world in which we live. The canon is chosen, not born.

Popular-culture literature, large-scale production, and economic hegemony

In direct contrast to high-culture literature is the second part of the literary field, that of popular-culture literature. Bourdieu locates popular-culture literature in the field of "large-scale cultural production" which is defined in explicit and hierarchical contrast to the field of restricted production (1985). The important attributes of the field of large-scale cultural production for my analysis are (1) the dominance of economic considerations, i.e., "investment profitability," over symbolic considerations and popular literature's resultant status as a commodity, and (2) the orientation of the culture industries toward the universal or widest possible audience as a necessary condition of profitability.[8]

Popular-culture literature is used primarily as a market commodity purchased and consumed by individuals (Cawelti 1976). Popular-culture literature is often written under conditions of mass-production (e.g., Radway 1984: 19–45). Rather than serving a symbolic, constitutive role in nation-building, popular-culture literature tends to be used and understood by

---

[8] Bourdieu also focuses on the external source of production and evaluation criteria in the field of large-scale production (1985: 28–33 especially; 1993). See also footnote 3.

both its producers and its consumers as a readily accessible commodity driven by market forces.[9]

Because the organizing principle of the field of large-scale cultural production is investment profitability, it is necessary to obtain the largest, and therefore the *least* differentiated, market possible. Popular-culture literary production is driven by homogenizing forces that embrace universal themes and interests in the hope of attracting the largest possible number of consumers. Thus the central evaluative criteria for popular-culture literature becomes its popularity, which serves as a crude measure of profitability, hence the importance of "bestseller" lists. Relative sales figures are even presented to readers as a central evaluative criterion through the use of cover blurbs such as "Ten weeks on the *New York Times* bestseller list."

As its economic value predominates, the determining forces for popular-culture literature are market forces. In the United States and Canada this has meant the domination of the relatively weak Canadian publishing industry by much stronger American publishers. Factors such as Canada's small population and concomitant small market, the historically distribution-oriented nature of Canadian publishing, the increasingly complex technology of publishing and hence ever greater economies of scale have all contributed to a situation in which American-authored and published popular-culture novels dominate the Canadian bestseller lists.[10] Despite government intervention in the form of protective legislation, subsidy, and tax incentive, Canadian publishers lag behind American publishers in control of their own national market.

Differences in literary content

In addition to my central focus on the uses and production contexts of high- and popular-culture literature, I am also interested in the question of what the substantive differences in the content of national literatures mean. As I noted, reflection theory suggests that what national literatures reveal is the difference between the American and the Canadian national character. Although Americans and Canadians may well have some degree of measurable difference on personality scales, I argue that what cross-national literary differences actually show is the legitimated vision of "Canada" and of being "Canadian" and a similarly legitimated vision of

---

[9] Stephen King demonstrates the dominance of this understanding of popular literature in his 1987 horror novel *Misery*, in which the narrator mounts a strong defense of popular-culture literature and a concomitant attack on the pretensions of high-culture literature.

[10] British publishers and British-authored books also have a significant presence in Canada.

"America" and of being "American."[11] This legitimated vision, although part of a political process, is also a meaning-making process. Canon formation and maintenance serve as a filter through which elite preoccupations and tastes manifest themselves in high-culture literatures. It is precisely because canon formation is influenced by concrete political processes, rather than abstract aesthetic principles, that high-culture literature tells us something important. High-culture literature codifies the legitimated vision American elites have about being American and the legitimated vision Canadian elites have about being Canadian (DiMaggio 1982; Greenfeld 1992). This codified vision of the nation and the national experience then helps to determine the content of American and Canadian national identities.

There are three central assumptions underlying my analysis of the source and uses of national literatures. I am arguing, first, that canon formation and maintenance are *political processes*: not natural or automatic occurrences, but socially constructed undertakings the historical basis of which is nationalism and which are undertaken by concrete persons with particular interests in specifiable contexts. Second, I am arguing that canon formation and maintenance are *meaning-making processes* shaped by the tastes and social locations of those who create and maintain canons. Therefore some texts and some social conditions will be ignored, while others are emphasized, and still others are mis-specified or only partially acknowledged. Given the contingent and political nature of the meaning-making process, it is not surprising that canonical texts will be read and interpreted differently over time and across audiences. Finally, I am arguing that canon formation and maintenance processes have a *reciprocal relationship* with the "social" world – they affect the construction of the nation and influence the imagination of the national population in addition to being shaped by the nation and its experience.

An empirical comparison of national literatures

The basis for my rejection of traditional reflection theory is a systematic comparison of three types of Canadian and American high-culture and popular-culture literatures: a selection of twenty central canonical novels taught in college courses, a group of twenty-nine contemporary literary prize-winning novels, and a collection of 135 recent, annual top ten, best-

---

[11] In fact, Seymour Martin Lipset (and others) have clearly shown American–Canadian differences in public opinion and self-reported values on religion, law and order, economic risk, state welfare policies, philanthropy, elitism/equalitarianism, etc. (Lipset 1990; see also Nevitte and Gibbins 1990).

selling novels.[12] I analyzed each of these novels, coding its thematic content, its narrative elements, and its literary style. Comparing across literary type and across nations allows me to show the inadequacies of reflection theory, the socially constructed and highly politicized relationship between high-culture literature and the nation, and the different uses and production fields of high-culture and popular-culture literature. This cross-national, cross-literary comparison provides empirical substantiation for my argument that national literatures exist not because they unconsciously reflect "real" national differences, but because they are integral to the process of constructing national differences.

Specifically, if literature was indeed read and valued because it reflects national character and articulates the collective ethos, there should be a close match between the themes and concerns, if not the literary style, of socially valued literature and widely read literature. But this is not the case. My data show that while elite-valued, high-culture literatures demonstrate a strong pattern of cross-national difference, widely read, popular-culture literatures do not. Furthermore, the cross-national differences that do exist in popular-culture literatures are frequently not the same as the cross-national differences in the high-culture literatures. That is, there is no pattern of cross-national distinctiveness that holds across different types of literature; thus there is no literary support for the idea of an underlying coherent national character in either the United States or Canada.

As an example, 100 percent of the Canadian canonical novels I analyze feature a protagonist whose family is important, either because the family is a formative influence on the protagonist, or because members of the family are important actors in the story that is told.[13] In contrast, only 40 percent of the American canonical novels I analyze have protagonists with important families. From a reflection perspective, this is a clear story not just of Canadian–American distinctiveness, but of a Canadian national character that is enmeshed within and strongly affected by family and of an American national character that is independent of and unconcerned with family. Indeed, several scholars have made very strong arguments along these lines (e.g., Atwood 1972; Baym 1985).

But expanding our account to consider popular-culture novels as well as high-culture novels disrupts this tidy story. When I compare American and Canadian bestsellers, I discover that an equal one-half of both American and Canadian novels have protagonists whose families are important. Not

---

[12] Appendices A through C list the titles of the three types of novels. Appendix D contains a copy of the coding sheet.

[13] "Family" here refers to either parental families (the parents and siblings of a protagonist) or conjugal families (the spouse and children of a protagonist).

only is there no cross-national distinctiveness in this comparison, but there is also no support for the Canadian-determined-by-family and the American-free-of-family thesis: Canadian or American, half are and half aren't. In the remainder of chapter 1, I explicate my critique of reflection theory, outline the political process of national canon formation, and describe the structure of the book.

The limits of reflection "theory"

The explanatory power of the reflection metaphor has been implicitly, if not always explicitly, questioned by recent theoretical developments in cultural sociology and related fields. Nonetheless, reflection-type arguments describing the relationship between cultural materials and society pre-dominate in journalism and in much of the recent work in cultural studies. At its most basic, reflection theory simply states that cultural products mirror or reflect the society that produces them (Albrecht 1954; Peterson 1979). This simple idea, that social context affects cultural works, is a battle waged and won, if indeed it ever was a battle (Holub 1984: 132; Griswold 1981). The problem is not the basic idea that the social world influences cul-tural objects, but that reflection "theory" is unable to function as a theory, since, as Noble points out, "it is never adequately explained how the 'optics' of reflection work . . . the relationship proposed between the real and fictive worlds remains obscure" (1976: 213–14).[14] Since reflection is used simply as a vague metaphor, the mechanics of the process remain unclear (Becker in Candido 1995; Griswold 1994: 21–43).

Frye provides a classic summary of the reflection perspective's inability to specify clearly how national character is translated into national litera-ture when he claims that during the process of writing "the writer . . . often has the feeling, and says so, that he is not actively shaping his material at all, but is rather a *place* where a verbal structure is taking its own shape" (1971: 233, italics added). National character as an alien force inhabiting the authorial body seems somewhat less than adequate as sociological explanation. In addition, the national literature as national character per-spective makes it difficult for us to understand cross-national literary commonality or intra-national literary difference. Nationalist theories of literature seem simultaneously to deny the universality and commonality of human experience and to deny the distinctiveness of ethnic, racial, and other socially constitutive groups that are smaller or larger than the nation.

---

[14] See also Wolff: "'reflection' is no longer a notion which theories of representation will allow. Cultural forms . . . do not just directly represent the social in some unmediated way. Rather, they *re*-present it in the codes and processes of signification" (1992: 707).

Furthermore, reflection theorists tend to assume both that the social and the cultural are clearly separable and that the former determines the latter (Clark 1983; Wright 1975).[15] More sophisticated formulations reject such notions in favor of a model of the relationship between culture and society that assumes an integrated social world within which social structures and behavior both shape cultural products and are shaped by them (Giddens 1984; Griswold 1986; Swidler 1986). Cultural products are not only affected by the social context, but are instrumental in the creation and modification of that context (Wolff 1992). As Smith stresses, this effect is especially powerful in the case of canonical works: the canonical work has special power "to shape and create the culture in which its value is produced and transmitted, and, for that very reason, to perpetuate the conditions of its own flourishing" (1983: 28–9). The ability of such texts to "speak" to us, she argues, stems from their having been "so thoroughly mediated . . . for us by the very culture and cultural institutions . . . by which we ourselves have been formed" (Smith 1983: 29). Reflection arguments that ignore the constitutive functions of cultural products cannot hope to explain adequately either cultural products or their social relations.[16]

Additionally, reflection arguments ignore the issue of the variability of meaning. That is, reflection theorists assume that they have access to the "true" and singular meaning of the texts. Textual meaning is simultaneously understood as inherent and preexisting in the text, and as fully accessible only to the trained critic. Reflection arguments, in other words, assume that the central power of a text or set of texts stems from psychological needs or social psychodynamics of which ordinary readers are not even necessarily conscious. Such a view does not allow for active readers who participate in the creation of meaning through their interaction with and interpretation of the text (Fish 1980; Jauss 1982; Griswold 1987b). Frye (1971), for example, assumes that Canadian readers understand and respond to Canadian canonical works because it is those works that capture the hostility of the vast North and of a malevolent Nature, conditions which

---

[15] The terms theorists use may vary. Reflection theorists often use "culture" in the anthropological sense of a total way of life, rather than the "social" as the determining and an idea of material culture or cultural artefacts as the determined. Similarly, Marxists employ the notion of the determining economic "base" and the determined cultural "superstructure" (Williams 1978). Nonetheless, the idea of two separate spheres, one of which determines the other, predominates.

[16] This criticism of reflection theory's implication of dual spheres does not mean that one cannot talk about cultural products and their immediate environment as distinct from the more distant social world. Although culture and society are intertwined and "engaged in ongoing mutual construction," they can be considered separately for analytic purposes (Griswold 1986: 6). Indeed, the very strength and complexity of the relation between the two virtually requires an heuristic distinction for analytic clarity.

have engendered a sense of terror in the Canadian national character. He does not consider that the meaning of these texts may be constructed differently across readers by, for example, social location, ethnic identity, or historical era. Similarly, Fiedler (1966) finds the very significance of American literary themes in their veiled character. It is meaning that is hidden from the ordinary reader which is most powerful, most important.

Finally, in the case of literature, reflection theory fails to take into account the inadequacies and partiality of literary reflection. Literature may provide an accurate picture of some aspects of society, but it also "presents structured misreflections, which magnify or diminish certain aspects of reality, twist some or leave others out altogether" (Desan, Ferguson, and Griswold 1989; see also Candido [1995: 149] on the "liberty" of even naturalist authors). The intuitive appeal of the equation "unique nation-state = distinct national character = distinct national literature" fails in the face of questions regarding the specifications of the reflection process.

The process of canon formation

Traditional formulations of the system of valorizing national literatures also fail to consider questions of the canon formation *process*. In traditional discussions of national literatures the composition of the canon is assumed; it is envisioned as an archive of "the best that has been thought and known" (Arnold 1949: 499; Leavis 1969; Brooks 1975). Canon formation is assumed to be a natural and automatic process in which the "Great Works" transcend time and place to become classics. In the past twenty years, however, scholars have developed more sophisticated analytic models of canon formation that focus on "the complex of circumstances that make texts visible initially and then maintain them in their preeminent position" (Tompkins 1985: xii). Scholars focusing on specific works and authors have attempted to "expose" the institutional and ideological biases of the canon and to "explode" the "myth of transcendentally 'great' literature" (Wolff 1992: 709).

Tompkins (1985), for example, investigates the development and continuation of Nathaniel Hawthorne's canonical status, demonstrating how political activity by interested factions first established his authorial reputation. In addition to arguing that his initial reputation was largely the conscious work of a small group of influential Boston literati, Tompkins argues that the aspects of Hawthorne's work that were admired by nineteenth-century critics are substantially different from those aspects of his work on which his current status rests. Thus the changing and indeed contradictory criteria for Hawthorne's canonical status make clear the contingent nature of literary judgments. The idealized assumption of a transcendent text appropriate to and resonant with all times and all peoples (or even all people within a specific cultural tradition) is belied by well-documented fluctuations in both authorial reputations and the bases for those reputations that may appear constant (von Hallberg 1984; DeNora 1991; Corse and Griffin 1996).

The process of canon formation, and of the establishment of artistic reputations generally, cannot fail to be a political matter (Lang and Lang 1988). As Tompkins notes, literary evaluation is "not an activity that is performed outside of political struggles and institutional structures, but arises *from* them" (1985: 23, italics in original). The judgments of the past influence present judgments precisely because "the text we read is never separable from its history of recognition" (Holub 1984: 148–9; Smith 1983). A group of specific people – academics, critics, editors, publishers – with certain class positions and specialized types of training select and value one group of texts over others (Ohmann 1987). The canon is a product of human choice and contestation, not a natural occurrence.

Cultural sociology has provided an increasingly sophisticated focus on the process of cultural valorization, or the establishment and functioning of evaluative systems for cultural objects (e.g., DiMaggio 1982, 1987; Griswold 1987b; Lang and Lang 1988). Viewed through such previous sociological work, the process of canon formation becomes indisputably recognizable as a process of cultural valorization and, therefore, as a political process mediated by elites rather than a "natural" acknowledgment of "the best." Furthermore, cultural sociology's acknowledgment of the importance of the broader conditions of production pertaining to cultural products and practices allows us to see the historical development of national canons as occurring within, and as promulgated by, the process of constructing the nation (Brubaker 1992; Greenfeld 1992; Hobsbawm 1992). Thus the insights provided by work in cultural sociology focus attention on and therefore make visible the "political" as opposed to "natural" character of canon formation, the ways in which the cultural practices of canon formation and literary nationalism create meaning as opposed to simply reflecting it, and the powerful, socially constitutive, rather than passive, nature of national literatures and the cultural practices that sustain them.

This recognition of the political and constructed nature of the canon raises the issue of mediation. Because the canon is chosen, because specific, political criteria are used to elevate the status of some texts while devaluing others, national literatures cannot serve as representations of the entire range of national experience (Ahmad 1992). Instead, what national literatures can provide is a sense of the national experience mediated through the interests and the concerns of *those who select and validate texts.* An analysis of canonical national literatures may be informative, but it is informative about the relationship between high culture and elite visions and preoccupations, not the relationship between literature and "the people."

The structure of the book

In chapters 2 and 3 I present an historical analysis of the timing and development of the national canon in the United States and Canada respectively. I demonstrate that national canon formation is triggered by political developments, i.e., the undertaking of the nation-building project, rather than literary developments. The conjoint processes of nation-building and canon formation are best seen in the United States in the eighteenth and nineteenth centuries and in Canada in the twentieth century.

In chapters 4 and 5 I present the findings on the cross-national comparison of the high-culture novels. Chapter 4 focuses on the structure and history of the canon and presents the results of the canonical comparison. The two groups of novels exhibit strong cross-national differences as is required by their use in imagining and constructing the unique nation. Chapter 5 analyzes the uses of contemporary high-culture literature and presents the findings on the comparison of the literary prize-winning novels. Most importantly, I argue, contemporary literary prize winners serve as an avenue for revisions to the national images created in earlier works and reaffirm the hierarchy of high culture and popular culture by positing a realm of "pure" literary merit. Both types of high-culture literature are best understood by their location in the "field of restricted production" and their concomitant primary status as symbolic, rather than economic, objects (Bourdieu 1985).

Chapter 6 presents the findings on the comparison of the best-selling novels and argues that the enormous cross-national similarity in popular-culture texts can be explained by an organizational and institutional analysis of the publishing industry in the two countries. Popular-culture literature is located in the field of "large-scale cultural production" where economic considerations outweigh symbolic considerations (Bourdieu 1985). Popular-culture literature, therefore, is not used as a forum for defining or negotiating the national identity, but is used instead as a mass-market commodity. As such, popular-culture literature is aimed at the largest possible audience and shaped by the requirements of "universal" appeal and mass-marketing techniques. Chapter 7 concludes the book by expanding my arguments regarding the symbolic and economic work performed by high and popular culture.

2

Nation-building and the historical timing of a national literature in the United States

> Can we never be thought to have learning or grace
> Unless it be brought from that horrible place
> Where tyranny reigns with her impudent face;
> And popes and pretenders,
> And sly faith-defenders
> Have ever been hostile to reason and wit,
> Enslaving a world that shall conquer them yet.
>
> "Literary Importation," Philip Freneau's lamentation on British cultural domination of the newly formed United States, 1788.

Freneau's poetic anguish over British cultural domination of the newly formed United States characterizes the historical self-consciousness of the nation-building process – and the clear sense that writers felt they had a role to play in the process. As I argued in chapter 1, newer work in nationalism has demonstrated the position of the nation as an "invented" or "imagined" construct supported by cultural stratagems that create and bolster the myths, traditions, and emotional ties that help constitute the nation in the mind of its citizens. Less work has been done, however, in specifying the role of high-culture literature and canon formation in that process. Chapters 2 and 3 rectify this omission through an analysis of the often quite deliberate construction and maintenance of national literatures in the United States and Canada respectively.

It is my argument that the emergence of a national literature in both Canada and the United States was concomitant with the initial period of nation-building. The identification and development of American and Canadian national literatures were used to help imagine the nation and to help develop a unique national identity. Canada and the United States present a powerful comparison for this thesis since, despite their many similarities, the two countries underwent the process of nation-building at significantly different times. Americans were concerned with developing a distinct nation to bolster and unify their new state formation from the earliest post-Revolutionary days. The political and military struggle of the American Revolution galvanized American nationalism. Canadians, on the other hand, faced both the problems of a divided founding tradition and, within the anglophone majority, the issue of defining themselves through their relationship to and status within the British Commonwealth until well into the twentieth century. Rather than a military separation, Canada's political independence from England evolved as a slow and gradual easing of legislative, legal, and ritualistic ties.

In the United States the search for a critically renowned "native" literature was a subject of concern to artists, journalists, and the cultural elite virtually from the moment of political independence (e.g., the Freneau poem cited above). In Canada, however, the subject of "Can Lit" was barely raised until the mid-twentieth century. The American need for a new nation, the deep desire for distinction from and parity with England, the cultural and constructionist process of creating the United States of America, meant that a national literature was eagerly sought, bitterly disputed, and loudly proclaimed from America's beginnings in the late 1700s. The concomitant Canadian interest in a national identity was subsumed in a persistent tension regarding the relationship between Québécois and other French-speaking citizens and the anglophone affiliation with England and her Empire for another 150 years. Canadian nationalism, and thus the identification and development of a Canadian national literature, was a creature of the twentieth century (Jenson 1995).

In short, an historical consideration of canon formation in Canada and the United States demonstrates the connection between nation-building processes and national canon formation. Despite the availability of Canadian authors and Canadian writings in earlier periods, despite formal unification of the Dominion of Canada in 1867, Canada did not "need" a national literature prior to its separation from the British Empire and the gradual emergence of a Canadian national identity which crystallized only in the post-World War II era. Thus existing early writings were simply not identified as part of a *Canadian* canon until many years after their initial publication. The United States, however, "needed" a respectable national literature as soon as possible.

Despite the many differences in Canadian and American national canon formation, this central similarity predominates: during the period of intensive nation-building, elites in both Canada and the United States focused attention and expended resources on the discovery, development, and praise of a national literature. The similarities between the American process of literary discovery and national canon formation in the 1800s and the Canadian process of literary discovery and national canon formation in the mid-1900s are very strong (Atwood 1982). At this point, before turning to the analysis of the specifics of canon formation in the United States, I would like to address the more general historical relationship between literature and the nation-state.

Literature and the nation-state

"Great" literature now seems irrevocably tied to the nation-state. As I have noted, literature is both interpreted and taught within national units. Course catalogues and anthologies feature such categorizations as "Chinese Imperial Poetry," "Nineteenth-Century American Literature," "Great Russian Writers." These are accepted and familiar literary categories. But they are not simply linguistic categories based on shared language type. This can be seen in the fact that anglophone Caribbean, Indian, or African writers, for example, are not taught in English Literature classes, despite the fact that they write in English and are, as likely as not, members of the erstwhile British Commonwealth. There is even continuing debate in Russian Literature departments about whether émigré Russian writers writing in Russian should be taught in Russian Literature courses (Henry 1990). Language alone does not explain our categorizations of literature within national units.

The seemingly primal connection of literature and the nation is in reality a modern historical phenomenon stemming from late eighteenth- and early nineteenth-century theorists of nationalism and the concomitant rise of political nationalism in Western Europe. These theorists made the connection between nation and national literature explicit. It was early nationalists who first promulgated the now accepted ideas that "literature comes in national units [and] . . . that a writer's work should be praised for embodying the distinctive features of [a] . . . people" (MacLulich 1987: 21). These theorists stimulated "new interest in the past and glorified the ideals of folk, 'race,' and nation" (Hubbell 1972: 7). By the early twentieth century these ideas had so taken hold that one social commentator could argue that: "A people may be great through many means, but there is only one measure by which its greatness is recognized and acknowledged. The final measure of the greatness of all peoples is the amount and standard of the literature and art that they have produced" (Johnson 1922: vii).[1]

---

[1] Johnson's statements were made in the preface of an anthology of African-American poetry, in reference to the importance of his "own people" producing a distinctive literature and art. Others writing at the time, however, found greater originality and "Americanness" in the writings of African-Americans than in any writing by white Americans:

the contributions of the Negro to American culture . . . [are] more striking and singular in substance and structure than any contributions that have been made by the white man

The German Romantic nationalists were the strongest proponents of the arguments linking the nation and its cultural products. Late eighteenth-century German ideas of nationhood were identified with a specifically literary national spirit, *Nationalgeist*. Brubaker describes the central vision of the nation in German Romantic thought:

In the social and political thought of Romanticism . . . nations are conceived as his-torically rooted, organically developed individualities, united by a distinctive *Volksgeist* and by its infinitely ramifying expression in language, custom, law, culture, and the state. Despite the emphasis placed on the state, the Romantic under-standing of nationhood is fundamentally ethnocultural. The *Volksgeist* is constitu-tive, the state merely expressive of nationhood (1992: 8).

Nationalism presumes the state and its formations are coterminous with "the people" and their culture – and the latter expressive of the former.[2] For nationalism, as Gellner notes, may be defined as "the striving to make culture and polity congruent, to endow a culture with its own political roof, and not more than one roof at that" (1983: 43). Thus the national charac-ter of literature came to be seen as a natural and primal characteristic arising from the natural and primal unit of the nation.

The nation, however, like the designation of literature as national, is not a "naturally occurring" phenomenon. As I have noted, recent scholars have amply demonstrated the socially constructed character of "the nation" (Anderson 1991; Brubaker 1992; Gellner 1983, 1994; Greenfeld 1992; Handler 1988; Hobsbawm 1992; Hobsbawm and Ranger 1983; Soysal 1994; Zerubavel 1992). As Gellner has so definitively written, nations are not "a natural, God-given way of classifying men" and:

nationalism is *not* the awakening of an old, latent, dormant force, though that is how it does indeed present itself . . . Nations are not inscribed into the nature of things, they do not constitute a political version of the doctrine of natural kinds . . .

> . . . In fact, they constitute America's chief claim to originality in its cultural history . . . the Negro . . . has developed out of the American milieu a form of expression, a mood, a literary genre, a folk tradition, that are distinctly and undeniably American . . . The white man in America has continued, and in an inferior manner, a culture of European origin (Calverton 1929: 3–4).

> Similarly, Parker argued that "there is one portion of our permanent literature, if literature it may be called, which is wholly indigenous and original . . . we have one series of literary productions that could be written by none but Americans, and only here; I mean the Lives of Fugitive Slaves" (1907: 37).

[2] Brubaker develops two models of nation-states, contrasting the German case and the French case: "In Germany the 'conceived order' or 'imagined community' of nationhood and the institutional realities of statehood were sharply distinct; in France they were fused. In Germany nationhood was an ethnocultural fact; in France it was a political fact" (1992: 4; see also Soysal 1994).

[Nationalism] is in reality the consequence of a new form of social organization, based on deeply internalized, education-dependent high cultures, each protected by its own state (1983: 48–9, italics in original).

The modern nation-state is not the natural embodiment of geographic and cultural singularity; it is an abstract entity created through political and military processes and sustained in the minds of people.[3] Nations are created, not "awakened," and that creation "must include a constructed or 'invented' component" (Hobsbawm and Ranger 1983: 14).

One of the central roles of a national literature is to assist in that "construction" and "invention" of the nation. National literatures are one avenue for the identification, legitimation, and maintenance of the nation (Spencer 1957; Ziff 1981; Griswold 1992). The nation and its cultural expression in literature underlies, unifies, and makes meaningful the political formation of the state. Literature helps to sustain the nation-state through its evocation and indeed creation of the unifying, emotionally powerful image of the nation and the national identity. If nationalism is an "emotive identity" with a "sovereign community" (McCrone 1992: 6), then national literatures are one method of fostering the emotion and forming the community. A national literature furnishes some of the "inventions or even . . . forgeries" that provide "substantial bases for psychological membership" in the national society (Schudson 1994: 26). Literary expression helps to construct common images of the nation and the generally available understandings of the relationship between the people and "their" nation.[4] Greenfeld makes clear both the constructed nature of "the nation" and the powerful role the creation of "national identity" plays in that construction:

a nation is first and foremost an embodiment of an ideology. There are no "dormant" nations which awaken to the sense of their nationality . . . rather, invention and imposition of national identity lead people to believe that they are indeed

---

[3] Brubaker (1993) uses the concept of the "nationalizing state" to emphasize the processual nature of the construction of the nation and the identification of the people with that tradition, image, and identity (see also Handler [1988]; also Tiryakian and Nevitte [1985] on "relational" and "dynamic" conceptions of nationalism).

[4] See Brubaker:

> particular cultural idioms – ways of thinking and talking about nationhood . . . were reinforced and activated in specific historical and institutional settings . . . once reinforced and activated, these cultural idioms framed and shaped judgments of what was politically imperative, of what was in the interests of the state . . . The more general analytical point is that cultural idioms are not neutral vehicles for the expression of preexisting interests: cultural idioms *constitute* interests as much as they express them. These culturally mediated and thereby culturally constituted interests are not prior to, or independent of, the cultural idioms in which they are expressed (1992: 16, italics in original).

united and as a result to become united; it is national identity which often weaves disparate populations into one (1992: 402).

The naming and development of a national literature is one process by which disparate populations can be symbolically "woven" into one.

National literatures are important because of their ability to create and sustain an identity and a national community that do not depend on direct relationships. Reading is a solitary activity, but an activity that can powerfully unite solitary readers in imagined communities. Reading a text that hundreds, if not thousands or even millions, of others are reading or have read invites the reader into the community constituted by those readers. Literacy allows a reader to participate in the experiences and feelings of groups and situations s/he could never encounter or participate in directly. Anderson understands the process of reading "the novel and the newspaper" as central to national identity formation (1991: 25–46).[5] Nation-states are rooted in the fact that although most "members of even the smallest nation will never . . . meet . . . [yet] in the minds of each lives the image of their communion" (Anderson 1991: 6). National literatures are instrumental in the creation and maintenance of that "image of communion."

In the modern world, "people have come increasingly to conceive of themselves as members of very large collectivities linked primarily by common identities but minimally by networks of directly interpersonal relationships" (Calhoun 1991: 95). Because of this lack of direct relationships, the ability of cultural media to envision and widely distribute images of those common identities becomes increasingly powerful. It is through the "mediation of the world of political symbols," represented in part by national literatures, that "people without direct interpersonal relations with each other are led . . . to imagine themselves as members of communities defined by common ascriptive characteristics" (Calhoun 1991: 108, in discussing Habermas). National literatures help to construct the "common identity" so paramount to the creation and preservation of the "large collectivity." National literatures, *unique* national literatures, help provide that extremely important piece of national life – "a conception of what makes Us into Us," and what separates "Us" from "Them" (Poggi 1978: 11–13; see also Mauss [1969] on national group boundaries).

Creating a common identity marked by a sense of unity, loyalty, and

---

[5] See also Greenfeld on the constitutive effect of literacy on nationalism. She argues that reading the Bible was one of the powerful factors stimulating English nationalism in the sixteenth century because it gave the masses a new sense of individual human dignity and allied them in their own world view with the small circle of new aristocrats and clergymen who were coming to understand themselves as "an English people" (1992: 53–4).

cohesiveness from the often disparate groups that form national populations is a difficult task that is attacked in part with a cultural artillery: Huxley
(1959: 50) proclaimed that "nations are to a very large extent invented by
their poets and novelists." Nation-building requires explicit campaigns to
create "a transcendent realm of essential identity," a vision of unity rooted
in a common national identity, overreaching all subsidiary differences and
overriding all other identities, such as ethnic or religious identities, which
may divide and polarize national populations (Lloyd 1987: x).

Although national literatures generally provide themes, character types,
and morals that lend substance to the national image, that may not be the
central basis for their influence in national identity formation. The *content*
of specific texts may well be of less importance than the *form* of their existence as a national canon.[6] Students reading *Huck Finn* or *The Stone Angel*
in a group, as students all across the country are doing, and as their older
siblings and maybe even parents (although not in Canada) did before them,
experience what Anderson calls "occasions for unisonality" (1991: 145; see
also Schudson 1994: 34). Although Anderson speaks of singing the
national anthem as the archetypal occasion for unisonality, the common
experience of the national literature – whether read with passionate interest, dutifully skimmed in school, or only experienced through study aids or
the illustrated comics version – is part of what sustains the image of
national communion. We experience participation in a national collectivity
because it is explicitly acknowledged that the national context of the
reading provides its significance.[7]

In addition to aiding internal processes of nation-building and national
identity formation, national literatures assist in these processes in the international community. National literatures have become identified within
both national and international communities as an essential characteristic
of nation-states. MacLulich and others (e.g., Lease 1981) have shown that
one of the "standard marks of nationhood" is "the possession of a national
literature" (1987: 24). In order to lay claim to full nationhood, nascent
nation-states need not only military and political independence, but cul-

---

[6] See for example Ahmad (1992 in chapter 3, especially pt. VII) on the difficulty of finding,
in many cultures, literature that specifically refers to, or even allegorizes, the nation. The
nation-building aspect of national literatures is not necessarily content-based, but may be
found in the form and in the production arrangements of national cultures. Berezin's
(1994b) argument regarding the fascist character of Italian theater under Mussolini makes
a similar point: the "fascist" nature of theater lay in its production structure and the viewing
conditions rather than in the particular content of dramatic productions.

[7] This is, in part, what so excites the debate about the canon. Many participants in the debate
have some experience of participation in a collective culture and whether they articulate that
clearly or not, it unsettles them to imagine no sense of the "image of our communion" being
transmitted through literature.

tural independence as well (Dominguez 1992). A viable national literature is one of the clearest signs of cultural independence. Once national literatures became understood as a basic requirement of a full-fledged nation-state, new nations had to have their own national literature or risk losing status in the international arena. In the nineteenth century, these ideals of cultural nationalism were so powerful that in their light "the lack of a national culture raised the question *as to the reality of the nation itself*" (Greenfeld 1992: 442, italics added).

Because national literatures play such a role in imagining the nation and inventing a tradition, an identity, and a unifying history, it obviously follows that each nation's literature must be distinct from other nations' literatures. National literatures differ from one another because the identity, and thus the uniqueness, of the nation is a central subtext of national canons (Spencer 1957; Neil 1975; Ziff 1981). National literatures both help construct the distinct nation and serve as markers of the very uniqueness they helped construct.

In short, the very existence of the nation is at least partially dependent on its cultural and literary manifestation. National literatures are used to help the process by which the new nation is "endowed with a sacred unity and made to seem a natural social unit" (Kertzer 1988: 179). National literatures are a central resource in the process of creating the necessary unity, loyalty, and patriotism of national populations. National literatures and their reading generate experiences of unisonality and help to mediate the indirect relationships required in the construction and maintenance of national communities.

In addition to helping with internal nation-building processes, national literatures also serve as markers of international status, promoting the legitimacy and status of the nation-state in the global arena.[8] To the extent that the world system has increasingly become the central determinant of national legitimacy (Meyer and Hannan 1979), two things occur. First, the requirements for being understood as an actual and appropriate nation-state become codified at the level of the world system (Thomas, Meyer, Ramirez, and Boli 1987). Second, nation-states conform to the definitions legitimated by the world system regardless of the appropriateness of requirements for specific national situations (e.g., Meyer, Ramirez, and Soysal 1992). Or, as Virginia Dominguez has noted regarding the current power of the value of culture:

---

[8] See Schroeder for a discussion of Weber's contention that international competition will increasingly be based on the honor and prestige of national cultures and that therefore "the increase in cultural prestige" is "the ultimate future aim of a nation" (1992: 119–20).

I am . . . struck by the apparent success European countries have had over the past 100 to 150 years convincing the rest of the world that culture is a "thing," that it has value, and that any self-respecting group of people must have it. People . . . are overwhelmingly buying into the elite European idea that there is such a thing as culture and that it is through one's culture that one's value is judged. We need only think about China's current "culture fever" or Japan's ongoing *Nihonjinron* or Papua New Guinea's panic about developing a national culture or the Quebequois insistence on Quebequois cultural identity (1992: 36).

Every respectable nation must be able to demonstrate its "own" culture – and national literatures are a standard method for so doing. Thus national literatures must be distinct in order to serve the twin duties of mobilizing national populations through the imagination of the nation and laying claim to full-fledged status as an independent and complete nation within the global community. I turn now to an analysis of the process of national literary development as it occurred historically in the United States and, in the following chapter, as it occurred in Canada.

Canon formation in the United States

The role high-culture literature plays in the national identity process can be seen most clearly in the United States in the nineteenth century, with its beginnings in the late eighteenth century. In the United States, a nationalist ideology and the desire to create national unity existed virtually from the Revolution that created American political independence. This situation was in sharp contrast to the situation in Canada. In Canada, strong ties with Britain and continued divisions between the "nations" of English-speaking Canada and French-speaking Canada kept nationalist sentiment at bay, at least for the majority of the population, until the middle of the twentieth century.

The historical demand for a national literature in the United States

The historical debate regarding the establishment of an American national literature provides a glimpse of the passion with which early American commentators regarded the establishment of a national culture. By 1780, the political existence of an American state was assured,[9] but as writings by statesmen, journalists, and men of letters of the time make clear, the establishment of an autonomous political state was seen as an obviously necessary, but clearly not sufficient step toward the creation of the United

---

[9] The exact shape of that entity, or entities, was not as definite, but it was clear that some form of independent state or states would exist.

States of America. As these men not only saw, but harped on, the United States needed to establish itself as a nation as well as a state: "political independence," it was argued, "only served to emphasize American cultural provincialism" (Ruland 1972: 48). America needed an independent identity and a separate cultural tradition in addition to political autonomy. Nationhood – cultural independence – required casting off the "state of colonial and provincial dependency upon the old world" which marked America despite her statehood and political independence (Ruland 1972: 294).

Nationalism, however, assumes that humanity is "naturally divided into separate units or nations, each unified by a common language and culture, and each possessing certain distinctive traits" (MacLulich 1987: 26). The newly formed republic of America, on the other hand, was from almost the beginning a conglomerate of diverse peoples with diverse languages, cultures, and traits (Greenfeld 1992). The building of the *nation* required a cultural unification, the establishment of an indigenous American "tradition," not simply political independence. Revolution and legislation may have created the States, but culture and literature were needed to make them United. Because the assumed congruity between state and some "natural, unified" human group was even more problematic in the American case than in earlier European cases, it was concomitantly more important that "the traditions . . . be provided and the sentiment of nationality kindled" (Hubbell 1972: 10; see Hobsbawm and Ranger [1983] however on the "invention of tradition" more generally).

Thus it is not surprising that the earliest desire for the establishment of an "authentic" American literature began to be expressed very shortly after the American struggle for independence. The widely varying conditions in America, especially between North and South, meant that while there was strong national feeling, there was also little assurance that the national would triumph over the regional – particularly once the external British threat was gone. Until the Civil War, forces for disintegration were "at least as strong as those which fostered unity" (Greenfeld 1992: 444). This situation was alarming to many who were committed to the establishment of a strong unified republic. Thus, "there was a conscious effort to forge a national consciousness that would admit of no doubt that the United States were indeed a nation, and a nation which more than any other deserved passionate commitment" (Greenfeld 1992: 444). A belief in and fostering of American exceptionalism, the sense that the United States had a unique destiny and history, was a strong part of this process (see Kammen [1993] for a review of the cross-disciplinary work in American exceptionalism; see also Lipset 1996). The forging of a "national consciousness" required both the creation of an articulated and materially available American culture *and* the rejection of English culture.[10]

By 1787, Noah Webster was already warning that the "authority of foreign manners keeps us in subjection" (Greenfeld 1992: 442; see also Bynack 1984).[11] American elites concerned with the transformation of their disparate populations into a nation saw the English literary tradition as "unsuited to the needs of the new republic" (Hubbell 1972: 7) and agitated for a new tradition that would free Americans from being "the literary vassals of England . . . do[ing] homage to the mother country" (Brownson [1838], quoted in Ruland 1972: 270). Lease cites an 1816 announcement in *The Portico* which makes the American understanding of this need clear: "Dependence, whether literary or political, is a state of degradation, fraught with disgrace; and to be dependent on a foreign mind, for what we can ourselves produce, is to add to the crime of indolence, the weakness of stupidity" (1981: 3). A concurrent article in *The Port-Folio* made the comparison between cultural and other claims to nationhood still clearer by urging American men of letters to emulate the drive and persistence of the military so that America would become "as renowned in literature as

---

[10] The early American interest in the identification and definition of a unique national litera-ture was primarily of interest to the elite groups operating at, and committed to, the national, rather than regional, stage (Greenfeld 1992). Nonetheless, literature was also of great interest to the general population – more so than we might reasonably suppose given certain stereotypes of American intellectual life. America had an early, and persisting, rep-utation for anti-intellectualism and disinterest in culture. The accuracy of this stereotype is challenged by Greenfeld (1992: 460–72) who argues that the stereotype of American anti-intellectualism obscured the historically high degree of literacy and interest in learning among Americans in all walks of life. For example, Greenfeld refers to Tocqueville's (1835) observation:

> Although America is perhaps in our days the civilized country in which literature is least attended to . . . still a large number of persons there take an interest in the productions of the mind and make them, if not the study of their lives, at least the charm of their leisure hours . . . There is hardly a pioneer's hut that does not contain a few odd volumes of Shakespeare (quoted in Greenfeld 1992: 462–3).

She then comments dryly that:

> Those who know "when Russia learned to read" or when French peasants turned into Frenchmen will no doubt for a moment that odd volumes of Shakespeare (or Zhukovsky, or Racine) in a peasant hut in Central Russia or Provence in the 1830s (or 1850s, or 1870s) would be an utter impossibility, and that whatever might constitute the charm of leisure hours in those parts, it would not be, by any stretch of the imagination, the productions of the mind (1992: 463).

Although the development of an American national literature was a process primarily directed by intellectual elites, it would be a mistake to consider that American cultural and literary activities in the nineteenth century were irrelevant to the general population.

[11] Webster helped the nationalist cause as he saw it with the publication of the *American Dictionary of the English Language* in 1828, making clear the distinctiveness of the American language from the English (Anderson 1991: 197).

she is in arms" (Lease 1981: 4). Nationalists clearly understood that a "nation could not be powerful or well regarded if it was not independent. Independence, therefore – economic, political, *and cultural* – was the para-mount concern" (Greenfeld 1992: 441, italics added).

The Americans were not the only ones to make note of this situation. The British were well aware of, and frequently commented upon, the absence of an American literature and what that meant:

> The literary independence of the Americans is far from being so complete as their political, for as yet they possess no national literature and invariably regard ours as appertaining also to them. By national literature we . . . mean . . . a literature that appeals directly to the national feelings . . . and above all, administers to the just pride of a nation, inspires a feeling for the national glory, and inculcates a love of country – a literature which foreigners may admire, but none can feel, in the deep sanctuary of the heart, but a native (*Athenaeum* [1831], quoted in Ruland 1972: 235).

The importance of a national literature was clearly recognized by both Americans and those in other nation-states. The absence of an American national literature was seen as a fundamental failure and a weakness with the potential to undermine the credibility of the American nation-state.

In the early 1800s came the decisive blows that galvanized American commitment to the development of an "authentic" national literature. In December 1818, the British critic Sydney Smith wrote: "Literature the Americans have none – no native literature, we mean. It is all imported . . . But why should the Americans write books, when a six weeks' passage brings them . . . our sense, science, and genius, in bales and hogsheads?" (quoted in Hubell 1972: 5). Smith contemptuously dismissed American claims to a "true," as opposed to merely political, independence from England. Smith also implied that the situation was inevitable. However worse was still to come. In January 1820, the Reverend Smith again wrote on the American literary situation, asking his now infamous question in the *Edinburgh Review*: "In the four quarters of the globe, who reads an American book?" (Ruland 1972: 157). The agonized response of American writers, publishers, and men of letters to Smith's second question demon-strated the considerable attention the issue of a new national literature com-manded in the States and further stimulated the growing quest for an American literature.

Spencer (1957: ix) notes that the "importance of the conscious pursuit of nationality" is indicated by the "fact that scarcely a native author of any importance before 1900 failed to engage in the inquiry and to declare himself publicly on its issues." James Russell Lowell summarized the prevailing attitude in the early part of the nineteenth century: "It had been resolved unanimously that *we must and would* have a national literature.

England, France, Spain, Italy, each already had one. Germany was getting one as fast as possible, and Ireland vowed that she once had one far surpassing them all. *To be respectable, we must have one also*" (quoted in Hubell 1972: 5, italics added). William Ellery Channing not only acknowledged the importance of literature to the national enterprise – "[L]iterature is plainly among the most powerful methods of exalting the character of a nation" – but lamented the American lack: "Do we possess indeed what we may call a national literature? Have we produced eminent writers . . . ? We regret that the reply to these questions is so obvious" ([1823] 1841: 248, 252). Similarly, the theologian and "publicist for ideas" Theodore Parker complained in 1846 that:

In England, the national literature favors the church, the crown, the nobility, the prevailing class . . . We have no American literature which is permanent. Our scholarly books are only an imitation of a foreign type; they do not reflect our morals, manners, politics, or religion, not even our rivers, mountains, sky. They have not the smell of our ground in their breath (quoted in Gates 1989: 30).

Herman Melville joined the "attempt of American authors, critics, and patriots to design and foster a national literature" (Spencer 1957: vii) and, thirty years after Smith's query, proudly responded "the day will come when you shall say who reads a book by an Englishman that is a modern?" (quoted in Lease 1981: xii).

Walt Whitman was also a passionate advocate of the attempt to cultivate a national literature. In a letter to Emerson written in 1856, Whitman berates Americans for their cultural dependence and reliance on "ready-made" English literature: "Where are any mental expressions from you, beyond what you have copied and stolen? Where are the born throngs of poets, literats, orators, you promised?" ([1856] 1982: 1328) He returns to the same theme of the need for a truly American literature in "Democratic Vistas," a long prose essay written in the late 1860s, in which Whitman defines as our "fundamental want to-day in the United States" a class of "native authors, literatuses" who are to breathe life into "the whole mass of American mentality." For without this literary foundation, Whitman tells us, "this nation will no more stand, permanently, soundly, than a house will stand without a substratum" for the "central point in any nation" is "its . . . literature" ([1868]1982: 932, 938).

The early American canon and canonical change

At approximately the same time as Whitman was complaining about the state of American writing, Nathaniel Hawthorne and Herman Melville were publishing what would eventually come to be seen as two cornerstones of the American canon. *The Scarlet Letter*, published in 1850, and *Moby Dick*, published in 1851 are, with their authors, now considered at the core of the American canon. Although Hawthorne's reputation was firmly established during his lifetime, Melville was to be canonized only by much later generations: "When . . . [Melville] died in 1891, there were few who remembered him, and many of those who had read his earlier books thought he had died long before" (Hubbell 1972: 59). Canon formation is an uneven process. Evaluations of texts and authors change over time, although part of the very cultural work canons perform is to deny or at least obscure the transitory nature of literary valuations (Chandler 1984; Kenner 1984).

Despite the aura of stability and the ideology of transcendent excellence surrounding canonical selections, canonical change is an essential aspect of canon formation (Gerson 1991: 46 especially). Canonical change generally follows a model of "punctuated evolution" rather than one of "continuous, smooth evolution" as substantial changes in canons are "usually indicative of a major shift in [literary-critical] values" (Bennett 1991: 134). The early period of canon formation in the United States was erratic and highly contested. The canon was accepted in one place before another, and involved ongoing and inconsistent processes of ignoring, valorizing, and delegitimating various authors and their works (e.g., Golding 1984, see also McCarthy [1991] on the Canadian situation). Canons are neither static nor monolithic.

Nonetheless, an outline of the initially accepted American canon was beginning to appear by the late nineteenth century. This burgeoning national literature had helped to create strong feelings of nationalism in the United States, especially in the post-Civil War era (Hubbell 1972: 10). Spengemann notes that the very first courses in American literature were offered in the:

workingmen's and mechanics' institutes and libraries that sprang up in the northern and midwestern states during the 1820s and 1830s and then in the land-grant universities created for the education of the American working class. Like Oxford and Cambridge, the old patrician colleges of the eastern seaboard were among the very last institutions to offer instruction in the literature of their own country (1989: 173).

The more formalized and elite institutions were unsure of the worth of American literature and unwilling to canonize it until much later than less formalized and less elite institutions.

Although the topic of American literature was not *institutionalized* in university curricula until the twentieth century, courses in American Literature were being given by the 1890s in a broad range of colleges and universities (Hubell 1972; Lauter 1991). These late nineteenth-century courses embodied the earliest judgments of the American canon. The courses featured "the 'Big Ten': Irving, Cooper, Bryant, Emerson, Hawthorne, Longfellow, Whittier, Holmes, Lowell, and Poe. Occasionally Thoreau or Mrs. Stowe might be included, but not Whitman or Melville" (Hubbell 1972: 245). By 1896, with a national literature beginning to be established within the academy, John S. Hart could publish his literary history, *Manual of American Literature* (Hubbell 1972: 245).[12]

Spencer argues that by the decade of the 1890s, the "major phase" of the literary "quest for nationality" was "termina[ted]" (1957: ix). Spengemann, however, claims that "doubts concerning the possibility of America's literary independence from the rest of the English-speaking world could still be heard as late as 1915" although the last of such doubts "were soon drowned out in the roar of national pride that greeted the American military triumph in Europe" (1989: 118). Although costlier and difficult to sustain in the long run, military nation-building often has a more rapid and powerful effect than literary nationalism. The initial work of establishing a national literature was thus concluded around the turn of the century. The pervasive American nationalist spirit of this period "was in great measure a literary achievement" (Hubbell 1972: 10).

The early part of the twentieth century was a period of relative stability for the American canon. The end of World War II, however, saw a significant adjustment to the canon as literary critical values experienced a sharp change. Using "New Critical," close-reading techniques, influential postwar scholars such as Henry Nash Smith, R. W. B. Lewis, and Richard Chase reconstructed a vision of the American novel that emphasized the free individual struggling to define himself against society and that elevated the twentieth-century writers Hemingway, Faulkner, and Fitzgerald to the company of Melville, Hawthorne, and Twain.[13] These writers have continued at the core of the American canon through the current period.

The 1970s and 1980s witnessed another wave of significant canonical dispute as the stability of the postwar canon was challenged. The most recent attempt to reformulate the canon has been largely led by feminist and African-American attacks on the very basis of the canon formation process (e.g., Showalter 1985; Baker and Redmond 1989). Although the

---

[12] Spengemann (1989: 153) cites Fred Pattee's *A History of American Literature*, published in 1873, as the very first history of American literature.

[13] By the 1920s, Hemingway, Faulkner, and Fitzgerald were all publishing to varying degrees of acclaim – Faulkner to little if any: "In the years 1929–1932 when William Faulkner was bringing out his best books, most critics were either puzzled, angered, or disgusted by what they found in them ... In 1945 all of Faulkner's seventeen books were out of print" (Hubbell 1972: 319).

project of "opening up" has resulted in some profound changes to the canon, and a large literature critical to and problematizing of canonical notions, the newest wave of change has not succeeded in completely dislodging the traditional canon as constituted in the 1950s.[14] Thus the cycle continues: as new critical theories and new textual strategies are constructed, the particular interests and capacities of their proponents privilege new authors and new texts (Corse and Griffin 1996). Periods of only minor canonical change are punctuated by the establishment of major new versions of the canon (Bennett 1991).

Thus the history of national canon formation in the United States demonstrates the powerful relationship between high-culture literature and the process of nation-building. The military struggle and political independence of the United States in the late eighteenth century stimulated the need for cultural independence and a national identity. The search for and desire to find an "authentic" American literary voice preoccupied journalists, authors, poets, and the intellectual elite in the States throughout the late eighteenth and nineteenth centuries. The voices of the time are explicit in their understanding of the necessity of a national literature as both proclamation of full national independence and catalyst for national identity development.

The development of an American nation and an American literature thus focused on the rejection of an English identity and the English nation. In Canada, as we will see in the next chapter, the same conceptual relationship between literature and the nation holds true, but the historical specificities of the Canadian case mean that the process of national canon formation occurs in a different period and plays out in a very different fashion. Separation from Britain, although an enduring theme in Canadian history, was not the single driving force in the search for Canadian national distinctiveness. Canadian nationalism, when it arose, involved a complex negotiation of French and English founding traditions, and a more ambivalent attachment to and identity within the British Commonwealth. In the United States, the central work of the nationalist project was to develop an identity separate from the Old World, to bring to life the City upon the hill.

---

[14] This canon may be exemplified by a 1962 MLA Committee on Priorities that named as the major American writers Hawthorne, Melville, Emerson, Thoreau, Poe, Twain, James, and Whitman in the nineteenth century, and Faulkner, Hemingway, Eliot, Frost, O'Neill, and Stevens in the twentieth century (cited in Hubbell 1972: 279).

3

Nation-building and the historical timing of a national literature in Canada

> Canadian identity is weaker in both the sociohistorical sense of Mexico
> . . . and the compactual or covenantal sense of the United States, which
> historically has required a unified political credo for its immigrant society.
> More regionalistic than the other two, Canada is still working out the con-
> sequences of having had two founding European cultures and of having
> followed the evolutionary path to state formation in 1867 and subsequent
> independence (Earle and Wirth 1995: 3).

Although the theoretical argument delineated in chapter 2 holds true for
the Canadian case, the specific historical circumstances in Canada generated a very different development pattern for Canadian national literature
than that which occurred in the American case. In Canada, several distinctive features of the political situation suppressed the search for and the
development of a national literature until the mid-twentieth century.

Early Canadian society faced three powerful threats to the possibility of
the national project. First, there was a strong division between English and
French Canada, rooted both in historical animosity between the founding
societies and in profound differences between anglophone and francophone in religion, language, occupation, orientation to modernity, and economic power. Canada's *sub*national division between the French and
English founding traditions generated an inherent tension in the attempt to
construct a unifying, fully national literature. Nationalist sentiment in
Canadian history has historically taken a wide variety of forms and refer-
enced many different visions of Canada – visions that are often incompat-
ible (Berger 1970; Cook 1986; Gougeon 1994). As the opening quotation
from Earle and Wirth makes clear, the historical conditions of Canada's
founding have continued to subvert both the development of a national
canon and the nationalist project more generally.

Second, the anglophone majority of Canada were possessed of a strong sense of British imperial identity with only secondary thoughts of an independent Canadian nationalist identity. Canada's ties to Britain determined the dominant anglophone Canadian identity in *supra*national terms vis-à-vis the British Commonwealth for much of Canada's history. This obviously precluded the necessity of developing a uniquely Canadian cultural expression of national identity. Thus the concept of Canada as a nation was from the beginning threatened both from below by the *sub*national division between the French and English founding populations, and from above by the *supra*national level identification with the British Commonwealth.

Finally, the vastly larger and more aggressive society poised along Canada's southern border threatened Canadian political autonomy and cultural distinctiveness from the beginning – a possibility imagined with horror by some Canadians, but with joy by others. The United States has been many things to Canada, but has rarely been irrelevant. The development, effects, and eventual success of the Canadian national canon can only be understood within the context of these persisting tensions between francophone and anglophone, between British imperial status and Canadian independence, and between continentalist and nationalist orientation.

For much of its history, in other words, Canada had no need for a Canadian literature because Canada had no overwhelming sense of Canadian-ness. Canadians were content reading British or French literature, and understanding their own cultural expressions as a development within one of these existent traditions. The tensions between the two founding traditions, the attachment to the mother countries, and the often beguiling presence perched on the southern border undermined a unitary Canadian identity. Thus it was that writings by Canadians were not identified as part of a Canadian national canon until the process of Canadian nation-building began in earnest. It was only then that Canadians began to worry about being Canadian – of one sort or another – first and foremost.

In contrast to the American struggles to establish a national literature in the nineteenth century, Canada largely ignored the issue of a national literature until over a century later. The post-World War II era is generally considered the beginning of canonical Canadian literature in terms of preliminary elite recognition, although a number of texts now considered canonical were originally published much earlier.

The difference between the development of the American and Canadian canons cannot be explained by a simple lack of writing in Canada. Like early British settlers in the American colonies, settlers in and visitors to Canada wrote essays, histories, poems, and novels from the earliest days. The first descriptive poem by a visitor to the Canadian colonies, William

Vaughan's *The Golden Fleece*, was published in London in 1626 – a mere six years after the arrival of the Puritan pilgrims to the shores of Cape Cod Bay. Other poems and essays describing the northern British colonies and aimed at a British audience were published in London throughout the seventeenth and early eighteenth centuries (Vincent 1983: 652). Frances Brooke published what has come to be considered the "first Canadian novel" in 1769. *The History of Emily Montague* was published in London after Brooke returned to England from a Canadian stay of five years (1763–68) and is chiefly set in then contemporary Canada. Histories and other non-fiction writing were also published in the late eighteenth century, e.g., John Reeves's *History of the Government of the Island of Newfoundland* in 1793 and Samuel Hearne's *Journey from the Prince of Wales's Fort in Hudson's Bay to the Northern Ocean* in 1795.

After the founding of Halifax in 1749 and the garrisoning of Quebec in 1760, poetry and other literary genres intended for a more local audience flourished (Vincent 1983: 652). A number of literary magazines and newspapers, such as *The Novascotian*, the *Acadian Recorder* (published in the 1820s), and *The Literary Garland* (published monthly in Montreal from 1838 to 1851), published short stories, sketches, and poetry, in addition to non-fiction materials. Early writers such as Susanna Moodie, Thomas McCullough, and Thomas Chandler Haliburton were published in these journals. The first Canadian-published novel by a Canadian-born author, Julia Catherine Beckwith Hart's *St. Ursula's Convent*, was published in 1824 (Edwards 1983: 565–6). By the mid- to late nineteenth century (during and after the period of the American Renaissance), Canadian novelists such as T. C. Haliburton, Susanna Moodie, John Richardson, William Kirby, James De Mille, and Sara Jeannette Duncan were publishing – not only, or even primarily, in local markets, but in London and New York as well.

Similarly, French-Canadian literature, although not extensive, began to appear shortly after the establishment of New France. The earliest French-Canadian writing was the literature of exploration detailing journeys to New France in the late 1500s and 1600s (Warwick 1983: 552–3). Other forms of writing from the early period include "occasional verse and prose" and annals detailing life as residents in New France, particularly in religious institutions (Warwick 1983: 556–7). The first French-Canadian novel, *L'influence d'un livre*, was a melodramatic adventure published in 1837 as an encouragement to the francophone population in the midst of the rebellion.[1] The climate of nineteenth-century French Canada was not

---

[1] *Les Révélations du crime*, by François-Réal Angers, was also published in 1837. It was, however, an account of a real incident (Dionne 1988: 1229).

conducive to novel writing, as fiction was often suspected of promoting immorality. Good novels were "soon defined as . . . didactic, patriotic, and edifying . . . [Therefore] historical novels and novels of the land – that is, novels promoting an agricultural ideology and fidelity to traditions – were largely favored in Québec" (Cotnam 1983: 595; Simon 1991). The first French-Canadian novel to be translated into English was the 1863 historical novel *Les Anciens Canadiens* by Philippe Aubert de Gaspé (O'Connor 1983: 796). The first psychological French-Canadian novel, *Angéline de Montbrun*, whose theme was self-sacrifice, was published in 1884. In 1895, the ultramontane nationalist Jules-Paul Tardivel wrote the first novel to promote a separatist ideology, *Pour La Patrie* (Cotnam 1983: 595).[2]

Given the availability of novels and other fiction written by both French-speaking and English-speaking Canadians and/or about both French and English Canada by the mid-nineteenth century, the question becomes why was Canadian canon formation delayed until the mid-twentieth century? Although Canadian materials were certainly scarcer than American works, the difference in volume is an insufficient explanation for the differential rate of canon formation.

The explanation for the timing of Canadian canon formation is found in the timing of Canadian nationalism. Canadian writing was not understood as *Canadian*, was not constructed as an importantly Canadian artefact, until the notion of "Canada" was meaningful in nationalist terms. As long as English Canadians primarily understood Canada through its incorporation in the British Empire, on the one hand, and French Canadians understood Quebec as part of the French-speaking world, on the other, the process of national canon formation was largely irrelevant. Keith describes the (anglophone) situation thus:

The Americans, of course, had a far greater stimulus to produce an alternative and distinctive literature in English. Since they had become an independent nation, it was a logical step to define the difference . . . in literary as well as other terms. But because Canada had not severed political ties, there was less reason to break literary connexions; the incentive to produce an independent national literature that might stand as both a foundation and a symbol was . . . weak (1985: 3).

Although Keith (1985: 41–9, especially) seems to believe that most early Canadian writing was of insufficient quality to trigger canon formation, I would argue that the far greater problem was the lack of any perceived reason to even have a *Canadian* literature. The division between

---

[2] For further information on early novels in French Canada, see Maurice Lemire's (1970) *Les grands thèmes nationalistes du roman historique canadien-français* and Aurelien Boivin's (1975) *Le conte littéraire québécois au XIXe siècle*.

anglophone and francophone Canada combined with the dominant Canadian identification with the British nation, and the concomitant de-emphasis of the Canadian nation resulting from these two very powerful influences, meant that the impetus for an independent Canadian canon was lacking. The American presence simply added a third complicating factor to the nation-building process in Canada.

"One state, two nations"

The very phrase "Canadian nationalism" is misleading in that it subsumes a problematic series of concepts within a naturalized phrase that gives no indication of the turmoil right beneath the surface (Bashevkin 1991: 30).[3] Most fundamentally, the phrase occludes the central division inherent in the notion of "Canada" itself. The concept of "nation" in Canadian discourse is used to refer (1) to a pan-Canadian nation; (2) to the "nation" of English Canada; and (3) to the "nation" of French Canada. Or, as Ramsay Cook notes:

Running through our history since the eighteenth century have been two, not one, real or potential nationalist impulses. First there has been the French-speaking Canadians' commitment to *la survivance*. Secondly, there is the English-speaking Canadians' will to survive. Sometimes these wills are united. That is to say, the survival of French and English culture in Canada has been interdependent . . . But even during the periods when the defence of the garrison [from Americans] kept most French- and English-speaking Canadians working together, there were always some who wondered if the wrong garrison was not being armed. In French Canada there has been a continuous nationalist tradition which has insisted on the special mission of the French-Canadian community and the clear and present danger which association with English Canada presented for French-Canadian survival . . . On the other hand, there has always been in English-speaking Canada a tradition . . . which has insisted that the Canadian mission must be viewed in essentially British-Canadian terms . . . In varying degrees spokesmen for the French-speaking nationalists and the English-speaking nationalists reject . . . the validity of the concept of

---

[3] Or, in Allen Smith's more pessimistic view, the phrase references a potential, but hardly existent, condition:

> To register . . . the absence of a nationalizing idea in Canada at the exact same moment that we remark the presence of one in the United States is . . . to look for the conditions which might explain this difference. And to do that is to see in an instant that while Americans, historically speaking, possess the principal materials – a common language, shared values, etc. – necessary to the building of such an idea, Canadians patently do not. Indeed, not only do Canadians lack what is necessary to put together a totalizing idea of the classically nationalist sort so clearly evident in the United States; they have not even been able to cobble something together from what they *do* possess (1994: 10, italics in original).

political nationhood and cultural duality which has been central to the Canadian experience. They do not believe that a culturally divided community can produce a common nationalist sentiment (1971: 193–5).

The degree to which this mutual distrust and mutually exclusive sense of nationality are present in any particular historical moment and the reasons for their presence are variable and hotly debated. It is generally agreed, however, that the historical conditions of Canada's founding are crucial to an understanding of the problematic nature of the national enterprise. In brief, the differential origins, modalities, and historical specificities of the French- and English-speaking founding communities have led to very different notions of what Canada is and how it should function. The source of these distinctive circumstances is seen most clearly in the early history of the accommodations and tensions between the francophone and anglophone populations in Canada.[4]

Canada was "more fully formed by its colonial experience than the United States" (Earle and Wirth 1995: 2), experiencing first French and then British colonial rule, and not achieving the degree of self-government normally associated with a nation-state until 1867. Canada's early history is a tug-of-war between competing colonial powers and among territorial claims advanced by the English, the French, a variety of native peoples, and the Americans. The first French peoples in the part of New France now known as Canada appeared in the mid-1500s. Between 1534 and 1632, there were only a handful of French settlers, but following the reinstatement of the French in the area through the Treaty of Saint-Germain-en-Laye in 1632, the population grew to approximately 2,500 non-natives by 1633. The first communities of *Canadiens*, however, in the sense of people born in Canada of French parents, became established in the 1670s (Lahaise, in Gougeon 1994: 4).

In 1759 the French in the New World, led by Montcalm, were defeated by the English at the Battle of the Plains of Abraham. This defeat, known as "la conquête," is generally understood as a paradigmatic event for the francophone population in Canada since it, and its subsequent formalization in the Treaty of Paris in 1763, cut off the *Canadiens* from their

---

[4] This historical discussion is obviously an extremely condensed version of a considerable, and complicated, history. Although it ignores many important matters, the discussion is intended to give some sense of the differential basis for francophone and anglophone nationalisms in Canada – a topic with which few non-Canadian readers will be familiar. I draw extensively on works by Sylvia B. Bashevkin (1991), Ramsay Cook (1971, 1986), and Gilles Gougeon's *Conversations with Seven Leading Quebec Historians* (1994) in my brief overview. Further information can be found also in Behiels (1985); Berger (1970); Birch (1989); Brunet (1969); Lahaise (1971); Monet (1981); Ouellet (1980); Rocher (1992); Séguin (1968); and Trofimenkoff (1983).

originating society (e.g., Cook 1986; Gougeon 1994). Unlike the ending of ties between the United States and its country of origin, the cessation of relations between French Canada and France was undesired and seen as highly detrimental. Because the French "did not cross the Atlantic estranged from the culture that gave them birth," and because the settlers of New France understood their mission as being "to extend in the New World the French and Christian civilization whose creatures they were" (Smith 1994: 28, 26), the abrupt detachment from the mother country was experienced as a great loss of both identity and meaning. The conquest also resulted in more immediate damages to the francophone community as a number of French elites returned to France and the remaining *Canadiens* lost rights regarding their language, law, and religion.[5]

The *Canadiens* became a minority community surrounded by British North America, as Canada was then called, on one side, and the British colonies soon to become the United States of America on the other. In 1774, in part to assure that the *Canadiens* cast their lot with the former rather than the latter, the British created the Province of Quebec through the Quebec Act, thus restoring francophone rights lost following the French defeat of 1759. Partially in response to the influx of English Tories following the American Revolution, Britain then granted the Constitutional Act of 1791 which created Upper Canada (the future Ontario) for an anglophone majority and Lower Canada (Quebec) for a francophone majority. The Constitutional Act also guaranteed voting rights and therefore parliamentary inclusion for the francophone popula-tion. At this historical point, much of the French-Canadian population, including members of the remaining elite, were content with the Canadian situation for two reasons. First, France was convulsed by the Revolution of 1789 and was then under the control of a government committed to the enactment of the republican and revolutionary principles that informed the Revolution. The French Revolution symbolized all that the conservative, agrarian, clerically ruled and messianic *Canadien* society condemned. Thus British rule seemed to many the lesser evil in a choice between French rule by an unrecognizable and antithetical France and rule by the foreign, but less revolutionary, British. Second, unlike the anti-elitist and anti-clerical nature of the revolutionary French government, the British government of Upper and Lower Canada did not challenge the role of the Catholic church and the established elite in Lower (French) Canada. At times, the French loss to Britain was even beneficently referred to by the francophone popula-

---

[5] The exact number of French-Canadian elites who fled following the conquest, and the meaning of this flight for the *Canadien* community, is debated (e.g., Gougeon 1994).

tion as the "glorious defeat" because of its function as a protective bulwark against the terrors of revolutionary France (Lahaise in Gougeon 1994: 5; Cook 1971: 103).

However, as time passed the francophones became an increasing minority in Canada and were stymied in their attempts to legislate an autonomous French Catholic society in Quebec. Increasingly restive, and spurred on by the new French Revolution of 1830, francophone *Canadiens* escalated a series of demonstrations and protests into final culmination in the rebellions of 1837–8. This led to the creation of a single Province of Canada as the British retaliated against the *Canadiens* by subsuming their identity within the larger anglophone majority. The Union of 1840 was important because it constructed the minority status of the French Canadians within Canada and encouraged the ever greater influence of the Catholic church (Bernard, in Gougeon 1994: 20–1; Cook 1971).

Finally, however, the British North America Act produced the Dominion of Canada in 1867 as a relatively autonomous and independent state created out of the four eastern provinces. Although the "French-Canadian population of Quebec saw the Act as a pact between two nations [the "English" and the *Canadiens*] . . . the Anglo-Canadian population saw it more as a pact of different provinces uniting for common economic benefits" (Tiryakian and Nevitte 1985: 77). The *Canadiens* understood Confederation as the construction of a bilingual and binational state – the union of two "races," or separate "nations" joined in equal partnership. This understanding of the essential bipartite nature of French and English contributions to the new Dominion was undercut by an almost immediate recognition of both the francophone population's and Quebec's minority status and by the denial of the rights of Catholic French Canadians outside of Quebec.[6] However, the conferral of full provincial status to the traditionally majority francophone area of Quebec altered the horizon of possibilities for French-Canadian autonomy within Canada. The events of 1867 thus mark the beginning of francophone understandings of Quebec's provincial status as the means to preserve the French-Canadian way of life in religion, language, avocation, and law (Bélanger, in Gougeon 1994: 29), and, eventually, although much later, through economic development, social welfare, and the nationalization of the energy industry as well.

[6] The issue of schooling became a particular sore point. In Manitoba, New Brunswick, and Ontario various tensions arose as Catholic schools (usually French) were refused public subsidy and the French language was outlawed in public schools. Ironically, the Constitution Act made education a provincial domain and contained a clause allowing for the expenditure of public funds in support of confessional schools at the behest of the *English* (Protestants) in Quebec who feared the Catholic French majority would compromise their rights.

Louis Riel, central Métis figure of the North-West rebellion, during which he served as the provisional head of the Red River settlement, was hanged on November 16, 1885. Riel's belief in and actions on behalf of the Catholic faith and the French-Canadian presence in Manitoba made him a hero in Quebec (Stanley 1988). His death was understood by many French Canadians as a martyrdom,[7] and thus became a catalyst for a broader and more radical French-Canadian nationalism, particularly in terms of the explicitly anti-federalist stance that has marked it since this period (Bélanger, in Gougeon 1994: 34–5; Bashevkin 1991). Although separatist notions of Quebec independence were rare, or at least considered wildly impractical in this period, ideas of French-Canadian autonomy within the federal structure began to become ever more prominent, particularly as the notion was developed by Honoré Mercier in the 1880s (Bélanger, in Gougeon 1994: 37).[8] Cultural nationalism, the idea of the survival of an autonomous and self-determining French-Canadian society within a Canadian federal structure, then dominated francophone nationalist thought for another sixty years (Cook 1986: 14).

The development of French-Canadian, and later Quebec, nationalism in the period since Dominion has hardly been straightforward. A wide variety of ideas about the relationship between Quebec and what has been called the ROC or "Rest of Canada" (Atwood 1995: 15), about Quebec's role in relation to the francophone population outside Quebec, and about the appropriate political mechanisms for enacting any of these ideas have been promulgated at various historical points. Pan-Canadian nationalism, although generally defined in Anglo-Canadian terms, has been advanced by a number of French Canadians, including Prime Ministers Laurier, Trudeau, and Chrétien. Leading Quebec intellectuals of the turn of the century, including Henri Bourassa and Olivar Asselin, subscribed to just such a vision of a united Canada within which a strong Quebec existed until they realized that "Canada for the English-speaking population was not autonomous of its ties to the British Empire (in the Boer War and in World War I) . . . [and] they turned their nationalist orientation to that of Quebec" (Tiryakian and Nevitte 1985: 79). Canada's participation in the British

---

[7] In 1992, a resolution was adopted unanimously by the House of Commons and the Senate recognizing "the unique and historic role of Louis Riel as a founder of Manitoba and his contribution in the development of Confederation" (Clark 1994: 81).

[8] Although a separatist ideology was drawn up by Jules-Paul Tardivel between 1885 and 1890, stimulated in part by incidents of provincial decisions not to allow Catholic francophone schools to operate and, more particularly, by Riel's execution. Tardivel's vision of an ultramontane fundamentalist Quebec nation independent of Canada did not attract much contemporary support, but was influential for the later development of separatist Quebec nationalism (Bélanger, in Gougeon 1994: 30–4).

conflict in South Africa and the conscription crisis of 1917 galvanized the further development of Quebec nationalism and even separatism. The conscription crisis so alienated Quebec that the Francoeur motion "to accept the breaking of the 1867 confederation agreement" at least symbolically raised the specter of dissolution of the federal pact of 1867 (Linteau, Durocher, and Robert 1983: 509; Trofimenkoff 1982). The development of francophone nationalism in this period is best understood within the enduring context of English-Canadian commitment to the Empire: "the imperial relationship represented a fundamental barrier between English and French Canadians" (see Cook [1971: 147], in his discussion of the English-Canadian historian A. R. M. Lower; also Trudeau [(1968) 1980] for a similar understanding of the effect of English-Canadian nationalism on French-Canadian nationalism in later periods).[9]

The remainder of the century has seen the cyclical diminishment and rebirth of the phenomenon of francophone nationalism through a long series of political and cultural events punctuated by the redefinition of "les Canadiens" into the "French Canadians" and then the "Québécois" (see Jenson [1993: 337] on the process by which "choices of names configure the political opportunity structure"). The rising and falling importance of francophone nationalism and the different ways it has been expressed can be seen in the eighty-year period since the World War I conscription crisis galvanized French-Canadian separatism: the calm of the post-conscription period followed by a radicalization of French-Canadian nationalism during the Great Depression; the emergence of Duplessis's Union Nationale in the mid-1930s, "the first real political party that was deeply Québécois" (Desrosiers, in Gougeon 1994: 72); the second conscription crisis of World War II; the rejection by large numbers of French-Canadian elites of French-Canadian nationalism as a conservative, Catholic relic in the 1950s; the Quiet Revolution of the 1960s, with its rallying cry of "Maîtres chez nous" (Masters in our own house), that transformed Quebec's old agrarian, conservative, and deeply religious society into a progressive, secular, urban, industrial welfare state (Behiels 1985); the 1969 Official Languages Act that made Canada, "at least symbolically," an officially bilingual country (Laferrière 1988: 551); the Front de Libération du Québec's separatist militancy culminating in the kidnapping of two politicians (and the murder of one) (Fournier 1984); Trudeau's pronouncement that Quebec nationalism was dead (Balthazar, in Gougeon 1994: 113; Trudeau [1968] 1980; Clarkson

---

[9] Lower felt that the "'colonial mentality' of English Canadians" was hindering Canadian national development, and that if only "English Canadians could become as 'North American' in their outlook as French Canadians, a large step towards a true Canadianism would be taken" (Cook 1971: 147).

and McCall 1990); the renewal of the Quiet Revolution's goals after the 1976 election; the rejection of the 1980 referendum on sovereignty followed by a ten-year period in which nationalism was "becalmed" and the idea of "even limited independence" was "hastily buried" (Cook 1986: 16; Desrosiers, in Gougeon 1994: 94–5); the Meech Lake constitutional negotiations; and, finally, the 1995 referendum on separatism that ended with yet another inconclusive vote on Quebec separatism.[10]

Although this exceedingly sketchy overview of English/French relations and the development of Quebec nationalism hardly does the topic justice, the main points for a consideration of literature and the nation-building process are threefold. First, francophone nationalism and pan-Canadian (English) nationalism have become mutually exclusive as the former has become Quebec nationalism,[11] that is, a territorial (and some would say ethnic)[12] nationalism irrevocably rooted in foundational notions of autonomous provincial authority and a concomitantly weak federal structure. In stark contrast is the pan-Canadian "conviction that [federal] state intervention, direction, and even ownership must be seen as fundamental" and that, therefore, provincial autonomy must be subsumed to the federal

[10] On October 30, 1995, 50.6 percent of Quebecois voted "no" to the independence referendum, 49.4 percent voted "yes" (Farnsworth 1995b:3). In 1980, 60 percent of Quebecois voted "no" to a differently worded, but broadly similar, proposal that asked for permission for the Quebec provincial leadership to begin independence negotiations with the federal government.

[11] Certainly the history of francophone–anglophone relations before and after the territorialization of the former has been marked by suspicion and dislike, sometimes virulent, sometimes subtle, on both sides. Cook (1986) presents a strong argument on the failings of English Canadians to understand French Canadians, Johnson (1994: 405) an equally strong argument about the "tribal anglophobia" and "myth of the ethnic state" that dominate Quebecois history and thought.

[12] Advancing the argument are, for example, Johnson (1994) and newspaper reports that Parizeau and other separatist leaders blamed non-francophone ethnic groups for the defeat of the separatist proposal in the post-referendum period:

> The Quebec separatist manifesto speaks glowingly of ethnic pluralism and diversity. It . . . refers to Quebec's English speakers as "part of the founding people of the new Quebec." It is part of the discourse of a nationalism based on territory, meant to differentiate Quebec separatists from ethnic nationalists . . . Yet . . . after his separatists had narrowly lost in the Quebec independence referendum, Premier Jacques Parizeau . . . revealed some of the fault-lines between territorial and ethnic nationalism in the separatist movement . . . nearly 20 percent of Quebec's population . . . are not old-stock Quebecers, but English speakers or immigrants whose basic language is neither English nor French. This relatively large multicultural community – English Canadians, Jews, Italians, Spanish, Portuguese, Chinese, Haitians – voted overwhelmingly against secession . . . Mr. Parizeau . . . urged his followers . . . "Let us talk about us – 60 percent who voted in favor" of separation, he said. "We will have our own revenge, and we will have our own country" (Farnsworth 1995a: 10).

For positions refuting the allegations of ethnic nationalism in Quebec separatist sentiment see Gougeon (1994, especially Balthazar 108–9). See also Breton (1988) for a larger discussion of the ethnic and civic components of Quebec nationalism.

project (Cook 1986: 121; Bashevkin 1991). Second, the question of the relationship between Quebec and the rest of Canada is not yet resolved. Quebec nationalism has ebbed and surged, with separatist sentiment ever more prominent in periods of strong nationalism.

Third, and most importantly for my purposes, cultural practices, most centrally language – thus including literature, literary criticism, and canon formation – were among the earliest matters to be "nationalized" within the two separate communities of English- and French-speaking Canada. The historical and persisting tension between pan-Canadian and francophone nationalisms has meant that the relationship between canon formation and nation-building has been enacted at what is, at least officially, the *sub*national level. Quebec literature and the Quebec literary tradition are generally understood by the francophone population as originating within the French tradition (e.g., Lemire 1970; Ethier-Blais 1973; Cagnon 1986), as deeply tied to issues of French-Canadian development and nationalism (e.g., Cotnam 1983; Dufault 1991), and as not necessarily closely tied to English-Canadian literature and its development. Canon formation in Quebec has thus occurred under significantly different conditions and has developed in significantly different directions than has English-Canadian canon formation.[13] Even a brief history of French-Canadian canon formation leaves no doubt as to the nationalist assumptions at the core of literary development in francophone Canada.

Early literary criticism in Quebec, as established by Fr. Henri-Raymond Casgrain and perhaps best exemplified by Mgr. Camille Roy, was focused almost exclusively on content, considering literature "to be essentially utilitarian and functional, a vehicle for ideology and a tool for propaganda" (Shouldice 1979: 4; Bayard 1991). Casgrain, Roy, and Roy's disciples dominated the "official" view of French-Canadian literature in the nineteenth and first half of the twentieth century. In this view, French-Canadian literature was, and should be, founded on a set of interrelated precepts including "Catholic morality, fidelity to the French heritage, nationalistic fervor, and an idealized, romantic conception of traditional farm life" (Shouldice 1979: 4). Casgrain makes clear the nationalist orientation of these early critics when he writes "notre littérature sera nationale ou elle ne sera pas" (our literature shall be national or it shall not be) (quoted in Bayard 1991: 125).

The *romans de la fidélité* and *romans du terroir* (novels of fidelity to tradition and novels of the land or earth), novels by writers such as Philippe

---

[13] Bayard notes the distinction between the "Anglo-American concept of canonization and the French definition of legitimization," to begin with, and goes on to remind the reader that "criticism in Quebec is historically grounded in cultural determinants" (1991: 124, 125).

Aubert de Gaspé (*Les Anciens Canadiens*, 1863), Patrice Lacombe (*La Terre paternelle*, 1846), Laure Conan (*Angéline de Montbrun*, 1884), and Louis Hémone (*Maria Chapdelaine*, 1916) emphasized these themes through their presentations of traditional French-Canadian life and the importance of its preservation (Dufault 1991: 16–17; Shouldice 1979). This kind of rural novel, and the attendant criticism valorizing the rural novel, dominated French-Canadian novel writing until the mid-twentieth century.[14] Another aspect of the same insistence upon tradition and preservation was the strong emphasis in the French-Canadian literary world on the preservation of the French language.[15] Ringuet's *Trente Arpents*, published in 1938, is considered by many to be the finest example of the rural novel (Dionne 1988: 1229). Unlike earlier authors in the genre, "Ringuet depicts neither an idyllic agrarian life nor a wholly adverse urban existence" and thus may be seen as a transition figure in Quebec writing, moving the novel from a conservative to more open genre (Cagnon 1986: 29; Dufault 1991: 17).

Both the focus of Quebec writers and the critical understanding of French-Canadian writing shifted during the 1930s to post-World War II period. More broadly humanistic principles of literary evaluation were advanced by a new group of critics, some of whom were associated with the journal *La Relève* founded in 1934 (later called *La Nouvelle Relève*). Critics such as René Garneau, Roger Duhamel, and Guy Sylvestre – although not revolutionary – focused on both content and aesthetics in their literary criticism, unlike either the traditional critics or the earlier "exotics," and applied a more "universal" perspective to the evaluation of French-Canadian writing (Shouldice 1979: 7; Dionne 1988). The focus in many novels shifted during this time from the "collective salvation" envisioned in the rural novels to "individuals searching for themselves" in the psychological novels of writers such as Robert Charbonneau[16] and André Langevin

[14] Shouldice notes, however, that it "would be wrong . . . to regard Mgr. Roy's hegemony as being total. Throughout the history of Quebec, and particularly after the founding of the 'Institut canadien de Montréal' in 1844, there has always been an undercurrent of free-thinking in some intellectual circles, and the minority, nonconformist view has always been given some degree of expression" (1979: 5). Shouldice cites the writer–critics Henri d'Arles, Marcel Dugas, and Robert de Roquebrune as part of the circle of "exotic" critics and the journalists Olivar Asselin and Jules Fournier as party to attacks on "the regressive tendencies of ultramontane nationalism in both politics and literature" (1979: 6).

[15] Institutions such as the "Ecole littéraire de Montréal," the "Société du parler français," and the literary magazine *Le Terroir*, and proponents such as Abbé Lionel Groulx, promoted the preservation of the French language, the Catholic church, and the nationalist ethos through regionalist literature (Cagnon 1986: 18–19).

[16] Cagnon (1986: 42) describes Charbonneau's *Connaissance du personnage* (1944) as "a seminal work" that "definitively refutes the ideological, moralizing prose that for so long had been called novelistic writing" in French Canada.

and the transformation of French-Canadian society in the first novels of "sociological analysis" by writers such as Roger Lemelin, Gabrielle Roy, and Yves Thériault (Dionne 1988: 1230).

In 1948, the artist Paul-Emile Borduas issued his "intransigently anti-conformist" *Refus global* rallying "artists, poets, and novelists in a call for total liberation in all domains" (Cagnon 1986: 142). The effect of the *Refus global*, in combination with the many changes that were starting to transform agrarian, Catholic, conservative French Canada into urban, secular, progressive Quebec at the end of the 1950s, revitalized francophone Canadian literature. French-Canadian literature began to open up, incorporating preoccupations with form and structure, experiments with techniques of the French *nouveau roman* (new novel), and a host of alternatives to the heretofore required religion, realism, and the rural (Dionne 1988; Cagnon 1986: 48–51). This literary expansionism and rejection of the ultramontane authoritarianism dominant in the conservative French-Canadian tradition included a new interest in language. The most radical aspect of this focus on language was the use of the Quebec patois *joual*, by the *Parti pris* writers in their eponymous journal. Use of the patois symbolized a linguistic rejection of the colonizing French, thus linking the social revolution to the linguistic (Cagnon 1986: 50–1, 142).[17] By the beginning of the 1960s, the Quiet Revolution has begun and "the poets named their country: no longer Canada, but Québec" (Dionne 1988: 1230).

In the 1960s and 1970s, the novels of Quebec come to "question, and often refute, many of the conventional and traditional modes, values, and aims attributed to the genre" and to allow a "far greater degree of autonomy to their characters, increased flexibility to time and space, and an ambivalent openness to the architecture of the novel" (Cagnon 1986: 50). Feminist writing and a renewed sense of francophone nationalism came to fruition in a number of novels that are committed to the reawakening of interest in and orientation to a French-Canadian future that stands in stark contrast to the oppressive tradition and the "long ethnic death process" that was Quebec's historical past (Cagnon 1986: 51). The relationship between the development of nationalist sentiment and the development of a national literature is clear to these novelists, many of whose novels "have at their heart a certain apocalyptic essence in the links they establish between writing and history in Quebec" (Cagnon 1986: 51). In literary

---

[17] Cagnon notes however that the embrace of *joual* was intended "not so much to sing its praises as to expose it deliberately as a reflection of a people's loss of native language" and that the approach failed to garner much success as it limited "audience receptivity and . . . [created] resentment and confusion among the many not intimately familiar with the intentions of 'Parti pris'" (1986: 51).

theory and criticism, the 1970s saw the establishment of "Quebec's answer to structuralism – cultural semiotics" (Bayard 1991: 128) while the 1980s and early 1990s saw the advent of post-structuralism, feminism, and post-modernism (Bayard 1991: 129–30; Simon 1991: 168).

The enshrinement of literatures in the university curriculum is generally considered a strong symbol of canonical recognition (DiMaggio 1991; Lauter 1991). French-Canadian literature was not taught as an academic subject in Quebec universities until the 1950s. Programs of "specialization in French-Canadian studies were established at Laval, Montréal, McGill, Sherbrooke" and Quebec in the 1960s and 1970s (Hayne 1988: 1231). Curiously, *outside* of Quebec French-Canadian literature was taught at the undergraduate level in the 1930s or 1940s, although on a more limited scale than is now common within Quebec (Hayne 1988: 1231).

Despite vast changes in both the French-Canadian novel itself from the nineteenth to late twentieth century and in the nature of literary criticism applied to the French-Canadian novel, recent literary theorists stress the persistent centrality of the relationship between "representation and value, between literary and social configurations," between the novel and culture in Quebec (Simon 1991: 167; Bayard 1991; Lecker 1991). Literature and literary criticism in Quebec have informed not only the social, but the national: "the nationalist component has varied considerably both in kind and in intensity, but it has almost always been an important and distinctive feature of the Quebec intellectual landscape" (Shouldice 1979: 8). There is an abundance of evidence demonstrating the conscious and self-reflective nature of the national canon formation process – or the national legitimizations (see footnote 13) – that have occurred in Quebec (see, however, Ricard [1989] for a strong statement against this unproblematic equation of literature and nation; see also Godard [1990] for additional discussion on this point).

Thus the path of French-Canadian writing and Québécois canon formation diverges from the path of Canadian writing in English and the development of an English-Canadian canon. Although there is certainly interest in the *relationship between* Québécois literature and Canadian literature in English, the approach to the relationship is usually comparative, as opposed to an approach that constructs the two literatures as pieces of a single national literature. Indeed, Canadian comparative literature is now seen as an accepted and popular field of study, with especially strong programs at the universities of Sherbrooke and Alberta (Hayne 1988: 1231). One indicator of this usual separation is the now famous 1978 Calgary Conference list of the ten "most important Canadian novels," that most formally named the emerging Canadian canon. The only French-

Canadian novel to be included was Gabrielle Roy's *The Tin Flute* (see footnote 21).

As the "primary thrust of *Canadian* nationalism has been predominantly a British-Canadian affair" (Tiryakian and Nevitte 1985: 78, italics added) the nationalist project of *Canadian* (rather than Québécois) canon formation has also been predominantly English-Canadian. Thus the study of "Canadian" canon formation is in fact the study of Anglo-Canadian canon formation with only occasional references to francophone literature.

Understanding the context of Canadian canon formation as situated within the enduring tension between a French-Canadian nationalism oriented toward "fending off the threat of assimilation by a conqueror," on the one hand, and an English-Canadian nationalism oriented toward "differentiating . . . [Canada] from nations with which it shares many cultural characteristics," i.e., Britain and the United States, on the other, provides the groundwork for considering the second major difficulty with the national canon formation project in Canada, the *supra*national identification of the English-Canadian majority with the British Commonwealth for much of Canada's history (Cook 1986: 14).

The British Commonwealth, pan-Canadian nationalism, and the demand for a national literature in Canada

> For I believe, in Britain's Empire, and
> In Canada, its true and loyal son,
> Who yet shall rise to greatness, and shall stand
> At England's shoulder helping her to guard
> True liberty throughout a faithless world.
>
> > General Brock, the loyalist hero of Charles Mair's *Tecumseh: A Drama*, 1886.

Nineteenth- and early twentieth-century Canadian identity was dominantly anglophone and was rooted in Empire and Commonwealth, not Nation. British settlers in Canada were not driven by the same motives as British settlers in America. The latter "arrived alienated from their society [having] left their land in protest" (Smith 1994: 28). In contrast, the "principal and overriding fact shaping the outlook of the English who first came to the northern part of North America was their reverence for continuity, tradition, and properly constituted authority"; they wished to "recreate . . . a society governed by modalities the very image and transcript of those at the heart of the British constitution" (Smith 1994: 29). The founding populations of the future United States and the future Canada thus began with very different outlooks. In addition, the Canadian commitment to

Britain was further encouraged by the American Revolution of 1776 and the concomitant influx of Tory Loyalists to Canada. The government agency Statistics Canada (1989) has estimated that 37,000 erstwhile American Loyalists moved northward into Canada during the time of the Revolutionary War.[18] This surge in population was composed of a group defined by its explicit opposition to American notions of anti-British ideology and independence from British rule. The Loyalist immigrants left the United States in order to remain British; they were not looking to trade American nationalism for Canadian nationalism, but were eager to maintain their ties to Britain (see Lipset [1990] for an extended discussion of the Loyalist effect on Canadian development).

Thus Canada remained both formally and culturally a British possession until the twentieth century. In World Wars I and II, Canada entered war with Britain, seeing herself as not just allied through loyalty, but partnered with the beleaguered British isle – thus triggering the ire of the Canadian francophone population. The legal, political, and symbolic ties between Canada and Britain were longer and stronger than those between the United States and Britain, and their dissolution much less definitive. To the extent that Canadian nationalism existed and was even prominent in the nineteenth century (e.g., the Canada First Movement of 1868) it was a nationalism defined as much by its imperial context and connection as by its Canadian-ness.

While the Revolutionary War in the United States was both an expression of and an impetus for a separate cultural as well as political existence, Canadian independence was a much later, less violent, and less absolute affair. Promising "life, liberty, and the pursuit of happiness" to its citizens, the newly created United States of America explicitly affirmed the principles underlying its recent revolution in the constitution ratified in 1789. Almost eighty years later, provincial unification or "Confederation" in the new Dominion of Canada in 1867 promised "peace, order, and good government." Rather than being submitted to the provinces for ratification, the Canadian constitution was sent to London to be enacted by the British parliament and proclaimed by the Queen.

Canada's commitment to the British Empire has meant that while the United States pursued a policy of isolationism throughout long periods of its history, Canada has seen itself and has acted – at least internationally – as a member of the British Empire. Canada's formal and legal relationship with Britain lasted centuries longer than those of the United States – something few Americans realize. Canadian citizenship was not legally distinct

---

[18] Estimates of the number of Loyalists who entered Canada during this period vary. Lahaise, for example, places the number of arriving Loyalists between 40,000 and 45,000 (Gougeon 1994: 13).

from British citizenship until 1947. Canada did not have a distinctive flag of its own until the mid-1960s.

It was not until the mid-twentieth century that rising Canadian nationalism sparked a desire to dissolve the remaining formal and legal connections to Britain. At that time the processes of deciding to adopt a national flag and selecting a design for the flag (the Maple Leaf was adopted in 1965)[19] simultaneously demonstrated and stimulated a powerful wave of Canadian nationalism. Canadian separation from Britain was still not completed in the 1960s, however. Canada did not request that the British parliament give up formal, if unexercised, control over Canada until 1982.[20] Even now, Canada maintains symbolic and ritualistic ties to Britain that have yet to be severed.

Given this long-lasting Canadian connection to Britain and the historical identification of most Canadians with the British Empire, it is not surprising that the Canadian desire for and establishment of a viable national literature occurred much later than it did in the United States. For, as Neil argues, "the genesis of a local literature . . . has almost always been contemporaneous with the development of a truly national sentiment" (1975: ix). Despite various short-lived bursts of enthusiasm for a nationalism that envisioned the development of Canadian interests only within the framework of the Commonwealth, most Canadians lacked "a truly national sentiment" until the twentieth century.

In the aftermath of World War II, however, the first stirrings of sustained Canadian interest in Canadian literature and the first signs of a coherent literary nationalism began to surface. Older notions of Canadian nationalism as simply the commitment to a more equal relationship with Great Britain *within* the united British Empire began to give way (Cook 1986: 123) and the connection between Canadian independence and Canadian culture began to be made explicitly. In 1949, the Canadian government requested that Vincent Massey lead an investigation of "education, the mass media, [and] the nature of cultural affairs" in Canada (New 1989). The 1951 report on "National Development in the Arts, Letters, and Science," more commonly known as the Massey Report, had an immediate and striking impact on Canadian culture. Action was most visible on the federal front. The National Library was established and various long-term literary projects such as the *Literary History of Canada* (published in 1965) were undertaken. Private-sector support for a burgeoning Canadian

---

[19] Interestingly, *in 1948*, Duplessis "decreed by Order in Council – it took some time before he could have this measure ratified through legislation – that the fleur-de-lys would be the flag of Quebec" (Desrosiers, in Gougeon 1994: 80).

[20] Of course, the delayed repatriation of the Canadian constitution was due in large part to provincial wrangling with the federal government for increased concessions.

national culture was also forthcoming. The Canada Council was established by two individual philanthropists in 1957 to help support and
develop the arts in Canada. The McClelland and Stewart New Canadian
Library Series which focused on the publication, and re-publication for
those out-of-print, noteworthy Canadian academic paperbacks began
appearing in 1957.

By the 1960s, Canadian mobilization against British and especially
American cultural domination was in full swing. The Canadian centennial
in 1967 provided additional impetus to the twin processes of nation-building and the development of a national culture. Telefilm Canada was created
by the federal government in 1967, joining the Canadian Broadcasting
Corporation and the National Film Board. Also in 1967, the federal
government began funding the Canada Council. In addition to federal and
provincial financial incentives to increase the Canadian content of culture,
government regulation helped to control the "Canadian-ness" of radio,
television, and magazine content (Daniels 1988; Bashevkin 1991). The legislative fight for Canadian content in the mass media occurred within the
context of the construction of an officially bilingual Canada. The Royal
Commission on Bilingualism and Biculturalism reported its findings in the
1960s on the difficulties encountered by French speakers, resulting in the
1969 Official Languages Act making Canada bilingual (Laferrière 1988:
550–1).

Pan-Canadian nationalism reached its zenith in the period of the late
1960s and 1970s, despite the leadership of Trudeau, an avowed anti-nation-
alist (see Trudeau [1968] 1980; Cook 1971: 26; Bashevkin 1988; Clarkson
and McCall 1990). The ideology of pan-Canadian nationalism was rooted
in the vision of a strong federal state whose preeminent powers were needed
to stabilize and unify the diverse provincial interests and east–west tensions
of Canadian regionalism and to resist American imperialism and the
north–south continentalist threat. Furthermore, the interventionist federal
state was to serve as a key distinguishing characteristic sharply delineating
Canadian public life, with its emphasis on public/private initiatives and the
collective good, from the laissez-faire market principles and individualistic
orientation of the United States (Atwood 1982; Bashevkin 1991; Barlow
and Campbell 1993).

Despite the growing interest in Canadian nationalism and in the cultural
expression thereof in the 1960s, the project of national canon formation was
hardly institutionalized in this period. Lucas published a study showing
that in 1967–8, eight colleges and universities – Carleton, Manitoba,
McGill, New Brunswick, Queen's, Toronto, Western and York – offered
"only a total of ten [undergraduate courses] in Canadian literature and nine

combining it with other literatures, out of a total of 250 or so courses. At the same time these schools offered fourteen courses in American literature and seven and twenty-two in which it was combined with Canadian and British literature respectively" (Lucas 1971: 58). The situation of Canadian literature began to improve rapidly in this period, however, and by 1970–71 a "survey of the offerings in literature programmes in twenty-seven Canadian universities . . . reveals [that] of the 1,119 undergraduate courses given . . . ninety-four were American literature and fifty-nine Canadian" (Lucas 1971: 58).

Lucas blamed the disregard for Canadian literature both on a Canadian lack of interest in its own literature and on the preponderance of Americans on Canadian teaching faculties. Daniels (1988) also reflected on this influence, noting that in the ten years of Canadian university expansion, from 1964 to 1973, much of the new faculty was recruited from the United States and brought with them a belief in the superiority of American critical traditions. This situation was in contrast to a previous domination of Canadian faculties by *British* academics (Surette 1991: 23). Not only has the disproportionate number of American faculty at Canadian universities since waned, but many of those who remained in Canada have become Canadian citizens (Daniels 1988).

In 1978 the now "'infamous' Calgary Conference on the Canadian Novel" was held (Keith 1986: 155; Steele 1982; Lecker 1990). The conference provoked a great deal of explicit debate about Canadian canon formation. The conference organizers surveyed potential attendees by mail prior to the conference, asking them to choose "1) the most 'important' one hundred works of [Canadian] fiction . . . 2) the most important ten [Canadian] novels[21] . . . and 3) the most important ten [Canadian] works of various genres" (Steele 1982: 150). Although many people were upset at the notion of such explicit evaluation and canonization – with its concomitant implicit *exclusion* of the bulk of Canadian writing – the conference stimulated debate on the state of Canadian literature and helped to further

---

[21] "List B," the list of the ten most important novels, was composed of the following (Steele 1982: 153–4):

Buckler	*The Mountain and the Valley*
Davies	*Fifth Business*
Laurence	*The Stone Angel*
Laurence	*The Diviners*
MacLennan	*The Watch That Ends the Night*
Mitchell	*Who Has Seen the Wind*
Richler	*The Apprenticeship of Duddy Kravitz*
Ross	*As For Me and My House*
Roy	*The Tin Flute* [originally published as *Bonheur d'occasion*]
Watson	*The Double Hook*

institutionalize the teaching and historical rediscovery of Canadian literature (Ross 1982). McClelland and Stewart's "New Canadian Classics" series, for example, stemmed from the conference. Malcolm Ross, then editor of the New Canadian Library Series with over one hundred titles, describes the point of the lists not as a desire for exclusionary canonization, but as an attempt to "widen the possibilities for the serious study of Canadian writing, create an interest in writers hitherto unread, and for the practicing contemporary novelist, enlarge and enliven the reading public" (Steele 1982: 138). Nonetheless, one of the main effects of the conference was to institutionalize both the subject of "Can Lit" in colleges and universities and the likely content of the syllabi of those courses.

Anglophone Canadian canon formation occurred in a situation both similar to and very different from the situation the United States faced in the 1800s. Like the literature of the United States, Canadian national literature needed to define itself as independent from Mother England. Building a Canadian literature, and a Canadian nation, meant rejecting the English model – as American literary nationalists had rejected it one hundred years earlier. Unlike the American situation, however, Canadian uniqueness could not simply be found in the embrace of the New World and the rejection of the Old World. Canada had a second powerful presence from which it needed independence – the United States itself.

Margaret Atwood (1982) makes an explicit comparison between the activities in the Canadian literary world in the 1960s and those in the American literary world in the post-Revolutionary periods. In writing about her graduate study at Harvard in the early 1960s Atwood noted how her exposure to the history of American literature illuminated her understanding of the struggle for a viable national literature which was then occurring in Canada:

I found myself reading my way through excerpts from Puritan sermons, political treatises of the time of the American revolution, and anguished essays of the early nineteenth century, bemoaning the inferiority not only of American literary offerings but of American dress design, and wondering when the great American genius would come along. It sounded familiar. Nobody pretended that any of this was superb literature. All they pretended was that it was necessary for an understanding of the United States of America, and it was (1982: 382).

They [Americans] weren't groping for their identities; they had gone through all that, I found, back in the post-revolutionary decades, with symptoms very much like ours – the short-run, little-read magazines, the petty literary squabbles, the adulation of foreign writers, the conflict between "native" and "cosmopolitan" schools, the worry over cultural imperialism . . . why is there no great American writer, etc. (1982: 87).

Canadian worry about national identity and the lack of a national canon in the 1960s echoed American self-consciousness regarding the same fears and lacunae in the early 1800s.

Lloyd (1987) discusses a similar situation in Ireland regarding the development of a national Irish literature. He argues that "the *de facto* political identity forged by France and America in their military struggles" (1987: 63) stands in contrast to the situation in countries without an identity-forging revolution, such as Ireland – and Canada to an even greater extent. Without a "*unifying* concept of Irish [or Canadian] identity" defined by the revolutionary process, the development of a national literature is stymied. An authentic voice and clearly articulated vision of national identity is common only in "a national literature uninterrupted by [prolonged] colonial power" (Lloyd 1987: 63). In Canada the situation was especially constraining since Canada's colonial status was largely voluntary.

The American threat

The final threat to the Canadian nationalist canon formation project was – and is – the ever present behemoth to the south. In addition to serving as a serious and sustained threat to Canadian economic and cultural independence, however, the United States has served as perhaps the greatest single spur to Canadian nationalism. Historically, the United States has been an ally in the Canadian attempt to distinguish itself from Britain and as a natural counterbalance to the weight of the British Empire. The process of defining itself as "North American," as similar to the United States rather than similar to Britain, helped Canada to become independent of Britain and British interests. By generating a North American identity that distinguished Canada from Britain and provided a rationale for looking away from the Commonwealth, the United States stimulated English-Canadian nationalism's vision of Canada as prominent on its own terms, rather than through its position in the Commonwealth. Anglophone Canadian history thus exhibits an enduring tension between continentalist ideas of Canada's true identity as North American and aligned with the United States, on the one hand, and an enduring imperial nationalism in which Canada's British connections provide for Canada's international prominence, on the other hand. The relative dominance of these ideas has fluctuated historically, often in response to whether Britain or the United States was perceived as most threatening at the time.

In a curious tension with its role as an ally against Britain, however, is the United States' role of threatening giant – a role famously referred to by

Trudeau.[22] Even in this role, however, the United States has sometimes served rather than undermined Canadian nationalist interests. In its role as the "other" against which Canada is defined and from whom Canada must be protected, the United States has mobilized Canadian nationalist sentiment in a uniquely powerful fashion (Bashevkin 1991; Cook 1971). The American threat, the overwhelming flood of American ideas, American television, American magazines, American money, and American corporations has often been one of the most effective triggers of nationalist sentiment – and nationalist legislation (e.g., see Bashevkin's [1991] analysis of the enactment of the C-58 bill and the [unsuccessful] battle against the free trade agreements).

Despite its occasional unintended and supportive effects on Canadian nationalism, the sheer size of the United States and its manifest destiny expansiveness have generally posed a serious threat to Canadian cultural, economic, and even political independence since the 1700s. The United States represented a military threat to Canada's continued existence throughout Canada's early history. Repeated territorial battles were waged along the then undefined "longest (unprotected) border in the world." French dreams of recovering lost territory fueled early skirmishes, as did a number of European conflicts that spilled over into the North American colonies, e.g., the War of the Spanish Succession between 1702 and 1713 and the War of the Austrian Succession, also known as King George's War, between 1739 and 1748. One of the most serious incursions into Canadian territory was the American invasion of Canada during the War of 1812, which resulted in the determination of the present shape of the United States–Canada border during the peace negotiations that ended in the Treaty of Ghent in 1814 (Berton 1980, 1988; Stanley 1983). Although the threat of military engulfment faded by the end of the nineteenth century, other kinds of American dominance have threatened Canada since.

In more recent history, the American threat to Canada has largely manifested itself as economic, involving issues of both investment and trade, and cultural. In the cultural arena, the pattern of events from the late 1800s to the 1960s remained essentially the same: "American culture, entering the country, generated concern, anxiety, and a search for ways to ensure that it did not overwhelm Canadian culture" (Smith 1994: 105), although the

---

[22] In a speech at the National Press Building in Washington DC on March 25, 1969, then Canadian Prime Minister Trudeau said: "living next to you [the US] is in some ways like sleeping with an elephant: no matter how friendly and even-tempered the beast, one is affected by every twitch and grunt" (quoted in *New Canadian Quotations* [1987: 54], edited by John Robert Colombo, Edmonton: Hurtig Publishers).

intensity of response increased dramatically over time.[23] There has been a substantial history of anti-American rhetoric in Canada, particularly in the arena of culture and particularly in the 1960s and 1970s. The size and aggressiveness not only of the American economy generally (e.g., Innis 1956), but especially of the American "culture industries" such as publishing, movie-making, and television, has, in various periods and among certain audiences, stimulated a strong sense of fear about the "Americanization" of Canada.[24] Bashevkin (1991) analyzes one of the signal successes of the Canadian cultural nationalists, their enactment of the C-58 bill which controlled certain American cultural exportation, and compares the successful enactment of the C-58 bill to the cultural nationalists' failure to block the free trade agreements. The various free trade agreements are seen by many left-wing nationalists as the final triumph of the United States over what remains of an independent Canada. Barlow and Campbell (1993), for example, feel that the very existence of any meaningful unit called "Canada" is well on the way to destruction once the North American Free Trade Agreement (NAFTA) is signed. NAFTA is seen by these authors and their popular books, *Take Back the Nation* and *Take Back the Nation 2*, published in 1991 and 1993 respectively, as simply an American takeover of Canada and destruction of all that makes Canada unique.

This long history of tension between an American identity and a British identity, of both reaction against and acceptance of the United States, is visible in the canon formation process. Canada was both Old and New World, and its identity lay in *both* the rejection and the incorporation of some aspects of each. Keith describes the evolution of Canadian literature as initially developing "as a continuation of what was being produced in Great Britain" but then having "to define itself against the American tradition as it developed in the United States" with an eventual maturity "as a distinctive literature related to but independent of both parent and neighbor" (1985: x).[25] Canadian canon formation occurred within the doubly

[23] Smith notes a change in the 1960s, however, as "new profit-oriented cultural entrepreneurs" became interested in "assistance (or at least a free hand) in bringing . . . [American culture] in" to Canada (Smith 1994: 106). He argues that this results in a struggle between those Canadians trying for the "traditional" government help in keeping Canadian culture protected from American imports and those trying to use the government to help them sell American culture in Canada (Smith 1994: 106).

[24] Cook (1971) cites the historians Donald Creighton (*Canada's First Century*) and, especially, Harold Adams Innis (*The Fur Trade in Canada*, *The Cod Fisheries*) as central figures in the mid-twentieth century underscoring both the historic and contemporary American threat to Canadian independence.

[25] Surette somewhat sarcastically details the competing cultural ideologies of Canadian canonization: a desire for British culture continuity and American rupture versus those who "still view British cultural hegemony with greater alarm than they do the apprehended American threat" (1991: 21).

constrained territory of a reaction against both British tradition and American cultural exportation (or "American imperialism" as many Canadians were to charge). Canadian response to American cultural exportation often took the form of government intervention: "The strongest influence making for a government presence in the cultural realm was . . . always . . . the United States" (Smith 1994: 104).

The role of government in Canadian literary development

The development of a Canadian national culture differed from the development of an American national culture because of the role played by the government in Canada. The Canadian government has provided, relative to the American case, enormous amounts of money to develop and support a national culture. In 1990–91 the combined expenditures for culture of federal, provincial, and municipal governments totaled $5.9 *billion*.[26] The federal share of that total was $2.9 billion, of which 77 percent was allocated directly to the operating budgets of cultural departments and agencies, e.g., the Canadian Broadcasting Corporation (Statistics Canada 1994: 622). However, financial pressures on the federal government and attempts to reduce the deficit have led to a decline in federal government culture funding. Federal spending on culture in 1995–6 will be $2.4 billion (Fagan 1996).

One of the largest government-supported culture agencies is the Canada Council, founded in 1957 to support artists and arts organizations in Canada. Originally funded by moneys from two individuals, the Council began receiving parliamentary funds in 1967. In 1992 the Council received $106 million from the Department of Communications and allocated roughly $98 million in artistic grants to approximately 1,200 artists and 300 arts organizations. The Council's impact on the nation's literary culture is profound. The Council makes direct grants to authors and publishers, supports associations such as the Canadian Children's Book Centre and activities such as the National Book Festival, and funds writer-in-residence programs and public readings by authors across Canada. Total Canada Council support of writing and publishing in 1990–91 was $21.8 million. The Council has also administered and funded the Governor-General's Awards for Literature since 1959.

Further, both federal and provincial moneys helped support the explosion of smaller presses concentrating on Canadian literature that sprang up in the 1960s and 70s. Presses such as the Coach House Press (est. 1965),

[26] All figures in this section are reported in Canadian dollars.

House of Anansi (1967), NeWest, and Oberon, to name a few, were helped by government money that in 1988 totaled over $500,000. Government moneys also helped fund a number of new literary magazines such as *Canadian Literature* in Vancouver (1959), *Liberté* in Montreal (1959), *Alphabet* (1960), and *Livres et auteurs canadiens* (1961). This support is generally considered one of the key sources of the extraordinary increase in literary activity in the years between 1960 and 1985 during which W. H. New estimates "some 400 new serious writers" appeared (1989: 214).

Finally, the repatriation of Canadian culture from American and British domination was not only addressed by funding in favor of Canadians and Canadian content, but also by legislation controlling foreigners. The Foreign Investment Review Board (FIRA) was established in 1974 as a screening body to advise the Cabinet on possible takeovers of large Canadian firms by foreign corporations, and was used to help protect Canadian control of the culture industries. In 1985, Minister of Communications Marcel Masse instituted the so-called Baie Comeau policy requiring foreign purchasers of Canadian publishers to sell 51 percent of their holdings to Canadians within two years (Hutcheson 1987). The recent NAFTA talks also revived strong nationalist sentiment in Canada, if in the end little actual protection for Canadian culture industries.[27]

Unfortunately, the federal efforts at preserving, stimulating, and funding culture have often been understood by the francophone community as an attack on French-Canadian traditions and mores. The funding of pan-Canadian "national" culture has become increasingly politicized in Quebec, especially since the renewed nationalist interest of the 1960s. Federal institutions and funding policies are often seen as "intruders in Québec" who are "eroding indigenous culture" (Marsh 1988: 552). Quebec has responded with a high provincial level of cultural spending, the institutionalization of cultural funding as a provincial matter, and the virtual takeover of the Quebec branches of federal cultural institutions such as the

---

[27] Despite the traditional strong government support for the arts, many commentators and culture producers feel that the federal government at least is backing off from its commitment to Canadian culture. For example, the Canadian parliament did not increase the Council's baseline allocation between 1986 and 1992, meaning that inflation accounted for a 20 percent drop in Council funding between 1986 and 1992 and a 30 percent drop since 1982 (Dwyer 1992: 47). Furthermore, the Council took a 10 percent cut to its $95 million grants budget in 1993–94 (Turbide 1994: 55). The Mulroney government proposed in 1993 that the Social Science and Humanities Research Council be merged into the Canada Council. Although the measure was defeated, it was seen by many as a move to vitiate federal arts funding (Crean 1993). Similarly, the 1993 move of federal responsibility for culture from the Department of Communications to a new Heritage Department is also viewed ominously (Crean 1993).

National Film Board (Telefilm Canada) and the Société Radio-Canada (the CBC French network), which Balthazar describes as "the Francophone instrument par excellence" (in Gougeon 1994: 111; Marsh 1988). Quebec has had a Department of Cultural Affairs (now called the Ministry of State for Cultural Development) since 1961, obviously with an attendant Minister of Cultural Affairs, a National Library of Quebec, and a Grand Théatre de Québec. Government funding of culture at the federal level has been yet another source of federal–provincial tension between the dominantly anglophone central state and the francophone Quebec. Nonetheless, both the federal government of Canada and the province of Quebec distinguish themselves from the United States by their reliance on governmental funding of the arts.

Of course, the United States also provides public support to the arts. Unlike the Canadian emphasis on direct aid, indirect aid in the form of tax expenditures (foregone taxes) has been a cornerstone of United States public arts funding. This complicates efforts to compare American and Canadian government funding of the arts. The extent of government funding support is a difficult measure to compare internationally given the multiplicity of types of arts support including direct and indirect subsidies, national, regional, and local funding processes, population and currency differences, and questions of equivalence of definitions of arts and culture. Nonetheless, one international comparative study of arts support commissioned by the United States National Endowment for the Arts estimated that total direct public expenditures for the arts and culture totaled $1,157 million (Canadian dollars) in Canada in 1981–82 and only $702 million (US dollars) in the United States in 1983–84 (Schuster 1985: 43).[28]

In an attempt to provide more easily comparable figures, Schuster constructs a measure of "US Equivalents," which considers only those categories of expenditure found in the United States (Schuster 1985, especially Appendix A). Even with this extremely conservative measure,[29] Canadian expenditures per capita were almost triple those of the United States (Schuster 1985: 45, table 4). Canadian per capita expenditure on public support for the arts at all government levels was $32 (US dollars) in direct government support. Comparative figures for the United States were $13

---

[28] Remember both the currency difference – in 1985 the average exchange rate was $0.896 Canadian per US dollar (*World Currency Year Book* 1989: 257) and the comparative population figures – Canada has approximately 11 percent of the population of the United States.

[29] The "US Equivalents" figure drops total Canadian funding from $1,157.3 million (Canadian) to $939.6 million (Canadian), by ignoring such expenditures as support for national TV, radio, film development, libraries, and museums.

with estimated tax expenditure included and a mere $3 if only direct government support is considered (Schuster 1985: 45, US dollars).[30]

Government involvement, whether at the federal level or the provincial level, strongly differentiates Canadian and American understandings of the contemporary role of culture and delineates profoundly different parameters within which the creation, dissemination, and reception of cultural materials occur. Smith focuses on the sharp distinction between American and Canadian understandings of government's role in culture and on the centrality of state-supported cultural activity to Canada in his assessment of the difficulties over cultural provisions in the free trade talks:

When . . . journalist Bronwen Drainie notes that "Canada has a tradition that says artistic and cultural activity is necessary to our well-being and sense of identity," and when, further, she underscores the Canadian determination that "we will support such activity out of public funds," she is not simply making a casual reference to a minor phenomenon: she is – and the significance of this point can hardly be exaggerated – expressing a view that many Canadians consider cuts to the heart of national survival (1994: 107).

Or, as the author of the "Cultural Policy" entry in the Canadian Encyclopedia writes:

The values of the "free-market" economy . . . are often anathema to art . . . For those who believe that artistic expression is critically important to society and for those who acknowledge that the potential of communications technology lies beyond expanding the market for consumer goods, it is unacceptable to leave culture to a "free market" that is overwhelmingly dominated by a few foreign corporations. The disparities between . . . the US and Canada would, in a "free market," quickly reduce the smaller nation to passive consumers (Marsh 1988: 553).

Thus Canadian canon formation and literary activities, both historically and contemporaneously, need to be understood within a context of significantly different founding conditions and assumptions than those that hold sway in the American case. The central role of the state is one of these important differences.

In summary, the story of Canadian canon formation is a story of a nationalist project under pressure from subnational, supranational, and international pressures. Unlike the relatively straightforward relationship between a revolutionary political independence and the desire for and pursuit of a

[30] Schuster estimates that the US provides "indirect aid in the form of foregone taxes" at "three times the level of direct public support" for a total of $2,356 million in 1983–84 although this includes "arts and humanities for individual and foundation donations" (1985: 43–4). This brings total US "expenditures" to $3,058 million for 1983–4.

concomitant cultural independence in the United States, the Canadian relationship between nationalist sentiment and canon formation is subverted by specific historical circumstances including the binational character of Canada's founding, the long-standing identification of English Canada with the British Commonwealth, and the alternately protective and threatening relationship with the United States.[31]

I now turn our attention from the historical accounting of the conscious and political character of national canon formation to a discussion of the first empirical comparison – the American and Canadian canonical novels. As we progress to the consideration of textual differences, it will be helpful to keep the historical context in mind. In particular, the differential timing of national canon formation in Canada and the United States, and the explicit, conscious nature of the belief in and promotion of nationalistic canon formation by elites in the United States and Canada, provide the context for situating the cross-national differences and similarities in the form and content of the canonical novels.

---

[31] Or, as Ramsay Cook has described the situation: "the theme of survival in English-Canadian history has several variations [and] is . . . nearly as all-pervading as it is in French-Canadian history. Its variants include the struggle for survival against the pressure of the United States, the struggle of a colony to achieve nation-hood, and, finally, the struggle to maintain Canadian unity" (1971: 162).

4

The canonical novels: the politics of cultural nationalism

Gatsby turned out all right at the end; it is what preyed on Gatsby, what foul dust floated in the wake of his dreams that . . . closed out my interest in . . . men . . . careless people . . . [who] smashed up things and creatures and then retreated back into their money or their vast carelessness . . . and let other people clean up the mess they had made (Fitzgerald [1925] 1953: 2, 180–1).

True resignation meant accepting . . . the burden of leadership; and the moment he saw that he felt at one with the district, with his brother-in-law who had told him his story, with Ruth in her sorrow, and, strangely, with himself; for here was something to do once more . . . His own life had been wrong, or all this would not have happened. He had lived to himself and had to learn that it could not be done (Grove [1933] 1965: 264).

In chapters 2 and 3 I showed that historical patterns of national canon formation clearly demonstrate the relationship between literature and nation-building in the United States as far back as the eighteenth century and in Canada in the nineteenth, and particularly, twentieth centuries. In chapter 4, I turn from a consideration of the historical contexts of canon formation to an empirical comparison that demonstrates how the idea of unique national literatures is manifested in the canonical texts of the United States and Canada.

These quotes from the American *The Great Gatsby* and the Canadian *Fruits of the Earth* respectively exemplify the central thematic difference between the American and Canadian canonical novels that I will discuss – the contrast between American individualism on the one hand and Canadian social identification on the other. These differences, I will argue, are not "natural," but part of a process of national distinction. Just as the content of these canonical novels is constructed, so too is the form of the canon. Therefore, before focusing on the description and analysis of the canonical novels, I present data describing the structure of the national canon in Canada and the United States and the role of educational institutions in canon formation. In addition to providing a context within which to situate the analysis of the specific textual differences between Canadian and American novels, these data provide a comparative analysis of the differences in the form of Canadian and American national literary canons that complements the analysis of differences in canonical content.

The canonical novels

Defining the canon

The canon, although "known" to "everyone," is notoriously difficult to define precisely. One source of the difficulties inherent in a definition of the content of the canon is the contested nature of canonical authority. Bourdieu discusses how the "multiplication of authorities having the power to consecrate but placed in a situation of competition for cultural legitimacy" is a historical intensifying process (1985: 14). Canons, and other institutions and practices of cultural authority, are rarely monolithic, but instead fields of contestation, struggles among diverse groups, practices, and institutions which "propose and contest canons in order to enhance their own social standing" (Davey 1990: 676). Although I will speak of "the" canon of American and Canadian literatures, and provide some justification for my choice, I acknowledge that the canon is not static and that the more complex reality of canon formation is as "the scene of *competition* for the power to grant cultural consecration" (Bourdieu 1985: 24, emphasis added; see also Guillory 1993).

Despite more and less successful claims by various groups for the right to determine canonical status, the cultural authority for the designation of literary canons has in the contemporary period resided in universities. As Lauter notes, "canons . . . are made manifest in particular social and educational practices . . . institutional forms like curricula are central to the maintenance or modification of canons" (1991: 149; Lecker 1990). DiMaggio reiterates, arguing that in the modern period it is "universities [who have] substantial influence over the definition of 'official' culture. As keepers of the canons, universities and liberal arts colleges play the key role in disseminating cultural hierarchies" (1991: 138; also 1982b). Similarly, Bourdieu (1985: 13) sees the education system as an "institution of consecration" with the authority to "rank [cultural objects] on a scale of legitimacy."

The canonical novels analyzed in this chapter are drawn from a survey of college and university syllabi for introductory level American Literature and Canadian Literature courses in the United States and Canada respectively. I chose college syllabi because they provide access to that part of the canon that is both the most legitimated and the most widely disseminated. A canon drawn from college and university curricula represents both the "official" version of the canon and the version inculcated in the general, college-educated population. Colleges and universities do more than "validate" and "inculcate" the canon, however. Universities are also "authorized to . . . – within limits – expand the high-culture . . . literary canons" (DiMaggio 1991: 139).[1] The syllabi I collected demonstrate this, providing indications of both a powerful preservation of the canonical status quo and the persistent reworking of canonical change. Cultural contestation is evidenced by the competing versions of the canon represented in the various syllabi.

Data collection

The American canonical novels are selected from a group of twenty-nine syllabi representing introductory American Literature courses taught at liberal arts colleges, private universities, and public universities. I collected syllabi in spring of 1989 through a mailed request to English departments in February. I wrote to the departments associated with the top twenty doctoral programs in English and the ten undergraduate programs graduating the largest proportion of students seeking doctorates, asking for their most recent syllabi from introductory level American Literature courses. I received syllabi from Amherst, Brandeis, Oberlin, Pomona, and Williams Colleges, Princeton and Yale Universities, and the Universities of Chicago, California-Berkeley, Michigan and North Carolina-Chapel Hill. Schools generally sent the syllabi from all sections of the course taught in a year. I received over fifty syllabi, twenty-nine of which met my criteria.[2] The twenty-nine American syllabi I used reflect a wide range of philosophies regarding the canon. Some rely on anthologies and short stories, others on novels. The syllabi vary across depth versus breadth, tradition versus

---

[1] DiMaggio believes however that the authority of universities has been "eroding" (1991: 142) since 1960 because of the reorganization of cultural control from kinship elites to organizational elites, the increased consumer demand for cultural goods due to rising education, the shift from elite/private patronage to government/corporate sponsorship, and the managerial revolution that rewards arts managers for inclusive and expansionary models (see also Griswold 1991: 156). Nonetheless, university curricula are still the most common definition of the "official" literary canon (cf. Davey 1990).

[2] I required that the syllabi be dated 1988 or 1989 and be from general introductory level American Literature classes. Thus syllabi from classes such as "American Literature in the South" or "Nineteenth Century Women Authors" were not included.

reform, thematic versus survey orientations, the amount of reading and thus the average number of works possible to consider canonical. The syllabi from *within* schools represent no greater degree of similarity than those *across* schools – individual professors' training and preferences drive text selection more than institutional affiliation, at least at the elite level represented in my sample.

Both the extreme positions in the current battle over the canon and, more generally, a middle ground between the two poles are represented in the syllabi. The syllabi present strong evidence of the cultural contestation underway in American literature as their offerings range from a conservative or "traditional" vision of American Literature to a more revisionist picture. An example of the postwar "traditional" vision is an introductory "American Novel" course taught at one of the large, highly ranked public universities in the sample. The course assigns six novels: Nathaniel Hawthorne's *The Scarlet Letter*, Herman Melville's *Moby Dick*, Mark Twain's *Huckleberry Finn*, F. Scott Fitzgerald's *The Great Gatsby*, William Faulkner's *Light in August*, and Ernest Hemingway's *The Sun Also Rises* – six "classic" novels by six white men.

An example of a more revisionist syllabus is a course – offered at the same university – and entitled "Introduction to American Literature" that also assigns six novels. In this case, however, the novels are Harriet Beecher Stowe's *Uncle Tom's Cabin*, Mark Twain's *Huckleberry Finn*, Kate Chopin's *The Awakening*, Ralph Ellison's *Invisible Man*, Ernest Hemingway's *The Sun Also Rises*, and Alice Walker's *Meridian* – two "classic" novels by white men, three novels by women (written more than a century apart), and two novels by African-Americans. Although two of the assigned novels overlap, students reading *Huck Finn* and *The Sun Also Rises* in these two classes probably "read" very different novels given the profound differences in the context of other novels read in the class and what I assume to be the very different interpretive frameworks of the two classes. The understanding of "American Literature" constructed in these two classes frames the students' readings of the texts in specific ways, creating different strategies for reading the novels and for positioning them vis-à-vis one another and the American literary tradition more generally.

Despite these differences, and their roots in the current upheavals over the definition of the canon, what appears most clearly in these syllabi is a wide-ranging consensus regarding the core of the American canon – at least in its pedagogical form.[3] This can be seen in the broad consensus regarding

---

[3] The authors and texts most analyzed, written on, and praised by scholars may form a more elite version of the canon than that taught – and one less generally accessible.

the most frequently assigned novels. Even the two courses juxtaposed above overlap in one-third of their selections – Hemingway's *The Sun Also Rises* and Twain's *Huckleberry Finn*. I return to this point regarding consensus in the section on the canonical "core."

The Canadian canonical novels are selected from a group of forty-six syllabi for introductory Canadian Literature courses taught at a range of private and public universities. The syllabi were collected at the same time and in the same manner as the American ones. The sixteen Canadian schools that responded with syllabi are Carleton, Concordia, Laurentian, McGill, McMaster, Queen's, and York Universities, and the Universities of Alberta, British Columbia, Calgary, Manitoba, Toronto, Saskatchewan, Sherbrooke, Western Ontario, and Winnipeg.[4] The Canadian syllabi represent much less of a tension between "classic" and "revisionary" visions of the canon than the American syllabi, primarily because of the relatively recent date of canon formation in Canada.[5] Although there is some discussion between classicists and revisionists in Canada, the recency of canon formation mitigates against it.[6]

Once I had collected the syllabi, I selected the novels for analysis based on the frequency of their assignment in introductory level courses. I took into consideration both the frequency of authorial assignment and the assignment of particular novels. So, for example, Kate Chopin's novel *The Awakening* was assigned in 38 percent of the syllabi, but only one other work by Chopin was ever assigned. In comparison, *Light in August* was only assigned in 11 percent of the syllabi, but one of Faulkner's novels was assigned in a full one-half of all courses. Thus although no single title by Faulkner was assigned in more than 11 percent of the syllabi, Faulkner the author is clearly centrally located within the canon as 50 percent of the syllabi assign one of five different novels by Faulkner.[7]

The canonical "core"

The twenty canonical novels I analyzed represent a roughly equal percentage of assignments in each country. The twenty-nine American syllabi

---

[4] The three schools that did not respond were Montréal, Université du Québec, and Simon Frasier.

[5] One interesting further comparison between the two nations is the generally greater number of works assigned in the Canadian courses.

[6] The canon, however, is always contested terrain *in any location* and my operationalization of it as relatively monolithic is heuristic only. Canadian debates regarding the canon are presented in Lecker (1990, 1991, 1993) and Davey (1990).

[7] In cases such as Faulkner's, I selected the single most frequently assigned title, or, in the case of a tie, flipped a coin to select a single title.

generate a list of 105 works by forty-nine novelists. These works are mentioned (assigned) a total of 242 times. The ten authors of the American
novels represent only 20 percent of the forty-nine novelists listed in the
syllabi, but the writings of those ten authors account for 53 percent of the
total number of assignments in the syllabi. The central importance of these
ten authors is demonstrated by the disproportionate number of assigned
readings authored by the ten. For example, 7.4 percent of *all* assignments
in introductory American Literature courses are works by one man –
Nathaniel Hawthorne. The ten American novels I analyze represent 9.5
percent of the total number of novels listed, but account for one-third (32.7
percent) of the overall assignments.

The forty-six Canadian syllabi generate a list of 120 works by sixty-nine
novelists. These works are mentioned a total of 384 times. The importance
of the ten core Canadian authors is even more disproportionate than was
the case with the American authors. The authors of the ten Canadian
novels represent only 15 percent of the sixty-nine novelists listed in the
syllabi, but their writings account for 55 percent of the total number of
assignments in the syllabi. The importance of the ten core Canadian novels
is as equally disproportionate as was true in the American case. The ten
novels in my Canadian core represent just 8.3 percent of the total number
of novels, but again account for almost one-third (31 percent) of the assignments.

Thus, although I present analyses of only ten novels for each country, it
can be seen that these ten novels represent an extremely influential core of
the canon. These novels define the most frequently assigned, most central,
and most important core of the national literary canon in each country.
The ten novels I analyze for each country account for about *one-third* of
the novels assigned in introductory national literature courses across a
wide range of schools in each country. The authors of the novels are even
more centrally located than are the novels themselves. Works by these
authors account for over *one-half* of all of the assigned works in such
classes.

The most immediately visible difference between the American and
Canadian core novels underscores the argument of chapters 2 and 3: the
median publication dates for the American novels is significantly earlier
than for the Canadian novels. The American canonical novels have original publication dates ranging from 1850 to 1933. Six of the novels were
originally published in the nineteenth century and four of the novels were
originally published in the twentieth century. The median publication year
is 1887; the average of the American novels' publication dates is 1889. The
Canadian canonical novels were all originally published in the twentieth

century.[8] Four of the novels were originally published in the first half of the century and six of the novels were originally published in the latter half. The median and average publication year for the Canadian novels is 1953. The difference in these dates is directly correlated with the differential timing of nation-building processes in Canada and the United States. Canadian canon formation occurred much later than American canon formation. Although a significant part of the Canadian process involved the discovery and rehabilitation of older texts, the timing of canon formation processes nonetheless affected the texts on which attention was focused.

Canonical structure: margin and concentration

Before discussing the particular differences between the Canadian novels and the American novels, I want to mention a difference in the structure of the Canadian and American canons that is noticeable from an examination of the entire collection of syllabi. The number of titles and authors generated by amassing the syllabi varies across the two countries. This is partly an artefact of the larger number of Canadian syllabi, but it is more than that. The structure of the Canadian canon appears both broader and denser than the American canon. That is, although the Canadian canon has a wider margin than the American, there is also greater concentration about the core. As evidence of this we can compare two measurements: the number of novelists mentioned only once versus those mentioned more than once (a measure of the margin width) and the disproportionate assignments from core novelists (a measure of core concentration).

The American sample contains thirty-six novelists assigned on more than one syllabus and thirteen novelists mentioned in only one syllabus, for a total of forty-nine novelists in the sample. The Canadian sample contains thirty-eight novelists assigned more than once (a very similar number to the American, especially given the much larger number of syllabi), but an additional thirty-one novelists assigned on only one syllabus (2.5 times the number of Americans mentioned only once). Thus the Canadian canon seems to include many more authors than the American canon, although those authors appear to be located at the perimeter of the canon and their status may be indeterminate or in flux.

In contrast to this image of a Canadian canon that is expansive at the margins, a comparison of the core novelists shows greater concentration in the Canadian canon compared to the American canon. The ten most

---

[8] Although the syllabi listed several Canadian texts with earlier original publication dates, none of these were novels.

frequently assigned American novelists (what I designate the "core") represented 20 percent of all novelists, while accounting for 53 percent of all
assignments. The Canadian core ten novelists represented only 15 percent
of all novelists, while accounting for 55 percent of all assignments. The ten
authors in the American core thus accounted for 2.6 times more assignments than an "average" ten American authors would have. The Canadian
core ten accounted for 3.8 times more assignments than an "average" ten
Canadian authors would have. Thus there seems to be even greater agreement about the core Canadian authors than there is about the core
American authors.

The twin Canadian finding of both greater concentration and greater
expansiveness at the margins of the canon is perhaps indicative of several
things. First, Canada's historical development as a bipartite nation has
meant not only a long-standing image of Canadian cultural dualism as
incorporating two nations (French and English), but often an openness to
the incorporation of other groups as well, e.g., the 1971 adoption of a
federal multiculturalism policy or the image of the Canadian "mosaic" in
contrast to the American "melting pot." In addition, the timing of
Canadian nation-building in the postwar period meant that notions of
"cultural diversity" were already firmly encoded in international, e.g., the
United Nations and other global organizations, discourse. These pressures
may account for the expansiveness of the canon, while the greater
concentration, or agreement about the core, of the canon may be accounted
for by the relative youth of canon formation efforts in Canada. Recall from
chapter 3 that national canon formation is only a creature of the postwar
period, that the Calgary Conference only took place in 1978, and that
courses in Canadian literature were not fully institutionalized in Canadian
universities until the mid to late 1970s.

Canonical titles and canonical change

The canonical novels and their dates of original publication for the two
countries are as follows:

Canadian

Duncan, Sara J.	1904	*The Imperialist*
Grove, Frederick Philip	1933	*Fruits of the Earth*
Ross, Sinclair	1941	*As For Me and My House*
MacLennan, Hugh	1945	*Two Solitudes*
Buckler, Ernest	1952	*The Mountain and the Valley*
Laurence, Margaret	1964	*The Stone Angel*

Davies, Robertson K.	1970	*Fifth Business*
Munro, Alice	1971	*Lives of Girls and Women*
Laurence, Margaret	1974	*The Diviners*
Atwood, Margaret	1976	*Lady Oracle*

American

Hawthorne, Nathaniel	1850	*The Scarlet Letter*
Melville, Herman	1851	*Moby Dick*
Stowe, Harriet Beecher	1852	*Uncle Tom's Cabin*
James, Henry	1881	*Portrait of A Lady*
Twain, Mark	1884	*The Adventures of Huckleberry Finn*
Chopin, Kate	1899	*The Awakening*
Dreiser, Theodore	1900	*Sister Carrie*
Fitzgerald, F. Scott	1925	*The Great Gatsby*
Hemingway, Ernest	1926	*The Sun Also Rises*
Faulkner, William	1933	*Light in August*

The American canonical novels represent authors and titles established by the influential post-World War II critics, and some changes brought on in the ensuing years, particularly those created by the current debate on "opening the canon."[9] On the one hand, comparing the 1989 novels above with a poll conducted by twenty-six members of the American Literature section of the Modern Languages Association (MLA) in response to a 1949 UNESCO request for the top twenty American books demonstrates the persistence of the canon (Hubbell 1972: 301–2). In the 1949 poll, Hawthorne, Melville, James, and Twain were the novelists listed among the top five, Dreiser was listed in the top twenty, and Hemingway was listed among the top twenty-five.[10] These six authors are also in the core in 1989.

---

[9] One hundred years after the original "Big Ten" were taught in the initial American Literature courses of the 1890s, my sample looks significantly different. Partly this is due to my emphasis on *novelists*, a label appropriate to only a subset of the "Big Ten" – Irving, Cooper, Bryant, Emerson, Hawthorne, Longfellow, Whittier, Holmes, Lowell, and Poe, and occasionally Thoreau or Mrs. Stowe (Hubell 1972). Two authors overlap: Hawthorne and Stowe. Washington Irving and James Fenimore Cooper are the other Big Ten novelists. Bryant, Longfellow, and Whittier are poets. Lowell and Poe are poets and literary critics, the latter also author of short stories. Emerson and Thoreau are poets and philosophic essayists. Poe, Emerson, and Thoreau have remained strong American canonical figures; reputations of the rest have fared much less well.

[10] The other novelists in the top twenty (who were not included in my 1989 canonical core) were J. F. Cooper, Washington Irving, Willa Cather, W. D. Howells, and Sinclair Lewis. Stephen Crane and Edith Wharton were also included with Hemingway in the top twenty-five (Hubbell 1972: 302).

Fitzgerald, Faulkner, Stowe, and Chopin were nowhere mentioned in the 1949 poll. Some fifteen years later, however, a poll asked 182 scholars of American Literature to name the top ten American authors of the twentieth century. The top four novelists they named in this case were Hemingway, Faulkner, Fitzgerald, and Dreiser (Hubbell 1972: 281) – all corresponding with the 1989 core.

The most recent additions to the canonical core, on the other hand, demonstrate the perpetual flux of canonical inclusion and exclusion. Both Harriet Beecher Stowe and Kate Chopin have only recently attained canonical status. In the twentieth century American women novelists have tended to be seen as only minor figures. Writing about her earlier experience collaborating on an American literature anthology, for instance, Nina Baym reported that "as late as 1977, that canon [major American authors] did not include any women novelists" (1985: 63). Another comparison is provided by Lauter's (1981) survey of fifty course syllabi at twenty-five colleges/universities. Of the first fifty authors listed by frequency of appearance, only six are women. Emily Dickinson, a poet, is the twelfth author listed, Edith Wharton is, at number twenty-seven, the first female novelist listed (similarly, see the survey in *Chronicle of Higher Education* 1982).

Stowe's reputation has waned and waxed over the years. She was an extremely popular and widely admired writer in the 1850s and 60s, and was sometimes considered worthy of inclusion in the canon in the 1890s (Hubbell 1972: 245). In the twentieth century, however, her writing became seen as emblematic of the sentimental pap nineteenth-century American women writers were known for (Hawthorne's "damned mob of scribbling women") and was completely beyond "serious" consideration. It was primarily the feminist and African-American reconsiderations of the 1970s and 80s that raised Stowe's profile once again (Baym 1985; Tompkins 1985).

Chopin, on the other hand, was not considered even at the fringes of the canon until the 1960s. Prior to that time, Chopin was seen only as a regional colorist, known for her short stories utilizing creole characters and settings and published in popular magazines of the 1890s. *The Awakening* was not well received by contemporary reviewers; it was considered not only a bad book, but quite scandalous. One reviewer even described it as "sex fiction" (*Chicago Times-Herald* 1899: 9). *The Awakening* was out of print between 1906 and 1964. Chopin was resurrected by the feminist critics of the 1960s and gained increasing stature through the 1970s and 1980s (see Corse and Westervelt [1995] for an analysis of the changing critical reception of *The Awakening*).

The Canadian novels provide much less of a possibility for such long-term historical comparison. This is first because the canon is recent, and second because of a scarcity of *novels* in early Canadian literary history. Canadian literature is notable in comparison to American for the more important role played by genres such as humorous sketches and short stories. Early writers such as Stephen Leacock (*Sunshine Sketches of a Small Town*, 1912) were less likely to write novels than a variety of sketches or short stories. My selection criteria work against this tradition in Canadian literature.

In sum, the novels contained in the canonical core are products of particular canonical histories and are embedded in particular canonical structures in Canada and the United States. Canon formation processes occurred in both countries, but these processes were influenced by particular historical circumstances and have resulted in distinct structural configurations. The form of the American and Canadian canons is the product of specific historical contingencies and is not based in a reflection of some monolithic or stable or inherent Canadian or American culture. Having provided at least an initial sense of the structure of the American and Canadian canons, and having briefly considered the history of canonical change, I turn now to the comparative analyses of the core canonical novels.

A comparative analysis of American and Canadian core canonical novels

The question of meaning

The most important aspect of the comparison between the American and Canadian canonical novels is the simple fact that they do indeed differ. The specific content of those differences is also important, but the *meaning* of the differences in content is ambiguous. This ambiguity does not mean, however, that the content differences are *without* meaning. Cross-national literary differences in meaning matter, but not in the way we usually think of it. That is, the meaning of literary differences is not obvious, or "natural," or necessarily following from "reality." Instead, cross-national literary differences in meaning matter because they are part of a complex process of advancing claims about the identity and uniqueness of the nation. The terms under which such claims are advanced and the substance of the claims themselves, however, vary over time and across audiences.

Literary meaning is always subjective since it is a function of audience interaction with the text (Fish 1980; Radway 1984; Griswold 1987b; Shively 1992). Although readers participate in the construction of meaning, they do so under social circumstances. Readers encounter texts in social contexts laden with both explicit formulae and implicit cues for constructing meaning (Smith 1983; Long 1986, 1987). While readers engage in the construction of textual meaning, they do so within the constraints – and opportunities – created by both their own interpretive repertoires and the social contexts within which texts are encountered (see Swidler 1986; DeVault 1990; Press 1994 for a review of the literature on "reception").[11]

Traditional reflection theory argues that the meaning of national literatures lies in their revelation of national character. But, as I noted in chapter 1, cross-national literary differences mean something less unconscious, less deeply psychological, but *more* compelling than a difference in American and Canadian national character. Cross-national literary differences show us the difference between what vision of "Canada" and of being "Canadian" is accepted and legitimated by Canadian national elites and what vision of "America" and of being "American" is accepted and legitimated by American national elites. National literatures are not reflections of the national character, but manifestations of the "invention" of the nation, of the strategies used to create national identities.

It is precisely because canon formation is influenced by concrete political processes, rather than abstract aesthetic principles, that high-culture literature tells us something important. What we find in these novels are not so much "powerful examples of the way a culture thinks about itself" (Tompkins 1985: xi), but rather powerful visions of the way national elites *construct* the nation and national identity. The driving force behind that

---

[11] This is particularly true of canonical novels as they are generally read within a well-defined, even rigid, interpretive framework. Critical opinion of these novels is extensive, pedagogical instruction of them codified, and the result is a dominant paradigm within which readers encounter and understand these texts. This point was brought home to me most forcefully after I reread *The Scarlet Letter*, a novel I had not read in fifteen years. In high school I found the novel most unsympathetic, but my re-reading of it left me profoundly moved and filled with horror at my youthful callowness. Some time later, I was reading an article by Nina Baym in which she discusses traditional critical perspectives on American Literature and the feminist response to them. In shock I read:

> And in one work – *The Scarlet Letter* – a "fully developed woman of sexual age" who is the novel's protagonist has been admitted into the canon, but only by virtue of strenuous critical revisions of the text that remove Hester Prynne from the center of the novel and make her subordinate to Arthur Dimmesdale (Baym 1985: 73).

I had, as was completely obvious to me, coded Hester as the protagonist of *The Scarlet Letter*. I was amazed that one could read *The Scarlet Letter* as Dimmesdale's story. And then, slowly, I began to remember being taught this, that *The Scarlet Letter* is Dimmesdale's story, that the character I envision at the heart of the story is only relevant by her effects on Dimmesdale. Hester is, as Henry James said in the Norton edition of *The Scarlet Letter* that I used in high school, "an accessory figure" (Bradley, Beatty, Long, and Gross 1978: 288). When a dominant paradigm renders a text unintelligible, readers with sufficient resources will fight for their "own" meaning, but many more, like myself at age seventeen, will be disaffected (Showalter 1985).

process, as I have argued, is the ability to lay claim to national distinctiveness or uniqueness. Those who construct the canon, therefore, do not simply construct a *random* canon. Rather the canon needs a basis for cohesion and that cohesion must say something about national uniqueness. For my purposes, the interesting aspect of national literary differences is not their "truth" as social description, but their use as a means of identifying the nation and defining the national identity.

It is the crude and obvious process of deploying terms such as "American literature" and "national literary character" that performs the important cultural work of unifying nation and literature. The specific details about how nationality is manifested in one novel or another, or why this characteristic rather than that one defines American or Canadian literature, are relatively unimportant once the connection between literature and the nation is taken for granted. The academic debates regarding this novel or that interpretation are simply specific manifestations of the crucial cultural work that has succeeded at making the nation literary and literature national.

My own understanding of what American and Canadian differences in content "mean" is obviously a single interpretation, although one grounded in my study of American and Canadian literature and society and by my participation in specific shared social locations (Geertz 1973). It is marked by my training as a sociologist, by my American citizenship, by my gender, and by my comparativist perspective – among other things. Although I recognize the importance of audience in the construction of meaning, I wish to address the question of what the American–Canadian differences mean by offering my own, I think plausible, account of them (see Berezin 1994a: 1240–5 on plausibility). I will return to the issue of meaning in greater length in chapter 7.

Canonical differences

There are a number of differences between the Canadian and American canonical novels that strike one upon reading them as comparative blocks. Authorial gender, family life, the social class of the protagonists, the relative importance of the protagonist's work, the role of religion, the narrative tone of the novels, the conflicts and rebellions of protagonists; all of these characteristics differ across the Canadian and American novels. But there is a stronger, more overarching difference that makes itself strongly felt. Furthermore, a number of other differences, such as the relative importance of families, social class, and work, are related to this initial difference. Therefore, I begin my comparative analysis with a consideration of the

Canadian emphasis on social connection and the contrasting American emphasis on self-reliant individualism.

Connection versus individualism

As a group, the Canadian canonical novels are marked by their attention to and emphasis on interpersonal connection and social identity. Human connection, it is implied, is the only truly meaningful aspect of human life. Although it may be fraught with difficulty, peril, and heartache, connection is, in the end, the only true measure of a worthwhile life. American canonical novels, on the other hand, stress the dangers of social identity and social location, the constraints of interpersonal connection, and the potentially destructive power of the social. An individual identity, a strong and autonomous self-definition, are the hope offered by the American novels.

Consider for a moment the two novels I quoted from at the beginning of the chapter: the American novel *The Great Gatsby* written in 1925 by F. Scott Fitzgerald and the Canadian novel *Fruits of the Earth* written in 1933 by Frederick Philip Grove. Both are novels about powerful, self-made men who, having attained material wealth and success, then pursue personal relationships in an attempt to construct a fulfilling life. But this is where the similarities end.

Fitzgerald's Gatsby seeks to regain his one true love, the rich, beautiful, and now married Daisy Buchanan. But Gatsby's faithfulness to Daisy, his desire to marry her, brings him only ruin. She and her husband and their society – the throng of party-goers and hangers-on who flocked to Gatsby's mansion – disappear in their "vast carelessness." Gatsby is left alone, a sacrifice to Daisy's carelessness and the cold, exclusionary contempt of the very society that once surrounded him. His disastrous, solitary death and funeral are acknowledged only by a disillusioned and grieving Nick, Gatsby's uncomprehending father, and the one member of Gatsby's erstwhile entourage who bothered to show. Gatsby's belief in love, his belief in the deepest and most powerful of human connections, and through love his attempted integration and location in the social world, destroy him.[12]

In contrast to Gatsby's destruction by others, Grove presents Abe Spalding as a driven, obsessed workaholic and pioneer whose pursuit and eventual attainment of material success serve solely to alienate his family and leave him miserable and alone. Spalding only finds some hope of happi-

---

[12] Nick assures us that the degradation and death of Gatsby are due to the corrupt Eastern society that destroys people, juxtaposing his own more pure and free Western environment, to which he returns (sadder but wiser) at the end of the novel, but Fitzgerald never directly shows us this "better" society.

ness when he refocuses his attention on people – on service to family and community. Spalding's son dies, bringing him heartache, but he does manage to reconnect with his wife (through his other children's problems), and to turn toward his community – not through his previous self-aggrandizing political career, but through dutiful, though unpleasant, community leadership against the town's immoral elements. For Spalding there is no utopian familial picture, but there is a hope of redemption through his connection to family and community. For Gatsby, connection and (false) community lead to destruction.

A similar subtext regarding the danger of the social and the necessity of a strong, individualistic self underlies most of the American novels. *The Scarlet Letter* describes Hester's indomitable individual strength in the face of extreme social sanction, and her ultimate survival and even rehabilitation into the very hypocritical society that initially ostracized her. In contrast, her seducer Dimmesdale's individual weakness and fear of social condemnation drive him to madness and death. *Moby Dick*, *Huck Finn*, and *The Awakening* all portray as heroic, or at least most interesting, those who defy, ignore, and escape from society, from interpersonal connection, and from the rigid constraints of social identity. Underlying both *Sister Carrie* and *Portrait of a Lady* is a sense of the destructive power and falsity of society and social relations.

The Sun Also Rises and *Light in August* contain more ambivalent messages. *The Sun Also Rises* clearly warns of the futility of finding oneself and ones life's purpose through others – but it also suggests that the rare, dangerous, and fragile moments of communion may be all that keep you from death. *Light in August*, while emphasizing the dangers and difficulties of human connection, also suggests that the individual alone cannot succeed. *Uncle Tom's Cabin* is the least typical American novel in this regard. Indeed, *Uncle Tom's Cabin* – for all its focus on the quintessentially American institution of slavery – is very like the Canadian canonical novels. Stowe unabashedly proclaims that our salvation lies only in our deep love for God and for each other. This message, no doubt, at least partially explains the critical contempt for the novel so prevalent in the twentieth century.

In contrast, the Canadian novels, like *Fruits of the Earth*, stress social identity and the redemptive power of family, community, and human connection. A fascination with "human isolation" and "its causes, its effects, [and] the possibilities for a cure" permeate the Canadian novels (McGregor 1985: 105). The underlying struggle for connection is clear in *The Stone Angel* in which Hagar's deathbed redemption comes through her finally loving others more than herself; in *As For Me and My House* which details the senselessness of life without human connection and warmth; in *Two Solitudes* which is a paean to the possibilities of connection and identity through mutual recognition; and in *The Diviners* which details Morag's quest for true connection and the communion of mutual respect. In *The Imperialist* Lorne's character and identity are forged in the strength of the tightly bonded family and Canadian community – which is contrasted to the falseness of English and American society. *The Mountain and the Valley* describes David's happy childhood in the closeness and love of his family and community and his loss of that and his concomitant loss of identity and purpose. *Fifth Business* shows Dunstan's humanization through his loving, if somewhat unconventional, connection with Liesl.

Lady Oracle* and *Lives of Girls and Women* provide the ambivalent messages in the Canadian group – both balance their concern for connection and social identity with a fear of and warning against the loss of self. While autonomy may not be the goal, a strong self in the midst of connection is clearly a necessity. Overall, however, the Canadian canonical novels emphasize the importance of connection without an equal concern for autonomy – in sharp contrast to the American novels and their focus on autonomy and individualism.

Many observers and critics of American and Canadian literature have remarked on the individualist nature of the former and the desire for human connection expressed by the latter (e.g., Fiedler 1966; Atwood 1972; Lipset 1990; McGregor 1985). However, most commentators have been interested in the distinction as a reflection of "real" differences between American society and Canadian society. The meaning and importance of these distinct literary tropes, however, is their use in the complex process of advancing claims of literary uniqueness as a key indicator of national uniqueness. In the process of claiming itself a nation, the United States used as a central component the idea of individualism and the pioneering spirit (Lipset 1963, 1990; Greenfeld 1992). American claims of individualism are a central characteristic of the myth of American uniqueness, a cornerstone of the national identity. This does not mean that individualism in American society is necessarily "true" or "real," but that literary individualism constitutes a powerful statement regarding what is advanced as unique, new, and special about the United States.

Canadian national identity, on the other hand, was – and is – constructed in counterpoint to myths of American independence and individualism. During the process of Canadian nation-building there was a clear rejection of American notions of a pure market, of pure freedom, of pure, rampant individualism. The Canadian national identity was in part a reaction against the image of American identity as perceived by Canadians: the self-interested and dangerous gun-toting, Wild West-taming loner bound by no social code and controlled by no laws (Atwood 1972; Lipset 1986, 1988).

The geographic realities of Canada and the United States became mythic terrains from which national identities were drawn and upon which national identities were carved. Whereas the wilderness in America became a chance for the redemption of the strong individual, the wilderness in Canada became the external threat necessitating the strength and comfort of the social. Canadians, in their imaginations at least, were "geograph-ically confined within the habitable fringes of a vast northern hinterland that constantly raised the question of physical and social survival in the Canadian mind" (Earle and Wirth 1995). In the United States, on the other hand, there is a long tradition in which "forest, cave, and savage, Nature itself, and the instinctive aspects of the psyche they represent are read as beneficent, taken to symbolize a principle of salvation" (Fiedler 1966: 149).[13]

Where the central American myth celebrated individualism, the central Canadian myth celebrated the reliance on a community that would help sustain frail human life in the face of Nature's fearful forces (see, for example, Frye's [1971: 225] description of the Canadian "garrison mental-ity"). Canada was "a society more collectivist in outlook than the United States" (Earle and Wirth 1995: 2). McGregor has summarized the literary facet of the use of individualism to create the American identity and the use of social connection to construct a Canadian identity thus: "While the [literary] American's greatest fear is the loss of identity consequent upon acquiescence to social definition, the [literary] Canadian . . . believes that it is in terms of social definition that he is most likely to find himself" (1985: 436). As we move on to look at the other cross-national literary differences, I will return occasionally to a consideration of this predominant difference in the canonical novels.

Familial importance

The second significant difference between the Canadian and United States canonical novels is clearly connected to the initial difference. The role and importance of literary families vary dramatically between the American and Canadian novels. I coded each novel based on whether the protago-nist's parental family (the parents and siblings of the protagonist) and con-jugal family (the spouse and children of the protagonist) were "important."

---

[13] Fiedler also notes, however, the earlier American gothic tradition with its "heathen unre-deemed wilderness" as the symbol of evil and cites James Fenimore Cooper as the pro-genitor of the later "naturalization of the historical romance" (1966: 149).

Table 4.1   *Familial patterns in the canonical novels (in percentages)*

	USA (N=10)	Canada (N=10)
Protagonist has/had conjugal family	40	60
Conjugal family important:	30	60
positive	10	10
negative	10	10
ambivalent	10	40
Protagonist has/had parental family	30	90
Parental family important:	10	80
postive	0	20
negative	10	20
ambivalent	0	40
Either conjugal or parental family important	40	100
Neither family important	60	0
Both families important	0	40

I define important families as those that play a significant role in narrative development or are described as central to the protagonist's character and psyche, rather than families that are mentioned, but are largely irrelevant to the narrative. I further coded each important family as being portrayed as "positive," "negative," or "ambivalent," based primarily on the family's impact on the protagonist.

The first comparative difference, the Canadian focus on connection versus the American focus on individualism, finds partial roots in the difference between Canadian and American literary portrayals of family. The Canadian emphasis on human connection leads us to expect the prevalence and importance of family in Canadian novels. Concomitantly, the American emphasis on individualism leads us to expect a dearth of important families. In fact, families, and the relationships within them, play a much more important role in Canadian canonical literature than they do in American canonical literature. Table 4.1 displays the analyses of familial role in the twenty novels.

Six of the Canadian novels feature a protagonist with a conjugal family and virtually all of the Canadian novels, nine of ten, at least mention the protagonist's parental family. The American novels demonstrate less of a literary concern with families – four protagonists have conjugal families, three mention parental families. The greater Canadian concern with families becomes even more apparent when we compare the prevalence of important families: six Canadian protagonists have important conjugal families and eight Canadian protagonists have important parental families, only three American protagonists have important conjugal families and only one has an important parental family.

Laurence's *The Diviners* exemplifies the Canadian novels in terms of family. The novel focuses on a middle-aged Morag Gunn as she struggles to come to terms with her life, the people she loves, and the influences that shaped her. Morag is particularly concerned with her eighteen-year-old daughter Piquette and her relationship with Piquette's now dead father, and with her long-term foster parents, Christie and Prin. Although Morag's reflections on her life range across a variety of influences, loves, and desires, her families, parental and conjugal, actual and possible, occupy a central place in her life, memory, and understanding of who she is. I coded Morag's relationship with both her parental (foster) family and her conjugal family as important and ambivalent.

In contrast, Twain presents us with the archetypal individual American protagonist, the runaway Huck Finn floating down the Mississippi with no mother, a feared and despised father, a rejected parental substitute (Aunt Polly), and only Jim as a companion. I coded Huck's parental family as unimportant (because absent from all but the precipitating action) and negative. American individualism is also shown by Hemingway's Jake Barnes, who never even mentions family, by Melville's Ishmael who describes his long and convoluted adventures with only passing reference to family, and by Fitzgerald's Nick Carroway who mentions, but only barely, his loving and authentic midwestern family. I coded the parental families of the protagonists in these novels as unimportant.

Families are very clearly more important in Canadian canonical literature than in American literature. The importance of families in Canadian literature lies in the role they play in constructing the protagonist's identity. *All* of the Canadian novels present either conjugal or parental families as important and four of the novels present both families as important. The emphasis on connection, on social identity, begins with the family in Canadian canonical novels. The family is a primary source of identity, and the resolution of the relationship between self and family crucial.

In contrast to the Canadian situation, the American novels provide little emphasis on familial role and identity. Only four of the American novels present either family as important, none present both families as important, and six of the novels present neither family as important – something none of the Canadian novels do. The American novels' concern with individualistic identity and self-definition undercuts the role and importance of families. Atwood's remarks on the American family do indeed seem an apt description for the American canonical novels: "The family . . . is something you come from and get rid of . . . something the hero must repudiate and leave; it is the structure he rebels against, thereby defining his own freedom, his own Frontier" (1972: 131). Atwood's (1972: 132) understanding of the negative and entrapping nature of Canadian literary families, which she describes as the "ingrown-toenail family-as-trap," is, however, equally clearly *unsupported* by my analysis.

Gender

A third important difference between the Canadian and American canonical novels seems related to the first, although in complicated ways. This is the recurring issue of gender. Social commentators, sociologists, and literary critics, both American and Canadian, have commented on the issue of gender in American and Canadian literature. The general argument is that Canadian literature is more likely to be written by women and to focus on women's experience while American literature is more likely to be written by men and to focus on men's experience. The reasons given for this are varied – but all rely on reflection metaphors. For instance, Fiedler (1966) argues that the typical American protagonist is a man fleeing the confines of society and adult, heterosexual relations for the wilderness and relationships with other (dark-skinned) men.[14] Brown (1980) argues that American national experience in relation to Britain resonates to the myth of Oedipus, the violent and final rejection of his male parent by a male child, and that male experience is thus resonant. Green (1984: 2; 1986) posits that the mother–daughter relationship of "rejection and reconciliation" is the personal-level enactment of the Canadian relationship with the past. MacLennan (1949) and Brown (1980) see the female literary experience as resonant with the Canadian national experience with the United States – a relationship of low power, passivity, and accommodation.

Eight of the American canonical novels were written by men, two by women – and, as I have noted, the two women represent the most recent additions to the core. Five of the Canadian canonical novels were written by women and five by men. Although the Canadian authors have only an equal gender division, the comparative prevalence of female authors is clear. Further evidence for the comparatively stronger canonical position

[14] See also Anderson (1991: 202–3) on the importance of the "imagining of that fraternity, without which the reassurance of fratricide can not be born, [which] shows up remarkably early, and not without a curious authentic popularity." Anderson cites Cooper's *Pathfinder* novels, *Moby Dick*, and *Huck Finn* to support his point.

of women writers in Canada is provided by an analysis of the complete group of novels assigned in the forty-six Canadian syllabi and twenty-nine American syllabi. In the American sample, 33 percent of the assigned novelists were women and 26 percent of the assigned novels were written by women. In comparison, in the Canadian sample, 42 percent of assigned novelists were women and 39 percent of the assigned novels were written by women.[15] Women writers don't achieve parity with men in either case, but the Canadian canon is certainly more inclusive of women's writing.

The gender of the core novels' protagonists is a more complicated affair than that of their authors. Although the gender of author and protagonist generally matches, two American novels by male authors feature female protagonists – Dreiser's *Sister Carrie* and James's *Portrait of a Lady*. Hawthorne's *The Scarlet Letter* features Hester Prynne and Arthur Dimmesdale whom I will count as joint protagonists (see footnote 11). One of the two American novels by a female author features a male protagonist, Stowe's *Uncle Tom's Cabin*. One American canonical novel written by a male author features multiple protagonists encompassing both genders (three males and one female): Faulkner's *Light In August*. Thus I count three and three-quarters female protagonists and six and one-quarter male protagonists in the American canonical novels.

The gender of protagonists in the Canadian novels is simpler to calculate. One novel by a male author features a female protagonist, Ross's *As For Me and My House*, and one novel by a female author features a male protagonist, Duncan's *The Imperialist*. The gender of author and protagonist otherwise matches. Thus there are five female protagonists and five male protagonists as well as five female authors and five male authors in the Canadian canonical novels. While the Canadian canonical novels do feature more female protagonists than the American (five versus three and three-quarters), the difference is slight. The issue of what perspective on female experience is provided by an American canon that is both exclusionary of women writers and tends to present female experience primarily through the lens of male authorship is another question – and one that returns us to a consideration of the first comparison between American individualism/fear of connection and Canadian socialness/fear of lack of connection.

[15] This implies one further comparison. In both Canada and the United States, male novelists had more titles assigned than did female novelists, but the disparity is much greater in the United States. In the United States, women novelists had an average of 1.69 titles assigned while male novelists had an average of 2.36 titles assigned. In Canada, women novelists had an average of 1.64 titles assigned while male novelists had an average of 1.82 titles assigned.

The relationship between gender and the two poles of connection/affiliation versus individualism/self-definition has been posited by a long line of research. Parsons (1949; Parsons and Bales 1955) argued that men specialize in individualistic achievement and women in affiliative connection. Later, a line of research in feminist study, generally rooted in essentialist perspectives that assume the clear-cut distinctiveness of men and women and of male and female experience, has argued that connection, affiliation, and the definition of the self in terms of one's social relations are hallmarks of a feminine perspective. In comparison, competition, achievement, and a sense of self rooted in individual autonomy are hallmarks of a masculine perspective (e.g., Gilligan, Ward, and Taylor 1988; Gilligan 1982; Chodorow 1978). As Chodorow describes it: "The basic feminine sense of self is connected to the world, the basic masculine sense of self is separate" (1978: 169). Using this analysis, we might then be able to explain the Canadian focus on connection by the comparatively strong presence of women in the Canadian canon and the American fear of connection by the concomitant, disproportionate number of men in the American canon. Unfortunately, there are three major problems with such a line of argument.

First, it is unclear that the hypothesized relationship between gender and affiliation–connection versus achievement–individualism are correct. A number of researchers critical of the maximalist or essential positions of Gilligan, Chodorow, and others, have argued that there is little relationship between gender and the connection versus individualism perspectives (Colby and Damon 1987; Cochran and Peplau 1985; see also Tavris 1992: 79–90). Even Gilligan's own work has suggested both the dominance of the justice (male) perspective among women, *and* the ability of both men and women to move between perspectives (Gilligan *et al.* 1988).[16] Second, there is little data regarding the cross-cultural, international applicability of such notions of gender differences. Even if such a relationship holds in the United States, the construction of appropriate masculine and feminine behavior varies dramatically across different societies (Hofstede 1991).

Finally, and most crucially in the context of this study, the data simply aren't congruent with such an argument. The Canadian concern with affiliation and connection is manifested in all five of the novels by male authors and in three novels of five novels by female authors. In fact, it is two novels by female authors that exhibit the most ambivalence regarding the purely desirable nature of connection. Atwood's *Lady Oracle* and

---

[16] Cf. Swidler's (1986) argument that culture acts as a tool kit providing people with a wide range of capacities, some of which may be contradictory. Swidler stresses the "active" nature of individuals' use, and choice, of culturally available materials (see also Sewell 1992).

Munro's *Lives of Girls and Women* both provide cautionary messages about the danger of losing the self in an unthinking over-identification with another individual or with one's general social identity. Similarly, although Stowe strikes the "feminine" note of redemptive human connection in *Uncle Tom's Cabin*, Kate Chopin's *The Awakening* is a celebration of an overriding concern for the self, for individual autonomy, and for the denying of affiliative claims on that self. In addition, both the male-authored *The Sun Also Rises* and *Light in August* sound cautionary notes about the viability of the purely autonomous individual. Thus there does not seem to be any simple correspondence between gender and affiliative versus individualistic perspectives in either the Canadian or the American novels.[17] Although I will refrain from a detailed discussion of why the necessity for a unique, nationally distinctive literature takes the *specific* forms it does in Canadian and American literature until chapter 7, let me note here that I do not think these differences are arbitrary. The differences draw in complex ways upon available systems of meaning that are tightly connected to the larger political and economic environment in which they are found.

Social class and work importance

A fourth difference between the Canadian and American novels also helps create the connection versus individualism difference – the protagonist's social class. In coding social class, I used an eight-point scale with the following categories:

1. upper class/aristocracy
2. upper-middle class/professional
3. urban middle class (more educated)
4. agrarian middle class (less educated)
5. working class
6. lower class/poor
7. criminal/social outcast
8. prisoner/chattel/slave

The social class of the protagonists in Canadian novels are clustered in categories 3 and 4. *Eight* of the Canadian novels' protagonists are in those two

---

[17] McGregor argues that the role of gender in Canadian literature is profound, primarily because of the contrary evaluation of masculinity: "Quite contrary to the central and especially the American model, in a great many Canadian novels it is the *relinquishment* rather than the rediscovery or reassertion of a protagonist's masculinity that signals the achievement of emotional/aesthetic equilibrium" (1985: 143).

categories. The remaining two Canadian novels have protagonists in category 2 and 5. A typical Canadian protagonist is Dunny Ramsay in *Fifth Business*, a child of lower-middle class parents who becomes a schoolteacher and hagiographer, or Mrs. Bentley in *As For Me and My House*, the educated wife of an impoverished small town minister. Canadian novels in short are novels of the middle class.

The American novels, on the other hand, are novels of either outcasts or the very privileged. The class categories of the protagonists in the American novels are distributed in an *inverse* pattern to those of the Canadian. *None* of the American protagonists are in category 3 or 4. The social class of the protagonists in the American novels were clustered at the two ends at of the continuum in either categories 1, 2, or categories 5, 6, 7, 8. In the American novels, typical protagonists are the rich and well-educated Nick of *The Great Gatsby* and Chopin's wealthy and leisured Edna Pontellier or, conversely, the runaway Huck Finn and enslaved Tom of the eponymous novels.

This contrast in protagonist social class is clearly related to the issue of connection/affiliation versus autonomy/individualism. Middle-class lives are much more likely to be lives in which connection and affiliation play a large role. The lives of outcasts are defined in large part by their very lack of connection. To be an outcast, a criminal, a slave, is to be an isolated individual. Huck's status as a runaway, and a "dead" runaway at that, guarantees his isolation except from Jim and those to whom Huck lies. In the same way, the privileges of extreme wealth *may* serve to distance one from others. Fitzgerald positions Jay Gatsby in this way – he is alone in part because his wealth sets him apart; his interactions are inauthentic, he has only sycophants and hangers-on about him. Similarly, James shows Isobel's great wealth, combined with her pride, as an available barrier to be used against the attempts of others to get too close. In contrast, the middle-class protagonists typical of Canadian literature struggle to find lovers and mates, to care for their children and parents, to situate themselves within webs of friendship and family.

Another difference between American and Canadian canonical novels is related to this social class distinction and also to the connection versus individualism difference: the relative importance to the protagonist of his or her work. Only three American novels feature protagonists to whom paid employment is important. Eight of the Canadian novels, however, feature protagonists to whom such work is important. So, for example, the American *The Great Gatsby* has a protagonist who learns about bonds in a desultory fashion and a title character whose work is only vaguely identified, and only then because his success at that socially suspect work allows him access to the woman of his dreams. In contrast, the Canadian *Two Solitudes* features a fallen French-Canadian aristocrat whose work as a laborer awakens him to an understanding of the English-Canadian indifference to and exploitation of French Catholics and whose work as a writer crystallizes his vision of Canada's dual populations and the possibilities and pitfalls inherent in their relations.

For the Canadian protagonists work is important because of its dual nature: it is necessary to support oneself, to find a place and to function within society, but it is also an activity that helps shed light upon the self and its relation to society. The preponderance of protagonist-writers in the Canadian novels is one indication of this. Five of the ten Canadian novels feature protagonists who are writers or would-be writers. In *Lady Oracle*, *Fifth Business*, *The Diviners*, and *Two Solitudes* the protagonist uses writing to help order the world and his or her own place in the world. In *The Mountain and the Valley* David dies before he can act on his realization of the importance writing should play in his life. Throughout the Canadian novels the thought and care people put into their work, or the very conditions of its alienation in certain cases of menial work (notably in *Two Solitudes* and *The Diviners*), are rewarded.

In contrast, for the typical American protagonist, the project of the self *is* "work." The self is not enlightened through the conditions of paid employment; the exploration and development of the self is *itself* work. This emphasis on the project of the self has frequently been noted by writers such as Whitman, by critics, and by sociologists: the "great writers of . . . the 'American Renaissance' . . . put aside the search for wealth in favor of a deeper cultivation of the self" (Bellah *et al.* 1985: 33). Chopin's Edna Pontellier is one of the best examples. The story of *The Awakening* is, completely and solely, the story of Edna's search for and discovery of herself. Edna is joined in large part, however, by Hester and Dimmesdale in *The Scarlet Letter*, by James's Isobel Archer, by Nick Carroway in *Gatsby*, by Melville's Ishmael, and by Huck. The oblivious protagonists of *Light in August* and *Sister Carrie* are partially a warning of the perils attendant upon the inadequate cultivation of the self. None of these protagonists discovers his or her place in society through the struggles attendant upon paid employment, but all of them focus on the "deeper cultivation of the self." Only *Uncle Tom's Cabin* preaches the doctrine of subjugation of the self.

Generic distribution

A final difference that is clearly related to the overarching difference between connection versus individualism involves the generic distribution

of the Canadian and American novels. Genre analysis refers to the group-
ing of texts on the basis of form and content-driven categories such as
romance, action-adventure, or farce. In brief, generic designation is an
heuristic practice which assists the researcher in making sense of the
comparative patterns and capacities of the cultural objects under
consideration (Griswold 1987a). My typology of generic categories was
created both from traditional literary genres such as those listed above and
inductively from a series of summary sentences describing the primary
action of each narrative.[18] Although I acknowledge the difficulty of subsuming complex novels under a content-based system of generic designation (Kent 1986), I believe the practice of generic designation to be fruitful
(Rosmarin 1985).

The Canadian canonical novels fall into three genres – self-knowl-
edge/personal growth (S-K/PG), human condition, and coming-of-age.
The first category refers to texts focused on the personal development and
growth of the protagonist. This category contains six novels. An additional
three novels are in the category human condition, which contains narratives
focused on a more general examination of human society. The final
Canadian novel is in the coming-of-age category, which contains narratives
of adolescent awakening to the adult world. The American canonical
novels are also concentrated within these three genres; two within the S-
K/PG category, four within the human condition category, and one in the
coming-of-age category. In addition, two American novels were in the
morality tale category, containing narratives of moral caution, and one
American novel was in the allegorical adventure category, which contains
richly symbolic and allegorical action narratives.

The most interesting difference between the Canadian and American
novels is the greater propensity of Canadian canonical novels to focus on
narratives of S-K/PG. Six of the Canadian novels are narratives of S-K/PG
while only two American novels are. This genre of narrative focuses on the
growth and personal-discovery process of specific, idiosyncratic individuals. The genre is contrasted with the human condition genre which focuses
on individuals who are intended to be representative of some class, group,
or type. Even the most individually focused narrative obviously provides
morals, attitudes, and messages that may be extended to life outside of the
narrative itself. However, there is an observable difference between, for
example, Chopin's rendering of Edna's struggle to discover and define
herself despite the gender-bound conventions of society in *The Awakening*,

---

[18] It is important to keep in mind that generic specification in academic practice refers to heuristic devices, not immutable formulaic narrative structures.

and Drieser's depiction of Carrie's moral poverty and materialism in *Sister Carrie*. The former is primarily Edna's story, albeit a story with applicability beyond Edna's life, while the latter is much more a story about what happens to people like Carrie or Hurstwood, and how class and gender interact with morality and meaning in powerful ways.

Interestingly, the three Canadian novels in the human condition genre have original publication dates of 1904, 1933, and 1945, while the six Canadian novels in the S-K/PG genre have original publication dates of 1941, 1952, 1964, 1970, 1974, and 1976. The distribution of the Canadian novels across the two genres suggests a period effect on generic distribution with the S-K/PG genre seemingly a product of the late twentieth century. The generic distribution of the American novels, however, does not support this observation. The four American novels in the human condition genre have original publication dates of 1851, 1900, 1926, and 1933. The two American novels in the S-K/PG genre have original publication dates of 1899 and 1925.

The relationship between the Canadian emphasis on social identity and connection and the relative prevalence of novels of S-K/PG lies in the process of personal growth. In the Canadian novels, protagonists such as Laurence's Morag, Dunny in *Fifth Business*, Atwood's Joan, or David in *The Mountain and the Valley*, learn to understand themselves and their place in the social world through relationships with family, lovers, and friends. It is the processes of social interaction and the struggle to connect that drive self-knowledge, that illuminate personal growth. The American novels, even the two coded S-K/PG, lack such a sense of a socially situated personal development. *The Awakening* is one example of an S-K/PG novel whose protagonist finds self-knowledge *not* through social interaction and the intercession of family and friend, but through solitary introspection and self-scrutiny.

A second group of comparative differences

A second group of cross-national literary differences is less clearly related to the overarching difference of connection versus individualism. These differences include differences in narrative tone (the extent of optimism or pessimism in the novel), central conflict, rebelliousness of protagonists, presentation of religion, and the national identity of authors and protagonists. Although the reason for the difference in national identity of authors and protagonists is clear (the use of national literatures as "natural" expressions of the national character requires that they be written by national citizens) the meaning of the differences in tone, conflict, rebelliousness, and religion is less obvious. Previous authors working from a reflection perspective have nonetheless advanced a wide range of explanations for these differences.

Narrative tone

All novels express an emotional tone; reading them generates an emotional response. The narrative tone of a novel refers to this prevailing emotional attitude of the narrative.[19] The most interesting comparison between the typical tone of the American and Canadian novels is the difference between a tone of victory and fulfillment – a tone of success, optimism, and achievement – and a tone of despair and disappointment – a tone of failure, pessimism, and "mere survival" (Stouck 1988). Atwood, in her seminal *Survival* (1972), has most famously argued that Canadian literature is characterized by the latter and American literature by the former. I coded each novel as having either a "central" or "partial" tone of either type, a neutral tone, or a tone compounded equally of the two.

Canadian canonical novels are more likely to have a central tone of victory and fulfillment than are American canonical novels – four Canadian novels have such a tone while none of the American novels do. Typical of the Canadian novels with such a tone is Laurence's *The Diviners* or Munro's *Lives of Girls and Women*, in both of which the protagonist eventually comes to a fulfilling and meaningful life that incorporates and make sense of her past, although that may have been disappointing or unhappy. *Fifth Business* and *The Imperialist* are also fulfilled in tone. In contrast, the closest American canonical novels come to a central tone of victory and fulfillment is the *partial* victory of Stowe's *Uncle Tom's Cabin* and Chopin's *The Awakening* – in both of which "victory" is achieved only through the protagonist's death.

A central tone of pessimism and despair is common in both the Canadian and American novels, but is much more pronounced in the latter: six of the American novels and four of the Canadian novels have such a tone. Unlike the American novels, however, three of the four Canadian novels, *The Mountain and the Valley*, *The Stone Angel*, and *As For Me and My House*, end with an epiphany of some sort that softens the pessimism and despair of the rest of the story: David dies joyful at the top of the moun-

---

[19] What that tone and response are is not static. The construction of and response to a novel's tone is variable across readers, and across particular readers at different times. I have tried to explicate the reasoning behind my coding so that, despite the problems of textual interpretation and instability, readers may assess their accuracy. Obviously a familiarity with both the Canadian and American novels I discuss would be of enormous help to readers.

tain having finally understood his need and talent for writing, Hagar dies having made some small gestures of humanity and having repented of her pride and attendant loneliness, and *As For Me and My House* ends with some note of hope and renewed love for Philip and Mrs. Bentley. McGregor has argued that Atwood's (1972) famous insistence upon Canadian literary pessimism and despair ignores this ray of light that is so prevalent in Canadian literature:

A surprising proportion of Canadian writing, even when technically pessimistic on the level of plot or theme strikes a final note of limited or "contained" affirmation based . . . on a recognition of the double necessity imposed upon every individual simply by his own humanity of, firstly, accepting without either illusion or recrimination the existential "box" into which he is born . . . and secondly . . . taking full and free responsibility for what goes on inside the limited human space. According to what can be inferred from our literature . . . although the Canadian is well aware that man cannot choose his circumstances, he believes that one *can and must* choose how he will react to them; what, given his undeniable finitude, he will see, feel, *be* (1985: 440, italics in original).

To the extent the canonical Canadian novels are pessimistic, they do bear out McGregor's argument as to their "contained affirmation."

A corollary to the victory versus despair distinction is Atwood's (1972) seminal argument about the Canadian literary fascination with "mere" survival – as opposed to an American literary concentration on victorious fulfillment. My analysis does not support Atwood's argument, however. An equal one-half of the American novels and one-half of the Canadian novels feature protagonists caught in lives of "mere" survival.

Two American and two Canadian novels feature a protagonist who manages to find some improvement over mere survival. The two American novels are *The Scarlet Letter*, in which Hester Prynne is redeemed from her alienated and despairing isolation through Dimmesdale's confession and through her helping of other unfortunates and Pearl, and *The Sun Also Rises*, in which Jake faces his personal loss of both sexual function and Lady Brett with an ironic detachment, providing him some joy in the company of friends and other interests of his life. The two Canadian novels are *The Mountain and the Valley*, in which David realizes writing will be the salvation of his empty existence (but dies before he can act), and *The Stone Angel*, in which Hagar finally understands how pride has denied her a joyful life, allowing her to make some small amends.

Both the Canadian and American novels also feature one protagonist who recognizes and successfully triumphs over a life of mere survival. The American protagonist of *The Awakening* chooses suicide as a more honorable alternative than living a life of falsehood and self-denial while the

Canadian protagonist of *Two Solitudes* finds enough faith in himself to rise above the ethnically bounded social constraints and factional hatreds of pre-World War II Montreal. Although the latter protagonist makes a choice which seems more life-affirming, the former's choice is nonetheless an example of denying mere survival. Thus, my analysis is directly at odds with Atwood's *ad hoc* categorization of American and Canadian literatures as optimistic and fulfilling on the one hand, and pessimistic and despairing on the other.

Central conflict and rebellion

A second distinction focuses on the type of conflict central to the narrative in the American and Canadian novels. I coded the novels for type of central conflict. In order to be coded as the central conflict in a narrative I required that a conflict: (1) be crucial to the development of the narrative, and (2) be the primary conflict if more than one conflict existed. Therefore, a novel could be coded as having no conflict and, in novels in which multiple conflicts occurred, only the most important conflict was coded. For example, in *The Adventures of Huckleberry Finn* Huck is involved in a familial conflict with his father, a conflict within himself about hiding Jim or returning him to his owner, and an individual versus group conflict pitting himself (and sometimes Jim) against the larger world and its machinations. I defined the latter of these conflicts as the central conflict because it best matched both Huck's self-understanding and the central focus of the narrative.

The coding categories for central conflict were as follows: institutional (e.g., inter-national or inter-racial conflict), interpersonal (i.e., conflict between individuals), within-self, individual versus group, no central conflict, ideological, familial, and success struggle (e.g., a Horatio Alger scenario in which the protagonist battles a miscellaneous assortment of evils en route to success). All of the *canonical* novels are contained in the first six categories, none had either a familial or success struggle central conflict. The distribution of types of canonical conflict is shown in table 4.2.

The American canonical novels contain only three types of conflict. Four novels feature a central conflict which is within the protagonist's self, three novels feature a central conflict in which an individual is pitted against a group, and three novels feature an institutional central conflict. The Canadian canonical novels, on the other hand, include five types of conflict. Five of the Canadian canonical novels feature a central conflict within the protagonist's self, two novels have no central conflict, one novel features an institutional central conflict, one novel features an ideological central conflict, and one novel features an interpersonal central conflict.

Table 4.2   *Type of central conflict in the canonical novels (in percentage)*

	USA (N=10)	Canada (N=10)
Within self	40	50
Institutional	30	10
Individual versus group	30	0
No central conflict	0	20
Interpersonal	0	10
Ideological	0	10
Success struggle	0	0
Familial	0	0

One of the interesting results reported in table 4.2 is the distribution in the individual versus group category. Although none of the Canadian novels are in this category, three of the American novels feature individual versus group central conflicts. These novels, *The Awakening*, *The Great Gatsby*, and *The Adventures of Huckleberry Finn*, are all narratives in which the protagonist is confronted with the power of social groups or institutions rather than the power of individuals. The concept of a lone individual confronting a powerful group or institution is one which seems to resonate both with the mythic image of the lone American hero riding off into the sunset and with the descriptions of archetypal patterns in American literature offered by many theorists (e.g., Fiedler 1966).

However, the protagonists in these three narratives are not triumphant rebels winning through to victory and personal fulfillment. Instead, the three narratives feature protagonists on whom the cost of rebellion is clearly marked. The protagonist of the first narrative, Edna Pontellier, may find a certain fierce honor in her suicide, but few would describe her death as optimistic or particularly self-fulfilling. It is one thing to ride off all alone into the sunset and quite another to swim off all alone to one's death.

In Fitzgerald's *The Great Gatsby* Jay Gatsby not only loses everything he has or desires, but sees his own life and value debased by the "vast carelessness" of the Buchanans and others of their ilk. Huck Finn's optimistic desire for a life of freedom and personal happiness may not be quenched by his adventures, but the tale of his travels on the Mississippi make clear the compromises he is forced to make in a harsh and opportunistic world for the sake of the safety and survival of himself and his friend.

In addition to the three novels already discussed that have rebellious (if not victorious) protagonists, two American novels have semi-rebellious protagonists. Three Canadian novels have rebellious protagonists, e.g., Paul and Heather in *Two Solitudes* who rebel against their families and social classes to marry each other. There is also one Canadian novel in which the protagonist is an authority figure himself. None of the American novels contain protagonists who are authority figures themselves. The protagonist being in a position of authority, then, is equally *unlikely* in either the American or Canadian novels.

In those novels in which the protagonist is rebellious, both American and Canadian, much of the rebellion is directed against the climate of social opinion or social conventions, rather than individual people or institutions. Of the five American canonical novels with rebellious or semi-rebellious protagonists, three of them feature this type of rebelliousness: *The Awakening*, *The Sun Also Rises*, and *Portrait of a Lady*. The other two novels, *The Scarlet Letter* and *The Adventures of Huckleberry Finn*, also feature protagonists who rebel against public conceptions of proper behavior, but conflict in these novels also occurs with the people and institutions embodying those notions. Again, for the five Canadian canonical novels with rebellious or semi-rebellious protagonists three feature a type of rebelliousness directed against social expectation and convention: *The Stone Angel*, *The Diviners*, and *Lives of Girls and Women*. The other two novels, *Two Solitudes* and *As For Me and My House*, feature protagonists who, although also rebelling against public expectations or conventions, come into direct conflict with the people and institutions embodying such notions. Thus rebelliousness of protagonists, despite the arguments of Atwood and others, is not, in my analysis, a peculiarly American characteristic.

Religion

Four of the American novels and six of the Canadian novels present religion as important in some respect. Four of the American novels present characters to whom expressing personal beliefs is important and two of those same novels also present religion as an important institution. Canadian novels are more likely than American novels to present religious material in terms of the importance of the church in an institutional sense; four Canadian novels present religion in such a way. The Canadian and American novels are almost equally likely to present religion through characters expressing personal faith or beliefs; three Canadian novels do compared to four American novels. Previous theorists have argued that the public role of religious institutions is a more powerful force in Canadian social life while individual, privately held belief is more powerful in the American social tradition (e.g., Kollar 1989). The literary depiction of religiosity in the canonical novels does not support this distinction very strongly.

National identity

A final difference between the canonical novels is usually taken for granted. All of the Canadian novels have Canadian authors and all of the American novels have American authors. Although both Canada and the United States have large immigrant populations, only one of the canonical authors was not born a citizen of the canonizing nation. Frederick Philip Grove was born in Germany in 1879 and moved to Canada in 1912. Given the explicitly national functions of canonical novels it is not surprising that the canonical authors are native sons and daughters of their respective countries.

The national identities of the protagonists in the canonical novels also conform to such expectations. All of the Canadian canonical novels feature Canadian protagonists. Likewise, all of the American canonical novels feature American protagonists – with the technical exception of Hester Prynne in *The Scarlet Letter* since Boston was still an English colony at the time of the narrative's action. Again, it does not seem particularly strange that American literature would be by and about Americans and Canadian literature by and about Canadians. In order to use a national literature to advance the notion of the nation and its unique identity, one must be able to show the "natural" relationship between the nation and its people – embodied by authorial national identity. The importance of this point is underscored, however, in the comparison with the literary prize-winning and popular-culture novels.

Thus the canonical novels, when considered comparatively, display a strong sense of national distinctiveness and demonstrate sharp differences across national lines. The central point of the analysis is clear: American and Canadian canonical novels are different. The meaning of the specific differences that we see is, however, less clear. Although I have discussed the strengths and weaknesses of certain current understandings of some of the differences, I wish to reserve the detailed discussion of the meaning of specific differences until I have presented all of the empirical analyses. I will return to the question of meaning in chapter 7, but for now I wish to discuss one important factor affecting the construction of specific differences in American and Canadian canonical content – the role of canonical timing.

As should be clear from the discussions in chapters 2 and 3, the *timing* of the canon formation process in Canada and the United States affects the *content* of the canon in one very significant way – by highlighting the nation-state(s) that are considered the relevant "other." The nation-state, and therefore the national literature, in contrast to which the unique national identity must be established is made relevant by variant geographical, military, and historical conditions. Canada's need for differentiation from the United States as well as from Great Britain is but one example. Conceivably, had conditions been different, Canada may not have found the United States a relevant other. Such an historical contingency would have in turn affected the particulars of the form and content of the Canadian national canon. Similarly, if the Spanish–Mexican empire to the south had a more significant impact on nation-building in the United States, the literary context within which the American canon was selected would have been different – and therefore the form and content of American canonical novels may well have been different. Given the driving role of cross-national differentiation in national canon formation, the question of "different from whom?" is a powerful influence on canonical content. These "founding effects" (Stinchcombe 1965) in turn contribute to the development of specific national literary traditions which then establish the particular directions of national literary development.

I turn now to the second group of high-culture novels, the contemporary literary prize winners. The particulars of canon formation in Canada and the United States and the comparison of the canonical novels form the backdrop for my discussion of the prize winners. In addition to discussing the uses of contemporary high-culture novels and their patterns of cross-national difference, chapter 5 will return our attention to the issue of national literary traditions as the central theoretical context for understanding the content of contemporary high-culture novels.

5

The literary prize winners: revision and renewal

Where so many are excluded from access to our most distinguished literary decorations, what is wrong?
> Carlos Baker (1957: 63) in questioning the large number of "distinguished writers" who never won a Pulitzer.

The National Book Awards were founded in 1950 in response to widespread dissatisfaction with the Pulitzer fiction winners; the National Book Critics Circle Awards were founded twenty-five years later in response to widespread dissatisfaction with the National Book Award winners.
> James F. English (1993: 17) in his introduction to "An Economy of Prestige: Literary Prizes and the Circulation of Cultural Value."

The inclusion of contemporary Canadian and American literary prize-winning novels serves several purposes in this analysis. Most importantly, the analysis of prize winners provides a test of the competing unconscious-reflection-of-national-character and conscious-construction-of-national-identity arguments. The traditional reflection-of-national-character argument would expect contemporary high-culture literature to exhibit the same core cross-nationally distinctive characteristics as canonical literature since both types of literature are seen as reflecting *natural* national differences. An argument locating cross-national literary difference in the conscious construction of a unique nation, on the other hand, would not necessarily expect similar differences. Current literary prize winners, after all, are not contemporaneous with the nation-building process in the United States and Canada nor does their designation as worthy of a literary prize carry quite the same cultural authority as selection into the canon.

Second, the prize winners provide a comparison between Canadian and American high-culture texts that is unencumbered by period effects. That is, while the differences between the Canadian and American canonical novels may arguably be at least partially due to the differences in the period in which they are written,[1] the prize-winning novels provide a period-controlled, cross-national, high-culture comparison as all the novels were published during the period 1978–87. Finally, an examination of contemporary literary prize winners allows us to consider how the context within which novels are evaluated and accorded legitimacy alters as the importance of the initial nation-building process wanes and the concomitant need for national distinctiveness recedes.

The literary prize winners

Like canonical novels, contemporary high-culture novels are produced within the "field of restricted production" in which "economic profit is secondary to . . . symbolic value" (Bourdieu 1985: 13). And indeed the economics of contemporary high-culture fiction publishing would make it difficult for the field to be driven solely, or even primarily, by the profit motive since "most volumes of serious fiction, poetry, and drama do not sell many copies, even if they received excellent reviews. Publishing these works is typically a losing or marginally profitable proposition" (Zill and Winglee 1990: 81). There is, however, some evidence that the trade-off between symbolic value and low profitability is increasingly less attractive to publishers (see Max [1994] for a list of publishers reducing their role, or even no longer participating, in the trade book market despite their historical relationship with high-culture work; see also Coser, Kadushin, and Powell 1982).

Estimates of how many people actually read contemporary high-culture fiction are difficult to make and the reliability of the figures is unknown. Given that caveat, general consensus seems to be that the audience for contemporary high-culture fiction is quite small (Mann 1983; Yardley 1989; Zill and Winglee 1990). Philip Roth refers to a "drastic decline, even a disappearance, of a serious readership" (quoted in Yardley 1993: D2). In a review of public surveys on reading, Zill and Winglee's best estimate is that 7–12 percent of the adult American population has read "serious contemporary literature of all forms [novels, short stories, drama, and poetry] in the course of a year" (1990: 31).[2] In terms of novel reading alone, Zill and

---

[1] Note that this possibility does not weaken the argument regarding the national identity uses of high-culture literature. Regardless of the period in which they were written, the canonical novels I discuss are those currently considered canonical. Nonetheless, a comparison without the possible confusion of period effects adds to the analysis.

[2] Zill and Winglee (1990) base their estimates on two large-scale surveys; the Arts-Related Trend Study done in 1983–4 by the Survey Research Center at the University of Maryland and the Consumer Research Study on Reading and Book Purchasing done in 1983 for the Book Industry Study Group. The National Endowment for the Arts' nationwide Survey of Public Participation in the Arts (SPPA) (1982, 1985, 1992) reports reading, but does not, unfortunately, ask questions about the type of reading respondents report.

Winglee estimate that 11 percent of the adult American population has read either a classical or contemporary "serious" novel in the last twelve months and that perhaps 7 percent of the adult American population has read a "meritorious contemporary work" in that period (Zill and Winglee 1990: 25).[3] In comparison, Robinson found that 54 percent of adult Americans report reading *any* poem, play, novel, or short story in the past twelve months (Robinson 1993: 2).[4]

The approximately 50 percent of the American population reporting some fiction reading is not representative of the American population at large, however. The 1992 SPPA shows those who report having read literature in the past twelve months are disproportionately female (60.2 percent versus 47.2 percent of males), white (55.6 percent versus 45.3 percent of blacks and 41.5 percent of others), highly educated (70.5 percent of college graduates versus 48.8 percent of high school graduates), and have higher incomes (71 percent of those with incomes over $50,000 versus 57.6 percent of those with incomes between $25,000 and $50,000) (Robinson 1993: Appendix A.2). Zill and Winglee (1990: 11–12, 35–42) argue that the relative disproportion of women and those with higher incomes and more education increases the more exclusively one defines literatures. Thus American readers of contemporary high-culture novels are probably the most disproportionately female, highly educated, and with higher incomes of any readers.

The Canadian data on high-culture reading show somewhat higher percentages for novel reading and drama reading, and similar percentages for poetry reading. In the 1991 readership survey, *Reading in Canada*, 27.6 percent of adults reported reading "classic literature" in the last twelve months (Ekos Research Associates 1992: 22). Poetry and drama reading were reported by 12.2 percent and 12.9 percent respectively (Ekos Research Associates 1992: 22). Comparable American percentages for poetry and drama reading are 11–15 percent and 5–8 percent respectively (Zill and Winglee 1990: 26, 31). However, the Ekos authors caution that the Canadian report "*severely underrepresents the lowest decile of the Canadian population in terms of reading capacity*," resulting in an upward bias (Ekos

[3] They note the similarity of this figure to Mann's report on the 1981 Euromonitor readership survey in Great Britain that 6 percent of British adults were reading "modern novels" (Zill and Winglee 1990: 25; see also Mann 1982). However, Mann's estimate of the percentage of the adult British population who read "modern *literary* novels" actually ranges from 6 percent down to "no more than about 3 percent" (Mann 1983: 437, emphasis added).

[4] Many members of the publishing and literary world are even more pessimistic regarding the likely size of the audience for high-culture literature in the future given both the strong pull of the electronic media and the push of decreasing reading skills (Percy 1986; Max 1994; *New York Times* 1995: A18).

Research Associates 1992: 4, italics in original).[5] Unfortunately, the Canadian data do not include a category of contemporary high-culture novels, subsuming contemporary non-genre fiction in the category of "other fiction" which is reported by 35 percent of the respondents.[6] The Canadian data also indicate that women and the more highly educated are more likely to be readers (Ekos Research Associates 1992: 24).[7] Given the small size of audiences for contemporary high-culture literature, it is clear that understanding the field requires attention to processes and roles other than the purely economic.

Literary prize winners as precanonical texts

Literary prize winners are "precanonical" texts, educated guesses about what might survive the exigencies of time and caprice to become tomorrow's classics (Ohmann 1984: 398).[8] In their position as precanonical texts literary prize winners have several roles. One of these is to encourage the current elite version of literary aesthetics, otherwise known as rewarding "good" writing. Texts chosen as prestigious award winners must meet the aesthetic criteria of the critics, academics, and practitioners who make up the judging panels. However, this role, despite being the most frequently cited for the existence of literary prizes, is far from the only role literary prizes play.

A second important role played by literary prizes and the discourse surrounding them is the continued validation of notions of "pure" literary and aesthetic hierarchies of value (English 1993). The conferral of literary prizes and, *even more importantly*, the public discussions and disagreements about judges' decisions, the charges of evaluative idiocy and favoritism, the prize-bashing and "sneering condescension" about the process ultimately serve to confirm and affirm the existence and value of a cultural hierarchy:

[5] The report was based on a sample of 7,000 respondents from an initial telephone contact pool of 23,900 of whom 12,400 agreed to receive a questionnaire through the mail: a 52 percent response rate (Ekos Research Associates 1992: 2–3). However, the initial telephone contact precludes those without phones from the survey, and comfort with reading almost certainly affects the agreement to receive a questionnaire.

[6] The *Reading in Canada 1991* study reports "type" of fiction book read in the categories of mystery, romance, other fiction, science fiction/fantasy/horror, classic literature, cartoon books, Western, humour, drama, and poetry (Ekos Research Associates 1992: 22). Non-genre, contemporary fiction, that is high-culture novels that are not "classics," is subsumed under "other fiction."

[7] However, the Canadian data are reported in demographic groups by average number of books read, rather than percentage of group reporting any reading, so the data are not strictly comparable to the American data.

[8] Ohmann looks at precanonical texts slightly differently than I do. Although he defines precanonical texts as those "that are active candidates for inclusion" in the canon, he argues for best-selling status as a prime indicator (1984: 398). I would argue that winning literary prizes is a much better indicator of precanonical status.

The prize is a remarkable cultural phenomenon inasmuch as we could expect it to give the whole "cultural game" away, to expose the violent social and economic relations which are euphemized in the established canons, the aesthetic principles, and the special competencies of literature; and yet it manages, through a curious double-process, to do just the opposite, to frame its acknowledged material interests as dilutions or degradations of a pre-existing and purely *cultural* value, and thereby to affirm the very hierarchies of which it would seem to be a mockery (English 1993: 33, italics in original).

It is often the very attacks and criticisms that allow literary prizes to "keep the faith in a realm of 'pure' culture, in a cultural coin which is *not false*" because "prize-bashing is predicated, usually explicitly, on the possibility of true or uncompromised cultural valuations . . . [in a pure realm] *somewhere else*, somewhere above or apart from this circus-stunt vulgarity, [where] real distinctions between works of high and low literary value are still being made" (English 1993: 19–20, italics in original).[9]

Literary prize winners also serve as an international benchmark of the state of a national culture – a sign of the health and viability of current national cultures signaled across continents. In the jousting for national supremacy which takes place not only overtly through military aggression, but through subtler avenues such as Olympic medal competition, political rhetoric, and economic aid packages, literature often serves in part as yet another forum for nationalistic posturing. Like canonical texts, prestigious award winners also may serve political functions. Rather than contributing to the process of nation formation, however, highly visible award winners serve as an ongoing validation of nationhood, as markers of a flourishing national culture and identity. The production and possession of contemporary high-culture genres, perhaps especially literary, is one key avenue for participating in the increasingly global cultural arena, for demonstrating suitability for inclusion in the activities of the world system "core" (Meyer and Hannan 1979; Thomas, Meyer, Ramirez, and Boli 1987).

As precanonical texts, literary prize winners often serve as a "contemporary" canon, particularly through entry into the pedagogical canon in high schools and in contemporary literature classes in college curricula.[10] To the extent that the pedagogical canon is presented as a valued piece of

---

[9] Bourdieu makes a similar point when he stresses that "the two modes of production of symbolic goods [the field of restricted production and the field of large-scale production] . . . can only be defined in terms of their relations with each other"; they "coexist so as to be definable only in terms of their hierarchic . . . relations with each other" (1985: 29, 14).

[10] The term "contemporary" canon is somewhat paradoxical given the time-legitimated nature of the definition of a literary canon. Nonetheless, the pedagogical canon frequently reflects such a concept, turning to literary prize winners in its search for "relevant" or timely high-culture literature that will appeal to the notoriously ahistorical young.

the national culture, literary prize winners gain legitimation for their vision of the national experience. Literary prize winners, like canonical novels, become one of the representations of legitimated national experience available to society, although with less absolute authority. The status of prize winners, and thus their cultural authority, is more nebulous than that of the canon, the reception of such texts always open to charges of faddism, political favoritism, and the failure to past the "test of time."

Nonetheless, literary prize winners and their authors often occupy positions of significant cultural authority, which is well understood by the literary world. The acknowledged cultural power of literary prizes is most compellingly indicated by one recent example. On January 24, 1988, a statement signed by forty-eight African-American writers and critics was published in the *New York Times Book Review* protesting the failure of Toni Morrison to have ever won either the Pulitzer Prize or the National Book Award. The statement refers to the two prizes as "keystone honors" and advances a straightforward claim for the cultural authority of the undersigned: "The legitimate need for our own critical voice in relation to our own literature can no longer be denied" (*New York Times Book Review* 1988: 36). Morrison's *Beloved* won the Pulitzer Prize that year.[11]

Furthermore, literary prize winners and their authors are often centrally situated in the present-day literary world, granting further scope to their vision of national experience. But that vision, despite its possibilities for revisionary activity and its potentially wide dissemination, may well be a narrow one, created by an extremely small and arguably unrepresentative group of people and legitimated by individuals subject to the demands and constraints of their professions. Literary prize winners are not chosen by popular ballot, but by panels of "experts," experts with vested interests in the maintenance of a system which, among other things, strongly differentiates between high-culture literature and popular-culture literature (Ibsch, Schram, and Steen 1995).

Revisionary functions

During the initial period of nation-building, the need for a unique canon that helps construct the national identity dominates the canon formation process, so that the search for uniqueness drives canon selection. This process ignores, or at least subsumes, interest in literary themes and topics

---

[11] See Carol Iannone's (1991) scathing attack on this statement and literary prize juries' consideration of it for a good example of a counter-move in the "contestation" for the authority to determine cultural value.

that have already been the focus of other national literatures. Over time, however, a national literary tradition becomes established. Once a national literary tradition has been secured, the issue of differentiating "our" nation from others, while still important, no longer dominates literary considera-tion. The question "Do we have a unique national literature?" becomes less important and the focus shifts to reacting to *and against* the established national tradition. Internal development, rather than external differentia-tion, becomes the central context.

One aspect of reaction to an existing tradition is the inclusion of characteristics previously ignored in the interests of national uniqueness. That is, once the driving need for national uniqueness recedes, literature that addresses previously other-nation-identified issues can be valued. Thus for example, American literature may return to issues of money and mar-riage without fearing that the resultant literature will be too similar to British literature. Similarly, Canadian literature can turn to a consideration of the dangers of sociability and the importance of individualism without panicking that Canadian literature is indistinguishable from American lit-erature. Indeed, Sutherland (1977) has argued that a "new hero" emerged in Canadian literature in the 1970s, one whose individualism and sense of competence resembles the traditionally envisioned literary American more than the traditionally envisioned literary Canadian.

Canonical texts, I have argued, present a legitimated version of the national experience. The canon, however, is both representation *and con-structor* of what it means to be American or Canadian. Revisions to the canon, revisions to the rhetorical discourse about being a participant in the national experience, occur gradually. Literature which deals with tradition-ally marginalized or peripheral experiences enters the canon slowly, if at all. Literary prize winners are one avenue for experimenting with such poten-tial revisions.

Designating novels detailing marginal experiences as literary prize winners is one way of incorporating changes into the legitimated vision of the national experience.[12] Literary prize winners presenting non-main-stream or marginalized experiences make available possible revisions to the most broadly accepted understanding of the national experience. Such revi-sionist offerings then enter the field of canonical consideration, allowing changes in the presentation of the validated experience to occur. One of the most obvious examples of a revision to the American canon involves the gradual incorporation of novels dealing with racial and ethnic minority

---

[12] This is not to say that minority experience was not a part of the national experience, only that it was not part of the legitimated vision of the national experience.

experiences. But potential revisions to the canon involve many things other than a protagonist's race or ethnicity. A revisionary novel is also one that legitimates casual sex in a traditionally Puritan culture, or one that presents ennui and alienation as appropriate responses to the American Dream, or a novel that sanctions rebellion as a valid reaction to the Canadian emphasis on "order and good government."

Raymond Williams describes cultural tradition as "an intentionally selective version of a shaping past and a pre-shaped present, which is then powerfully operative in the process of social and cultural definition and identification" (1977: 115; see also McCrone 1992: 29–31). Hubbell makes reference to a similar, specifically literary action when he discusses how the "definition of a literary tradition . . . can be . . . only a kind of majority report. It stresses those elements in the older literature which at a particular time are felt to have value, to constitute a usable past" (1972: 7). As a national literary tradition emerges and is reacted to, the interpretation of the national tradition and the earlier texts that are included in that tradition change. Imagining the nation and naming its literature is a process in which the past both affects the present and is itself affected by the present (McCarthy 1991). In chapter 2, I described some of the canonical changes in American literary history. Often these changes, and those in other national canons, are generated by contemporary writing that highlights one strand of earlier work or a particular set of authors and makes others seem less central, less archetypally "American" or "Canadian." Contemporary high-culture literature not only changes the culturally validated vision of the national experience directly, but also indirectly through its effect on the preservation, interpretation, and evaluation of the literary past.

Because the canon is of necessity time-lagged, some mechanism for highlighting potential entrants to the canon is necessary so that the novels deemed worthy by today's selection elites are not lost to the arbiters of the future (see Griswold [1986] on the importance of cultural "archives;" also Schudson [1989] on "retrievability" and "retention"). Literary prizes are one such mechanism for marking contemporary novels as possible candidates for canonical inclusion. The labeling process in turn triggers the process of mobilizing support for canonizing specific texts and authors (see Tompkins [1985] for an historical description of the mobilization process in Nathaniel Hawthorne's case; see DeNora [1991] for a discussion of the process in Beethoven's case).

Thus, as I have described, the comparison of literary prize winners serves multiple purposes in this analysis. Most importantly, the comparison generates additional data as to the sufficiency of traditional arguments on national literatures. If the cross-national differences between the American and Canadian prize winners were the same as the canonical cross-national differences, this would provide support for a reflection of national character argument. Such, however, is not the case. The comparison of prize winners shows two areas of substantial difference from the canonical novels. One, the prize winners have a different primary focus than do the canonical texts. Two, those characteristics, such as family importance, that the prize winners share with the canonical novels show different patterns of variation. The differences between what is cross-nationally distinctive in the canonical compared to the prize-winning novels, between what each "reflects" about Canada or America, underscores the fallacy of assuming cross-nationally distinctive literary characteristics are "natural" or reflective of a coherent and unique national character.

In addition to providing data on this initial point, the prize-winning comparison helps to illuminate issues of canon formation, literary tradition, and cultural change. Neither canons nor nations are static. Canon formation is a process of struggle and competition – a competition in which the prize is the power of cultural authority. Revisions to the canon occur when new stakeholders achieve power in the competition for cultural legitimacy, when new readings, new critical strategies, vanquish older readings and older stakeholders, and thereby consecrate new texts and new authors (Bourdieu 1984, 1985; Corse and Griffin 1996; Corse and Westervelt 1995). Thus the process of prize giving and the attendant evaluative decisions provide not only the highlighting of possible future canonical texts, but also an arena within which the competition for both cultural consecration and the ability to confer cultural consecration are played out.

The literary prizes

The prize-winning novels I analyze are the winners of the two most prestigious literary awards in Canada and the winners of the two most prestigious literary awards in the United States for the ten years 1978 through 1987 inclusive. In Canada, the two prizes are the Governor-General's Award in English language fiction and the Canadian Authors' Association Silver Medal in fiction. In the United States the two prizes are the Pulitzer Prize for fiction and the National Book Award in fiction (briefly named the American Book Award).

The most visible literary award in the United States is the Pulitzer, in large part because most Pulitzers are for newspaper writing, which ensures extensive media coverage of the Pulitzer announcements. Joseph Pulitzer established the Pulitzer Prizes with money left in his will in 1911, although the first Pulitzer Prize for fiction was not awarded until 1917.[13] The Pulitzer in fiction is chosen through a two-tier system consisting first of a nominating jury of three "experts," generally academics, writers, editors, and critics. In 1990, there were a total of fifteen book jurors (three each for fiction, general non-fiction, biography, poetry, and history) of whom ten were college professors, and the remaining five were writers, editors, and critics (Bates 1991: 165–6). In 1990, the fiction jury, composed of Joel Conarroe, president of the Guggenheim Foundation and former executive director of the Modern Language Association, Diane Johnson, a San Francisco writer and critic, and Philip O'Connor, a Bowling Green State professor, read through 115 entries in their quest for the slate of three nominees or finalists (Bates 1991: 208). The names of finalists are then sent with a brief report to the Pulitzer Board, which has a three-person subcommittee assigned to the fiction prize. The subcommittee makes a recommendation to the full Board, whose decision is reported to and announced by the President of Columbia University. Since 1976, final decision about the prize rests with the Board – and that body has historically not been shy about exercising its prerogatives.

The Board has overturned the decision of the fiction jury on a number of occasions, particularly in the early part of the century. Even in 1974, however, the jury recommended Pynchon's *Gravity's Rainbow*, but the Board, finding the book confusing, would not concur and – ignoring books by Kurt Vonnegut, Joyce Carol Oates, John Cheever, Bernard Malamud, and Philip Roth among others – refused to award that year's Pulitzer in fiction. Similarly, the Board ignored the jury's recommendation of Norman Maclean's *A River Runs Through It* in 1977 and made no award.

The final decision regarding the Pulitzer Prize for fiction thus rests with a Board composed almost entirely of "white, male, senior journalists," most of whom would concur with the 1990 Pulitzer Board chairman Eugene Roberts, executive editor and president of the *Philadelphia Inquirer*, who views himself as a "career newspaperman, not as an arts critic" (Bates 1991: 194, 201). It was not until 1980 that the Pulitzer Board first included non-journalists, or for that matter women and non-whites (Shaw 1984: 183). In 1990, the sixteen voting members of the Pulitzer Board included only two non-journalists: Brandeis University professor Sissela Bok and Columbia University president Michael Sovern who serves *ex officio*.

The National Book Award (NBA) was created in 1950 in large part because of dissatisfaction with what were perceived as the obvious failures

---

[13] The Pulitzer Prizes have a long and complicated history. I relied on, and recommend for greater detail about that history, and the frequent scandals, changes in procedure, and politics contained within it, the following: Baker (1957); Stuckey (1981); Shaw (1984); and Bates (1991).

of the Pulitzer committees to honor key authors and titles in contemporary high-culture fiction. Originally three judges served on the NBA fiction award. In 1988, following the controversy over Toni Morrison's failure to garner the NBA for *Beloved*, the number of judges was expanded to five to "reduce the possibility of any individual judge casting a deciding vote" and to "broaden the award selection process by reflecting the expanded jury's diversity of opinion" (Roger Stevens, chairman of the NBA, quoted in *Publishers Weekly* 1988: 320). In 1988, the first expanded fiction jury consisted of chairman Joel Conarroe, president of the Guggenheim Foundation and former executive director of the Modern Language Association; Charles Johnson, chairman of creative writing and English professor at the University of Washington; Brad Leithauser, novelist and MacArthur Fellowship recipient; Joyce Carol Oates, author of short stories, poems, essays, and eighteen novels, including a previous NBA fiction winner; and Carolyn See, novelist, *Los Angeles Times* book reviewer, and English professor at UCLA (*Publishers Weekly* 1988: 320)

In Canada, the Governor-General's Literary Awards were first established by the Canadian Authors' Association (CAA) in 1936. In 1959, the administration of the Governor-General's Awards was undertaken by the Canada Council, the premier government funding body for culture. The Council appoints both an anglophone and francophone nine-member jury made up of experienced writers, academics, and literary critics. Seven awards are given in each language: fiction, poetry, drama, non-fiction, children's literature (both illustration and text), and translation. In 1990, the fiction jury in English was composed of chairman Leon Rooke, novelist, dramatist, and Governor-General's Award winner in 1983 for *Shakespeare's Dog*; novelist Sandra Birdsell; and Henry Kreisel, university professor at Alberta and the author of novels, short stories, and literary criticism (The Canada Council 1991: 96).

The Canadian Authors' Association Silver Medal has been awarded in the four fields of literature, prose fiction, prose non-fiction, poetry, and drama since 1975. Each year the awards chair of the CAA appoints a trustee for each prize category. The trustee may or may not be a member of the CAA, but is an "established" and "experienced" published author or academic. The trustee then chooses three jury members, also published writers or academics, who select the prize winner. Individuals or publishers may enter novels in the competition.[14]

---

[14] The information on the selection process for the CAA Silver Medal in Fiction was provided in a private communication with Alec McEachern, CAA administrator (December 7, 1995). Mr. McEachern was unwilling to provide the names of specific jurors as the CAA believes that the process should be kept confidential.

The composition of prize juries makes clear the location of literary prize competitions within the realm of high culture. The jury members are all located within the field of restricted production either as authors or as literary critics (de Nooy 1988). The juries are not just composed of high-culture experts, but of prestigious experts whose own achievements or institutional location makes their high status clear (van Rees 1989; Shavit 1989). No "ordinary" readers sit on famous literary prize juries, nor do the juries contain members tainted by undue commercial relationships.[15] Thus the boundary between high culture and popular culture, between the sanctified and the commercial, is faithfully reproduced.

Data collection

Because the awards may be given to short story collections, which I dropped from my sample in the interests of coding comparability, and because both awards are sometimes given to the same book or an award is not given at all, the literary prize winners number fourteen Canadian and fifteen American novels (rather than twenty apiece). The Canadian and American literary prize winners and the dates of their prizes are as follows:

United States

1978	Settle, Mary Lee	*Blood Tie*
1979	O'Brien, Tim	*Going After Cacciato*
1980	Mailer, Norman	*The Executioner's Song*
1980	Styron, William	*Sophie's Choice*
1981	Morris, Wright	*Plains Song*
1981	Toole, John Kennedy	*A Confederacy of Dunces*
1982	Updike, John	*Rabbit Is Rich**
1983	Walker, Alice	*The Color Purple**
1984	Kennedy, William	*Ironweed*
1985	DeLillo, Don	*White Noise*
1985	Lurie, Alison	*Foreign Affairs*
1986	Doctorow, E. L.	*World's Fair*
1986	McMurty, Larry	*Lonesome Dove*
1987	Heinemann, Larry	*Paco's Story*
1987	Taylor, Peter	*A Summons to Memphis*

[15] One clear indication of this was the dismay that greeted the changing of the National Book Award to the American Book Award with the concomitant change from the award being sponsored by the National Book Committee to being sponsored by the Association of American Booksellers (Hart 1983: 524).

* Won both the Pulitzer and the National Book Award that year. In 1978, 1979, and 1984 one of the American prize winners was a short story collection.

Canada

1978	Rule, Jane	*The Young in One Another's Arms*
1979	Engel, Marian	*The Glassy Sea*
1979	Hodgins, Jack	*The Resurrection of Joseph Bourne*
1980	Bowering, George	*Burning Water*
1981	MacLennan, Hugh	*Voices in Time*
1982	Kogawa, Joy	*Obasan*
1983	Kinsella, W. P.	*Shoeless Joe*
1983	Rooke, Leon	*Shakespeare's Dog*
1984	Robertson, Heather	*Willie: A Romance*
1984	Skvorecky, Josef	*The Engineer of Human Souls*
1985	Atwood, Margaret	*The Handmaid's Tale*
1985	Findley, Timothy	*Not Wanted On The Voyage*
1986	Davies, Robertson K.	*What's Bred in the Bone*
1987	Kelly, M. T.	*A Dream Like Mine*

In 1978, 1981, 1982, and 1986 the GGA was for a collection of short stories. In 1980 and 1987 the CAA Silver Medal for fiction was not awarded.

A comparative analysis of American and Canadian contemporary literary prize winners

The Canadian and American literary prize-winning novels are more similar in many ways than are the Canadian and American canonical novels. Although reading the two groups of prize winners does generate a feeling of distinctive Canadian and American literature, the contrast is much less stark than with the canonical novels. In substantive terms, this is perhaps primarily due to the abatement of the polarization between connection and autonomy. The primary difference between the Canadian and American prize winners involves instead a Canadian explicitness of attention to the issue of meaningful identity, both personal and national, and a concomitant American vagueness or cynicism about such possibilities. The *reason* for the decreased sharpness of the distinctions between Canadian and American prize winners as compared to canonical novels involves, as I will argue, both the central responsiveness of prize winners to *internal* literary traditions rather than *external* others and the increasing internationalization of the high-culture literary world.

National identity

The most striking difference between the Canadian and American prize winners is a difference so assumed that it was barely noticeable in the canonical texts – the national identity of the novels' protagonists. Like the American canonical novels, a resounding 100 percent of the American prize-winning novels feature protagonists who are American. Not only are the protagonists all American citizens, but the identity of their citizenship, the fact of their citizenship, is non-problematic; American citizenship is simply assumed in the American prize winners.

The Canadian prize-winning novels, however, are unlike either the American prize winners or the Canadian and American canonical novels. A full two-thirds of the protagonists in the Canadian prize-winning novels hold non-Canadian or only partially Canadian citizenship. Citizenship, rather than being a background assumption of the novel, is a substantive focus of narrative attention. In the Canadian prize winners, citizenship often involves a critical inquiry into identity, both personal and national or communal. Citizenship, both as an attribute of characters and as a process occupying narrative attention, serves as an avenue for exploring issues of personal and national development and for situating the self into a meaningful social world. The Canadian prize winners focus on the question of how "we" will live, of how "we" will order our society.

The nationality of the protagonists in the fourteen Canadian and fifteen United States prize winners is distributed as shown in table 5.1. Only five (36 percent) of the fourteen Canadian prize winners feature protagonists who are solely Canadian. Conversely, as already mentioned, all fifteen (100 percent) American prize winners feature American protagonists. In addition to the five protagonists who are solely Canadian, the Canadian prize winners feature an additional 21 percent of protagonists who become Canadian citizens, originally one German, one Czechoslovakian, and one American.

Of the remaining 43 percent of Canadian prize winners, 14 percent feature protagonists of unknown or unspecified nationality. One of these protagonists, Mrs. Noyes in *Not Wanted On the Voyage*, lives in the period before the founding of nation-states and the other, the title character in *The Resurrection of Joseph Bourne*, is never identified by his nationality. The remaining 29 percent of protagonists are non-Canadian. Two are British, one is American, and one is an ex-American turned citizen of Gilead – a

Table 5.1   *Nationality of protagonists in the prize winners (in percentages)*

	USA (N=15)	Canada (N=14)
Nationality solely same as that of prize-giving nation	100	36
Nationality becomes that of prize-giving nation	0	21
Nationality unknown or unspecified	0	14
Nationality different from that of prize-giving nation	0	29

future society in *The Handmaid's Tale*. The two British protagonists are the title character in *Shakespeare's Dog*, for whom nationality is an irrelevant characteristic, and George Vancouver in *Burning Water* who, although British, was an early explorer of Western Canada. The sole American protagonist is Ray Kinsella in W. P. Kinsella's *Shoeless Joe*, a novel revolving around the quintessentially American sport of baseball.

The variety of national identities exhibited by the protagonists of the Canadian prize winners compared to the assumed American nationality of the protagonists of the American prize winners is indicative of the difference between Canadian and American public discourses on national identity. The American national identity is a strong one. Fueled by pioneer and revolutionary myths (Daniel Boone and Paul Revere), supported by powerful symbols (the Stars and Stripes), and resonant with sturdy, if fuzzy, icons (the American Dream), the exact contours of the American identity may be debated, but nobody doubts its existence (e.g., Vandersee's "iconic" list 1994: 427; Lipset 1990; Doran and Sigler 1985).

In Canada, on the other hand, the overriding focus of the national identity debate is "Does Canada have a national identity?" (Lipset 1985, 1986; Howes 1988; Smart 1984). The central tension between the French and English founding traditions has made the construction of a unitary identity problematic. Canadian history is curiously lacking in the heroes, revolutionaries, and mythic figures that populate the American landscape (McGregor 1985). Rather than being an historically triumphant event, as was the American Revolution, establishing nationhood separate from Britain and the British crown was an historically anxious and certainly drawn out process for Canada. As I have shown in chapter 3, full national independence for Canada remained incomplete for a hundred years after the unification of the provinces into the "Dominion of Canada" in 1867. Because of its lateness and chronological alienation from Canada's assumption of statehood, the Canadian nation-building process had a certain diffuse and self-conscious quality that rendered the process less complete and more problematic than was true in the United States.

The timing of the national project was also important. Canadian nation-building largely occurred during a period of sustained inquiry and critical attention to the concept of "nation" and "nationality." Nation-building during a period often described as "post-national" clearly presents certain difficulties. Furthermore, Canada was a sophisticated political entity during its nation-building process, not a territory newly experimenting with independence and statehood. The Canadian national project occurred within a context of massive decolonization and an explosion in the number of new nation-states. Unlike many of the newly independent ex-colonies, Canada was an established state – but a state without a nation.[16] Unfortunately, the "imagined" and "constructed" aspects of an allegedly "natural" nationhood are both more visible and more problematic in the postmodern period, leaving the Canadian nation a somewhat hesitant beast. Thus the current debate about what it means to be "Canadian" is both much larger and more heated than the comparable debate about what it means to be "American."

Americans may believe that the United States has failed to live up to the promises of the national ideology. Partisan groups of one sort and another may lay claim to the "American Dream" or to what America promises with radically different images of what that entails. Nonetheless, Americans generally have a plethora of images about America, the American identity, the American Dream, the American Frontier, and a host of assorted other such concepts. Canadians, in contrast, are deeply and publicly involved in the process of determining a substance for their own national identity (Hedley 1994).

The discourse regarding Canadian nationalism and Canadian identity is common in both mass and elite communications. The issue is investigated legally and politically (e.g., the Meech Lake negotiations on the Canadian Constitution, the Canadian Content Laws, the Quebec separatist referendums), culturally (e.g., *Saturday Night*'s anniversary issue on the Canadian identity, the exploratory television documentary "Canada: The True North"), educationally (e.g., the creation and proliferation of "Can Lit" courses), and in just about every other forum of public life.[17] Literature is one of the central arenas for this discourse. The emphasis on national identity in the prize-winning novels contributes to the debate on the Canadian national identity – and serves as an indication of the depth of public concern with this issue.

---

[16] This is the opposite of the situation in Scotland, for example, described by McCrone (1992).

[17] Including, for example, stand-up comedy, common jokes, and other forms of humor.

National identity and communal life

The Canadian prize winners' concern with citizenship and national identity obviously echoes the Canadian canonical novels' concern with social identity and human connection. The level of concern is different however. The Canadian canonical texts, although focused on human connection, are generally engaged at an individual level. That is, the Canadian canonical texts are concerned with the question of how each one of us as individuals can live a meaningful life. The Canadian prize winners, on the other hand, are generally focused on the question of how "we" as a society, as a community, as a nation, can order our lives. So for example, *The Young in One Another's Arms* focuses on the creation of family out of human fragments, on the establishment of a social group that forms its own small society. *The Engineer of Human Souls* uses an explicit comparison with Czechoslovakia to ask how life in Canada is good or bad – and how it could be better. The Canadian prize winners ask a similar question to the Canadian canonical novels, but frame the issue at a group level of identity, rather than an individual (although an individual within a web of connections) level. The Canadian canonical novels address the question "How can *I* live a meaningful life," the Canadian prize-winning novels address the question "How can *we* live a meaningful life."

A strong majority (71 percent) of the Canadian prize winners focuses on this question, while only a quarter (27 percent) of the American prize winners address the question at all. None of the American prize winners have the question of how to order communal or national life as their narrative focus, although four make some reference to the question. Both *Sophie's Choice* and *Blood Tie* address the question indirectly through their comparisons of America to Europe and Turkey respectively. *Lonesome Dove* and *Ironweed* address the question even more indirectly through their often ironic engagement with traditional American myths of male isolation, violence, and "freedom" from conventional society and domestic life. Much more common among the American prize winners, however, is a narrative focus on the question of how *one* should live a meaningful life; 40 percent of the American prize winners and just 7 percent of the Canadian prize winners focus on this question. An additional 14 percent of both the Canadian and American prize winners focus on the issue of gender identity – how shall "we" live as women.[18]

---

[18] When this question is asked by male authors and protagonists it is translated as how shall "we" (all of us humans) live? The female authors and protagonists ask the question both as how shall "we" (all of us humans) live (e.g., Rule in *The Young in One Another's Arms*) and how shall "we" (women) live (e.g., Lurie in *Foreign Affairs*).

Human connection versus individualism

The difference between Canadian and American novels in the presentation of the importance of human connection versus individualism persists in the prize winners. Human connection is considered very important or of central importance in 54 percent of the Canadian prize winners and just 17 percent of the American prize winners.[19] Novels such as *The Young in One Another's Arms*, *Not Wanted on the Voyage*, and *The Resurrection of Joseph Bourne*, are premised on the centrality of authentic human connection for the construction of a meaningful life – and all portray a lack of care, concern, and love for others as evil.

Furthermore, in keeping with the emphasis on national/communal focus, an additional 29 percent of the Canadian prize winners note the importance of human connection, but set it within a broader critique of social relations, presenting human connection as important, but insufficient. In these novels individual connections are shown to be inadequate to the task of ensuring compassionate, tolerant, and equitable social organization. Kogawa's *Obasan*, for example, is concerned not only with the familial ties and explication of love between closely linked individuals, but with the broader issues of social connection and justice as they unfolded during the internment and dispossession of Japanese-Canadians in World War II. Similarly, *The Handmaid's Tale*, *Voices in Time*, and *The Engineer of Human Souls* all present individual love and connection as vital, but insufficient in a world in which the social order may be governed by hatred, intolerance, and a monumental disregard for people's lives.

American prize winners are more likely than Canadian to present human connection as important – but impossible, or at least dangerous and rare. Half of the American prize winners do so while only 11 percent of the Canadian prize winners do. In the American *White Noise*, for example, Jack and Babette love each other deeply, yet both are hounded and terrified by visions of death. Despite their shared terror, neither can confide in or comfort the other. Similarly, *Lonesome Dove*, *A Summons to Memphis*, and *Blood Tie* show people desperately struggling for communion, love, and understanding, but unable either to attain it or to pay the price it demands. The Canadian *A Dream Like Mine*, with its message of the impossibility of truly loving, understanding, or communicating with the "Other," is in this respect more similar to the American than to other Canadian prize winners.

An additional one-quarter (27 percent) of the American novels present

---

[19] Obviously, some novels were coded as both focused on the group level of national (or communal) identity and the individual level of human connection.

human connection as less important than attention to the development of or interest in the self. *Ironweed* seems almost elegiacal in its portrayal of Francis Phelan's estrangement from his wife and children, yet at the same time, the novel never suggests that Francis might be able to remain within the family to face his guilt and self-doubt. The possibility that his relationships within his family and within his community could enable forgiveness or heal his pain is never seriously considered. Similarly, Updike's Rabbit, although (finally) semi-content, always perceives familial life and his interpersonal relationships as entrapping and the notion of escape and personal freedom hovers relentlessly throughout the novel. This disinterest in both the importance of human connection and in the social level of analysis results in only one American prize winner, Styron's *Sophie's Choice*, that both views human connection as important, but also as insufficient without a broader critique of the social order. In contrast, four Canadian prize winners exemplify this mutual concern for interpersonal connection and a just social environment.

Familial presence

One set of particularly interesting results in the comparison of prize winners is the extent and content of the role played by families. Remember that the American canonical novels were marked by their absence of significant familial interactions – only 10 percent featured important parental families and 30 percent important conjugal families. Conversely, the Canadian canonical novels were strongly focused on family – 80 percent featured important parental families and 60 percent featured important conjugal families. All of the Canadian canonical novels feature at least one important family while only 40 percent of the American novels do. The relative importance of and focus on families is much more equally distributed in the prize winners, as table 5.2 shows.

The simple presence of conjugal families (families in which the protagonist is a spouse/parent rather than child) is higher in the Canadian prize winners; ten (72 percent) of the Canadian protagonists have/had a spouse and/or children versus six (40 percent) of the American protagonists. American prize winners are conversely more likely to feature single, childless protagonists; nine (60 percent) of the American protagonists versus three (21 percent) of the Canadian protagonists.

Despite being more prevalent in Canadian prize winners, protagonists' conjugal families are no more likely to be important to the narrative in Canadian prize winners than in American prize winners. Only five (36 percent) Canadian prize winners of the ten (72 percent) having conjugal

Table 5.2   *Familial patterns in the prize winners (in percentages)*

	USA (N=15)	Canada (N=14)
Protagonist has/had conjugal family	40	72
Conjugal family important:	33	36
positive	7	14
negative	20	14
ambivalent	7	7
Protagonist has/had parental family	60	64
Parental family important:	40	57
positive	13	14
negative	20	21
ambivalent	7	21
Neither family important	20	21
One or the other family important	67	64
Both families important	7	29

families feature the conjugal family as important to the narrative. This figure is equivalent to the American figure of five (33 percent) prize winners in which conjugal families are important to the narrative. The remaining five Canadian prize winners in which the protagonist has a conjugal family simply note the fact of a family without its presence having narrative significance. Kelly's *A Dream Like Mine* is the most extreme example of this. In the novel, the protagonist's only reference to his wife comes in a one-sentence thought that he will miss his wife and son if he dies during the events depicted. Canadian prize winners are equally likely to feature positive, negative, and ambivalent important conjugal families. American prize winners, however, are more likely to feature negative conjugal families (20 percent) than positive or ambivalent families (7 percent).

Parental family distribution is shown in the second half of table 5.2. Parental families are more equally present in American and Canadian prize winners than are conjugal families, although parental families are still somewhat more likely to be important in Canadian (57 percent) than in American prize winners (40 percent). Note that parental families are more likely than conjugal families to be important in both Canadian (57 percent versus 36 percent) and American (40 percent versus 33 percent) prize winners. In prize winners in which the parental family is important to the narrative, the distribution of positive and negative families is equal between

American and Canadian prize winners. Both Canadian and American prize winners are equally unlikely to consider neither family important to the narrative and equally likely to consider one or the other family important to the narrative. Canadian prize winners are more likely than American prize winners to consider both families important to the narrative (29 percent versus 7 percent).

Overall, this mass of data sheds some interesting light on the issue of families as depicted in Canadian and American literature. First, Atwood's (1972: 131) contention that the family is more important in Canadian literature than in American literature, that in America the family "is something you come from and get rid of" while in Canada the family is "a trap in which you're caught," must be reconsidered. Atwood does not distinguish between conjugal and parental families which generates some confusion in her argument. Furthermore, I believe it is important to distinguish between familial *importance*, more prevalent in Canadian than American high-culture novels, and familial *oppressiveness*, equally prevalent across the two countries.

The most interesting aspect of familial presence in the prize winners is in comparison to the canonical novels. The canonical novels clearly support an argument about national character difference – Americans are autonomous individuals defining themselves without reference to or need for familial context while Canadians are primarily family-identified and located. But the prize winners support a very different picture of familial significance – both Canadians and Americans are strongly identified by and located within parental families and to a lesser extent conjugal families. In other words, the national distinctiveness of familial significance in the canonical novels is not paralleled in the literary prize winners.

In fact, by other measures it is *American* prize winners, not Canadian, that are most likely to be centrally concerned with family. There are three American prize winners in which family conflict was the central conflict and two of those three novels are coded within the family drama genre. No Canadian prize winners, however, has a familial central conflict or falls into the family drama genre.

Generic distinctions

In chapter 4 I presented Griswold's (1987a) contention that generic designation is an essential part of the comprehension phase. I also detailed the process by which I created appropriate heuristic genres for the novels under study. The generic categories into which the prize winners were coded are as follows: self-knowledge/growth, life story, fable, science fiction,

Table 5.3   *Generic distribution in the prize winners (in percentages)*

Genre	USA (N=15)	Canada (N=14)
Self-knowledge/growth	27	29
Life story	20	14
Fable	0	21
Science fiction	0	14
Minority experience	0	21
War experience	14	0
Family drama	14	0
Other	27	0

minority experience, war experience, family drama, farce, coming-of-age, Western, and postmodern life story. The first two genres, self-knowledge/growth and life story, account for close to one-half of the prize winners; seven (47 percent) and six (43 percent) of the American and Canadian prize winners respectively. The remainder of the Canadian prize winners fall into three genres, two in science fiction, three in fable, and three in minority experience. The remainder of the American prize winners fall into six generic categories, none of which are fable, science fiction or minority experience; two in war experience, two in family drama, one in farce, one in postmodern life story, one in coming-of-age, and one in Western (see table 5.3).

The most obvious difference between the American and Canadian prize winners in terms of genre involves the distribution across specific genres. The Canadian prize winners were heavily represented in three genres, science fiction (14 percent), fable (21 percent), and minority experience (21 percent), in which no American prize winners occurred. Central to each of these three genres is the idea of alternative visions or experiences. Narratives in these genres deal with visions or experiences which are marginal or peripheral in some sense. The two science fiction narratives, *The Handmaid's Tale* and *Voices In Time*, posit possible future societies from extrapolations of recent social history. Two of the three fabulist narratives, *The Resurrection of Joseph Bourne* and *Shoeless Joe*, present miraculous visions of the transcendental nature of human faith and love, while the third, *Not Wanted On The Voyage*, reinterprets a Biblical story from a feminist and humanist point of view. The three minority experience narratives, *Obasan*, *A Dream Like Mine*, and *The Engineer of Human Souls*, all deal with the experiences of marginalized outsiders and the disparities between their lives and mainstream lives. As Hutcheon (1988) has argued vis-à-vis postmodernism, the experience of marginalization, the "ex-centric" narrative perspective, is uniquely suited to the Canadian novel as it is equivalent to the Canadian experience at a national and global level. Visions of marginality and successful alternative experience are suggestions for and investigations of the Canadian national experience.

Conversely, the American prize winners covered several genres in which no Canadian novels appeared. Although four of these genres contained only a single American novel, Western, coming-of-age, farce, and post-modern life story, two genres, family drama and war experience, each contained two American prize winners. The war experience narratives, *Paco's Story* and *Going After Cacciato*, are both concerned with the Vietnam War and its effects on the lives of the men who fought in it. Neither of these narratives falls into the traditional genre of war adventure with its emphasis on male bonding under conditions of courage and excitement. Instead, the two narratives concern the alienation and pain brought by war.

Gender

As noted in chapter 3, female authors comprised 50 percent of the Canadian canonical authors and 20 percent of the American canonical authors. In addition, 37.5 percent of the American canonical novels and 50 percent of the Canadian canonical novels had female protagonists. This comparative prevalence of female authors and protagonists persists in the Canadian prize winners compared to American prize winners, even though Canadian prize winners are less likely than Canadian canonical novels to feature women or to be written by women. Just over one-third (36 percent) of the Canadian prize-winning novels are written by women while one-fifth (20 percent) of the American prize-winning novels are written by women. Female protagonists are featured in 43 percent of the Canadian novels and 27 percent of the American novels.

Narrative tone

The Canadian canonical novels were more likely than the American to have a tone of at least "contained" optimism or fulfillment, while the American novels were slightly more likely to be pessimistic. The American and Canadian canonical novels were equally likely to feature protagonists trapped in lives of "mere" survival. Canadian prize winners are even more likely than the American novels to have a central tone of victory and fulfill-ment; 21 percent of Canadian prize winners do while *no* American prize winners do. These Canadian novels, *Shoeless Joe, The Young In One Another's Arms*, and *The Resurrection of Joseph Bourne* are all fables involving redemption by love. All three are narratives in which individuals and their emotional commitments to one another triumph over "the system."

Mere survival, however, is an evenly distributed theme: 21 percent of both Canadian and American prize winners have such a tone, in which the protagonist is incapable of improving his or her quality of life. In *Paco's Story*, for example, Paco has nothing and receives nothing from those with whom he interacts. He is without hope, he only endures.

Canadian prize winners are also more likely than American prize winners, however, to have a central tone of pessimism; seven (50 percent) Canadian and four (27 percent) American prize winners have such a central tone. Having a central tone of pessimism and/or despair is more likely than having a central tone of victory and/or fulfillment for both American (27 percent versus 0 percent) and Canadian (50 percent versus 21 percent) prize winners. The Canadian prize winners are likely to have a strong narrative tone, be it pessimistic or optimistic (77 percent), while the American prize winners are likely to have an ambivalent or emotionally muted tone (79 percent).

Central conflict

In chapter 2 I described the coding scheme for coding central conflicts, defined as both crucial to narrative development and primary. The central conflict categories are institutional (e.g., international or racial conflict), interpersonal (i.e., conflict between individuals), none, within self, ideolog-ical, familial, individual versus group, and success struggle (e.g., a Horatio Alger scenario in which the protagonist battles a miscellaneous assortment of evils). None of the prize winners were in either of the last two categories. The distribution of types of conflict is as shown in table 5.4.

The first four types of conflict, institutional, interpersonal, none, and within self, are equally prevalent in Canadian and American prize winners. Institutional conflict is by far the most common for both countries, accounting for 47 percent of the American cases and 50 percent of the Canadian cases. Interpersonal (non-familial) conflict and not having a central conflict accounted for an additional 7 percent and 20 percent respectively of the American and 7 percent and 14 percent of the Canadian

Table 5.4   *Type of central conflict in the prize winners (in percentages)*

	USA (N=15)	Canada (N=14)
Institutional	47	50
Interpersonal	7	7
No central conflict	20	14
Within self	7	0
Ideological	0	29
Familial	20	0
Success struggle	0	0
Individual versus group	0	0

cases. Although there were no Canadian novels in which conflict within the self was dominant, there was one (7 percent) such American case.

The central conflicts in the Canadian and American prize winners are more similar than different. The differences are centered in the categories of ideological and familial conflict. None of the American prize winners featured a central ideological conflict, while four (29 percent) of the Canadian prize winners involved ideological conflict as the central conflict. Conversely, none of the Canadian prize winners featured a central familial conflict, while three (20 percent) of the American prize winners did so.

The relative prevalence of ideological conflicts in the Canadian prize winners is largely a result of the emphasis in Canadian prize winners on alternative visions and experiences. The prize winners whose central conflict is ideological are *The Young In One Another's Arms*, *Shakespeare's Dog*, *Shoeless Joe*, and *The Resurrection of Joseph Bourne*. Three of these four feature some type of utopian, or at least redemptive, vision. *Shakespeare's Dog*, while not a utopian or redemptive novel, is at least partially a discourse on the possibilities inherent in the human condition and its potential superiority to animal existence. The nature of redemptive and utopian visions is such that they are generally defined through conflict with, or rejection of, traditional understandings of ordinary human experience. Each of these narratives has at its heart a rejection of the established understanding about human (and animal) relationships which prevails in general society. Unlike the Canadian prize winners, the American prize winners are less apt to feature conflict about possible ways of organizing human relationships than conflict about the division of existing power – a common theme in familial conflict.

Literary style

Another difference between the Canadian and American prize winners concerns literary style. The majority of both Canadian and American prize winners, eight (57 percent) Canadian and eleven (73 percent) American, are wholly or primarily realistic in style, totaling 66 percent of the prize-winning sample. The biggest stylistic difference between the Canadian and American samples involves the distribution of postmodern novels.

For the purposes of this research I define as postmodern those novels which have a "concern for form and language over subject matter" (Fraser 1989: 382), exhibiting most or all of these characteristics: (1) attention to the process of narration over the substance of the narration, (2) lack of attention to a logical, coherent, or meaningful plot, (3) shifting or ambiguous points of view, and (4) focus on the structure and use of language, particularly on word play. Using these criteria, four (29 percent) of the Canadian novels (*Burning Water*, *The Resurrection of Joseph Bourne*, *Shakespeare's Dog*, and *The Engineer of Human Souls*) and two (14 percent) of the American novels (*White Noise* and *Going After Cacciato*) are postmodern in style. I coded as realistic novels such as Atwood's *The Handmaid's Tale* which has certain postmodern aspects, most notably the narrator's self-consciousness in the prologue about the process of narration and the commentator's academic disassociation from Offred's narrative in the epilogue, but whose central text is realistic.

It is frequently argued in Canadian literary circles that Canadian literature is dominated by conventional literary styles, primarily realism, and is unwilling or unable to embrace the avant-garde, primarily the postmodern (Lecker 1990; Fogel 1984). This reliance on traditional forms of narrative is frequently cited as yet another reflection of the conventional, anti-revolutionary nature of Canadian society, particularly in comparison to American society (Lipset 1990). The prize winners, however, suggest otherwise, at least for the last decade, as there are twice as many Canadian as American postmodern novels among the prize winners of the 1978–87 period.

Hutcheon (1988) makes a very different argument about Canadian literature and postmodernism, one more compatible with the comparative Canadian prevalence in the prize-winning novels, although also a reflection-based argument. Hutcheon (1988) argues that literary postmodernism in Canada, while not necessarily inclined toward the American concern with formal, metafictional experimentation and "surfiction," is not only alive and well, but peculiarly suitable for narrating the Canadian story. Because postmodernism is at heart both paradoxical and problematic, because it "both sets up and subverts the powers and conventions of art . . . establishing and then undercutting prevailing values and conventions in order to provoke a questioning, a challenging of 'what goes without saying' in our culture," it is resonant with "Canada's own particular moment of cultural history" (Hutcheon 1988: 2–3). The paradoxical, questioning nature of postmodern writing "almost inevitably" places the writer, and thus to some extent the reader, into the margin, into the "ex-centric" position. And "since the periphery or the margin might also describe Canada's perceived position in international terms, perhaps the postmodern ex-centric is very much a part of the identity of the nation" (Hutcheon 1988: 3). Hutcheon's explanation of the postmodern in Canadian fiction is powerful because she connects the *inherent* qualities of the postmodern, its tone and consequent position, with Canadian social and literary concerns and because she distinguishes between the specifically American experimentation with postmodernism and postmodern literary forms more generally.[20]

Hutcheon (1988) and others (e.g., Kolakowski 1990; Kroetsch 1989) argue that when postmodernism entered the Canadian literary world, its form was influenced by the immediate and specific history of Canadian letters, and by the period of postmodernism adoption. It is not necessary that either the development or current state of Canadian postmodernism be synonymous with American postmodernism for the former to be thriving. For example, Pache (1985: 64) suggests that one feature of the paradigmatically Canadian postmodern lies in "the 'invention' of a collective past as a central concept." American postmodernism may be evolving in the direction of surfiction while Canadian postmodernism investigates issues of historical invention and marginal voice. That Canadian postmodernism is of a different style than others is not surprising given the specific historical influences and models available in the Canadian literary world compared to those in either the American or European context.

Rebellion

The American and Canadian canonical novels were equally likely to feature rebellious protagonists; the protagonists in one-half of each sample were

---

[20] See Weir, however, for a very different interpretation of Hutcheon's work, which, among other things, describes Hutcheon's writing as "[S]ubjecting Canadian as well as international modernism to a normalizing influence, domesticating deviance and inscribing it within her postmodern paradigm" and thereby converting "danger into safety, the marginalized into the mainstream, the non-referential into the referential" (1991: 181).

rebellious or semi-rebellious. The Canadian prize winners, however, are clearly more likely to feature protagonists who are defiant or rebellious toward authority than are the American prize winners: 50 percent of the Canadian prize-winning novels do so while 27 percent of the American prize winners do.

Protagonists from Canadian and American prize winners are equally unlikely to represent authority themselves; two Canadian and one American protagonist do so. The three protagonists coded as representing authority are all rather iconoclastic examples of authority. The American protagonist in McMurty's *Lonesome Dove* is Call, an ex-Texas Ranger and cattleman whose milieu is the wildest of the untamed West. The two Canadian protagonists are George Vancouver in Bowering's *Burning Water*, a British explorer who experiences a homosexual relationship with a Spanish explorer and who subsequently goes mad, and Francis Cornish in Davies's *What's Bred In The Bone*, a Canadian spy/forger/art critic whose life story is narrated by an omniscient spirit as no one else has the least conception of all its convoluted twists. All in all, authority figures are resoundingly absent as protagonists in both countries' canonical and prize-winning novels.

Rebellion, while part of the American mythos, is much less a part of contemporary American high-culture literature. The American prize winners were more likely to feature protagonists coming to terms with the restrictions and possibilities inherent to their individual lives than protagonists (successfully) rebelling against oppressive authority. Canadian prize winners, on the other hand, did feature protagonists whose actions were defiant and rebellious. The increased incidence of rebellious Canadian protagonists may be seen as part of the revisionary functions of literary prize winners. American and Canadian prize winners are both exploring non-traditional areas of national experience within their own national contexts. Interestingly, the movement onto non-traditional ground may bring each set of prize winners closer to the traditional territory of the other.

Religion

Religious literary content occurs in two forms in the novels: (1) an organized religion is depicted as an important institution and/or, (2) the characters express personal faith or spiritual belief. These two forms occur both alone and together. Religion is important in four (27 percent) of the American prize winners and ten (71 percent) of the Canadian prize winners. The comparative figures for the canonical novels are 40 percent of the American novels and 60 percent of the Canadian novels.

Organized religion presented as an important institution is the most common form of religious expression in the prize winners. Eight (57 percent) of the Canadian prize winners feature some type of organized religion as an important institution. These religions include Catholicism, Protestantism, and Judaism, as well as General, Fundamentalist, and Old Testament Christianity. Three of the novels, *The Handmaid's Tale*, *Not Wanted on the Voyage*, and *Shoeless Joe*, exhibit strong anti-established-religion sentiment. Four (27 percent) of the American prize winners also portray organized religion as an important institution, including Judaism, the Mormon Church, and Fundamentalist Christianity.

Interestingly, Kollar argues that while Canadians "accept the importance of historical continuity, ritual, national organization, and a public role for their churches, Americans give priority to belief sincerely held, strongly claimed and privately enjoyed at home or within the local congregation" (1989: 14; see Hadaway, Marler, and Chaves [1993], however, for a fascinating study providing dissenting data on the comparative religiosity of Americans). This distinction is not "reflected" in the prize winners (cf. Perkins [1984] on religious content differences in American and Canadian magazines). Although religious institutions are more central to Canadian prize winners than to American prize winners, the corollary, that Americans are comparatively more religious privately, finds no literary support. Personal faith or spiritual beliefs are important in 43 percent of the Canadian prize winners and 14 percent of the American prize winners.

Romance

One interesting difference between the Canadian and American prize winners is the relative frequency of central love relationships. Romantic or love relationships are much more likely to be central to the narrative in American prize winners than in Canadian prize winners. This is obviously *partially* because the majority (72 percent) of Canadian novels feature protagonists who already have conjugal families. While having a conjugal family does not preclude a protagonist from being centrally concerned with a love relationship, it does usually imply that protagonists have resolved their central love interest. In the American prize winners the pursuit or establishment of love relationships is central to nine (60 percent) of the narratives, while in the Canadian prize winners this is the case for four (29 percent) of the narratives. This finding is contradictory to Fiedler's (1966) argument that American literature rarely focuses on adult heterosexual love. The different emphasis on romance between American and Canadian prize winners is not replicated by the canonical novels. Canadian and

American canonical novels were equally likely to feature a central love relationship; four Canadian canonical novels and five American canonical
novels did so.

In both Canadian and American prize winners love relationships were
less likely to be central for *female* protagonists than for male protagonists.
This was especially true in Canada where three of eight (38 percent) male
protagonists have a central love relationships, but only one of six (17
percent) female protagonists has a central love relationship. It remains true
for the American prize winners, although less dramatically; two of the four
(50 percent) female protagonists have a central love relationship while seven
of the eleven (64 percent) male protagonists have a central love relationship.

This reversal of the traditional female concern with love or the establishment of a relationship as the central issue of one's life may be a prime
example of the revisionary function of prize-winning novels. The emphasis
on love in women's lives, and its lesser centrality in men's lives, is undergoing
a shift. Prize winners show female protagonists whose central concerns are
"untraditional" in that they are not relationship-based, and male protagonists whose central concerns are "untraditional" in that they *are* relationship-based. A second romantic revision is indicated by the one prize
winner from each country in which the central love relationship is homosexual. The American *The Color Purple* features a female sexual relationship that transforms the protagonist. The Canadian *Burning Water* features
a male homosexual relationship between an English and a Spanish
explorer–sea captain.

The high-culture novels

I began this chapter by arguing that literary prize winners are precanonical
texts which serve multiple purposes: as stimulants to "good writing," as
validations of a "pure" literary realm, as benchmarks of national vitality,
and as an avenue for revisions to the legitimated vision of national experience presented in the canon. I then described the main focal difference
between the Canadian and American prize-winning novels as a Canadian
explicitness of attention to the issue of meaningful identity, both personal
and national, and a concomitant American vagueness or cynicism about
such possibilities.

Although the Canadian and American prize winners are nationally distinctive, they are distinctive in *different* ways than are the canonical novels.
First, the prize winners have a cross-nationally distinctive focus that is not
only substantively different than that seen in the canonical novels, but also
different in its degree of opposition. While the central difference between

the canonical novels involved an American focus on individualism and a self-referential identity and a directly opposing Canadian focus on connection and social identity, the prize winners' central difference is of a less explicitly oppositional nature. Canadian prize winners did focus on meaningful identity through community and/or nation in a way that American prize winners did not. However, the American prize winners' central focus was not the opposite of the Canadian prize winners' central focus in the way that the canonical novels starkly juxtaposed human connection and self-reliant individualism. Rather, the American prize winners simply seemed more cynical and pessimistic than did the Canadian prize winners about the *possibility* of meaningful identity through community and connection.

Second, to the extent that the narrative focus of the prize-winning novels involved characteristics similar to those in the canonical novels, the patterns of cross-national distinctiveness often varied. Thus, for example, although one of the sharpest canonical distinctions involved the strong importance of families in Canadian novels and the concomitant lack of importance of families in American novels, the American and Canadian prize winners are equally focused on and concerned with families. At the same time, the American and Canadian prize winners diverged on the issue of national identity – American citizenship was a background assumption of the American prize winners, but Canadian citizenship was far from an assumption in the Canadian prize winners – whereas the American and Canadian canonical novels showed no difference on this dimension. Again this attests to the insufficiency of the "reflection of national character" model of national literatures. A model that understands cross-national literary distinctiveness as the reflection of natural, coherent, and unique national characters cannot be supported when the content of what is unique varies so widely across types of texts.

I interpret these differences between the two types of high-culture literature as indicative of the different uses of canonical and contemporary prize-winning literature. Canonical national literature is predicated on national uniqueness and used to help construct an image of the naturally unique nation. Canonical national literatures are chosen *against* other national literatures. They are used to make bold juxtapositions of "us" and "them." Contemporary high-culture literature, on the other hand, is part of a pre-existing, indigenous cultural tradition. Contemporary high-culture literature, in other words, is chosen *within* the context of an existing national culture.[21] Rather than being solely a marker of international uniqueness,

---

[21] See Griswold (1992: 723) on the establishment of one particular literary tradition in Nigeria: "publication established a powerful model . . . which Nigerian writers now respond to, either in imitation or rejection, but cannot ignore."

contemporary high-culture literature is in large part a reaction to or a dialogue with an established internal literary tradition. Contemporary high-culture literature is read and evaluated within the internal, national context as much as the international one. Contemporary high-culture literature is, of course, also used to help affirm the vitality of the national culture in an international context, but within an established nation-state the requirement for national distinctiveness above all else is muted. Canonical literature is driven by differentiation and chosen in opposition to the "other." Contemporary prize-winning literature is driven by an ongoing national cultural dialogue and chosen within that tradition.

6

The bestsellers: the economics of publishing and the convergence of popular taste

> The *truth*, should you insist, was that the increasing dismissal of his work in the critical press as that of a "popular writer" (which was, as he understood it, one step – a small one – above that of a "hack") had hurt him quite badly. It didn't jibe with his self-image as a Serious Writer who was only churning out these shitty romances in order to subsidize his (flourish of trumpets, please!) REAL WORK! Had he hated Misery? Had he really? If so, why had it been so easy to slip back into her world? . . . Perhaps all he had hated was the fact that her face on the dust jackets had overshadowed his in his author photographs, not allowing the critics to see that they were dealing with a young Mailer or Cheever here – that they were dealing with a *heavyweight* here. As a result, hadn't his "serious fiction" become steadily more self-conscious . . . *Look at me! Look at how good this is! Hey, guys! This stuff has got a sliding perspective! This stuff has got stream-of-consciousness interludes! This is my REAL WORK . . . Don't you DARE turn away from my REAL WORK!*
>
> Paul Sheldon, the writer-protagonist of Stephen King's *Misery*, re-
> considering his own unquestioning acceptance of the high-
> culture/popular-culture hierarchy (1988: 286)

In the first five chapters, my attention has been concentrated on the realm of high culture, with a concomitant focus on cross-national differences between American and Canadian literature. Chapter 6 turns away from high-culture literature and its location in the field of restricted production to an analysis of the field of large-scale production and the best-selling novels within that domain. Stephen King's challenge to the deeply embedded assumption of the hierarchical worth of popular- and high-culture literature, wittily incorporated into a "formulaic" horror story, raises the preeminent issue of the changing focus from canonical and literary prize-winning texts to bestsellers. Why is it that high-culture literature is "good" even when it's "bad," but popular-culture literature is "bad," no matter how "good" it is? The answer to this question lies, once again, in the production and consumption contexts of the novels in question. Popular-culture novels, *commercial* fiction, performs the necessary work of counterpoint to, and hence enabler of, the symbolic value and purity of high-culture literature.

The bestsellers

Popular novels and the mass market

Unlike high-culture literature, popular-culture literature lacks a *national*, symbolic value. Although popular-culture literature, like all cultural products, does have symbolic value, its economic value predominates (Bourdieu 1985). Because of its location in the "field of large-scale cultural production," popular-culture literature is best understood as "art-as-commodity" produced for its "commercial value" by a mass-market culture industry (Bourdieu 1985) and consumed by individual readers pursuing private needs. High-culture literature is defined in contrast as "art as art"; that is, the symbolic considerations outweigh economic considerations (Bourdieu 1985). Canonical literature is "produced," in the sense of chosen into the canon, for "public" readers, e.g., school children or national populations, engaged in "public" pursuits such as schooling regarding the dominant cultural hierarchy or enculturation as "citizens." Popular-culture novels, however, serve primarily as readily available, mass-market commodities purchased by individuals for their personal entertainment and enjoyment.

High-culture literature, especially canonical literature, serves powerful, publicly symbolic functions. Popular-culture literature, on the other hand, serves a variety of needs and uses. It may meet personal needs for experiences such as adventure and excitement within guaranteed, safe limits (e.g., Cawelti 1976). It may provide escape from or enhancement of dull and impoverished lives (e.g., Radway 1984). Or it may lend readers validation and reassurance about their own life choices through a comparison with other, fictional lives (Modleski 1982; Radway 1984). While high-culture literature may also be used by readers to meet these personal needs, it is the political uses of canonical literature that *require* national uniqueness. Popular-culture literature, by contrast, does not require national uniqueness.

Because popular novels are used differently than high-culture novels, they are also produced, consumed, and evaluated in a different context than are high-culture novels. The production of popular-culture literature is "dominated by the quest for investment profitability": thus it is driven by publishers' decisions about what will sell (Bourdieu 1985: 28).[1] Publishing is increasingly subject to a "blockbuster" mentality that concentrates attention on "big" books written by "stars" and produced as part of a "media package" (Coser, Kadushin, and Powell 1982: 29–30). The preponderance of authors such as Stephen King and Danielle Steel in the best-selling sample provides ample evidence of this strategy (see Appendix C for a full list of the bestsellers). The advertising, cover iconography, and review strategy for novels by these authors rely heavily on the similarity of the new novel to the previous novels. The product being marketed is "the new Stephen King [horror story]" or "the new Danielle Steel [romance]," not the [unique and particular] novel *Misery* or *Fine Things*.[2] Books by each of these authors, and others like them, are presented as "pre-established forms" that "correspond to a pre-existent demand" (Bourdieu 1980: 280).

The audience for popular-culture literature is certainly larger than for high-culture literature. However, accurate figures are still difficult to collect. Large-scale surveys generally ask whether a respondent has read any books in the period under investigation without distinguishing between high-culture and popular-culture novels (Robinson 1993; cf. Zill and Winglee 1990). In the United States, the National Endowment for the Arts Survey of Public Participation in the Arts asks: "With the exception of books required for work or school, did you read any books during the last twelve months?" (NEA 1992: 2, questions 11–12c).[3] There is reason to believe that the majority of respondents who answer "yes" are referring to popular-culture "bestsellers" or "genre" literature such as mysteries, romances, melodramas, and horror stories (Zill and Winglee 1990). In the 1992 SPPA, 52.1 percent of the respondents indicated they had read a novel or short story in the previous twelve months (Robinson 1993: 2).[4]

---

[1] Contemporary high-culture novels are also obviously published with an eye toward profit (cf. Bourdieu 1980 on the French situation in an earlier period). However, value is created by high-culture novels in other ways as well. The prestige of having high-culture authors and titles under contract or on the back list may offset their economic weakness (see Max [1994], however, for a strong argument that this is increasingly less true).

[2] Stephen King has written about his adventures under the pen name "Richard Bachman" as, in part, an attempted antidote to being simply the Stephen King package whose books are purchased without regard for their individual characteristics (King 1985).

[3] The survey was conducted in 1982, 1985, and 1992, and a 1997 panel is planned.

[4] The NEA trend data show a statistically significant decline in the number of respondents reporting having read any poems/plays/novels/short stories in the last twelve months. The 1982 figure was 56.9 percent, the 1992 figure 54 percent (Robinson 1993: 5). As a comparison, the Consumer Research Study on Reading and Book Purchasing found in 1983 that 39 percent of adults reported having read a book of fiction in the last six months and one-half reported having read a book "of some sort" during the same period (Zill and Winglee 1990: 9).

Canadian figures for reading are slightly higher. The 1991 Department of Communications readership survey, *Reading in Canada 1991*, found that 63.6 percent of respondents reported having read a book of fiction in the last twelve months (Ekos Research Associates 1992: 20). Mystery and romance novels were the most commonly read (Ekos Research Associates 1992: 22). However, the authors of the report note that "[O]ur analysis leads us to believe that our sample *severely underrepresents the lowest decile of the Canadian population in terms of reading capacity*" (Ekos Research Associates 1992: 4, italics in original).[5]

Popular-culture literature is generally ignored by individuals who judge high-culture literature – except for occasional animadversions on the baffling popularity of such trash and the failings of those who write it.[6] Popular-culture literature is judged instead on its popularity – meaning its profitability. Such evaluations are made by a wide range of institutions, e.g., the *New York Times*, that also evaluate high-culture novels. However, the evaluation of popular novels in these venues is commercially based (how popular/profitable is a particular novel this week) whereas the evaluation of high-culture novels in these venues is based on literary and aesthetic judgments. Reviews of "serious" novels in the *New York Times* or the *New York Review of Books* do not concentrate on sales figures.

The importance of bestseller lists is not lost on producers. The covers of popular novels frequently trumpet their sales through starbursts encircling blurbs such as "#1 *New York Times* bestseller" or, for those whose popularity may have been achieved in less culturally authoritative places, simply "Ten weeks on the bestseller list." Bruce Harris, president of trade sales and marketing at Random House, understands that consumers think a place on the bestseller list "means that a book is good," but he demonstrates a failure to understand why that should be so when he goes on to say, "It's the most powerful marketing tool you have – yet it really doesn't say anything, does it?" (quoted in Reilly 1995). As Bourdieu knows, however, "the successful get more successful," because "*in this market*," "success is intrinsically a guarantee of value" (1980: 284, emphasis added).[7] It is the commercial success of popular-culture fiction that demonstrates its "value."

Popular novels are, of course, substantively reviewed as well. However,

---

[5] See chapter 5 for a longer discussion on reading statistics.
[6] This tradition has a long history, e.g., Hawthorne's frustrated complaint that the country "is now wholly given over to a d—d mob of scribbling women" whose work outsold Hawthorne's own, despite what he felt was its manifest inferiority (contained in an 1855 letter to Wm. Ticknor, his publisher, and quoted in *Hawthorne and his Publisher* by Caroline Ticknor, Houghton Mifflin 1913).
[7] In comparison, of course, is the field of restricted production where "success is suspect and asceticism in this world is the precondition for salvation in the next" (1980: 284).

when popular novels are critically reviewed, the review location, language, and evaluative criteria used by reviewers is generally different from that used by reviewers of high-culture novels.[8] For example, popular novels are often judged on their narrative engagement, their excitement level and ability to "grab" the reader, while high-culture novels are more often evaluated on the author's language and stylistic skills.[9] When popular-culture novels are reviewed in high-culture venues, the review may be bounded in some way, e.g., a column on "Mysteries" that clearly identifies the formulaic parameters of the evaluation, or the review may take a patronizing or gently bemused tone (see for example, Towers [1987], the *New York Review of Books'* review of Scott Turow's *Presumed Innocent*).[10] The form, content, and uses of popular-culture fiction, and the contexts within which these novels are produced and consumed, are thus quite different from those pertaining to the high-culture prize winners and canonical works.

Data collection

The best-selling sample is composed of the ten novels which spent the greatest number of weeks in each calendar year from 1978 to 1987 on the weekly hardcover bestsellers list in *Publisher's Weekly* in the United States and in *Maclean's* in Canada.[11] This sample is intended to be representative of the most popular novels, i.e., those novels read by the most people in each country. Truly measuring which novels are read by the most people, however, is close to impossible since people read books checked out of libraries, buy books they never read, read books they never buy, and otherwise circumvent systems designed to identify how many people read any particular book. Number of weeks on the bestseller list is a proxy for overall popularity.

[8] See for example Corse and Griffin (1996) on the changing evaluative criteria used to judge *Their Eyes Were Watching God* as the novel moved from being understood as popular entertainment to being taken seriously as a high-culture novel.

[9] Selection by entities such as the Book-of-the-Month Club also serve as evaluative mechanisms for popular and "middlebrow" literature (Radway 1989).

[10] The reviewer for the *New York Review* was not particularly impressed with Turow's first novel. He describes the prose as "serviceable," and berates the author for his conclusion, which commits "an act of literary bad faith that any serious writer of such fiction would scorn" (Towers 1987: 21–2). Of course, the mere fact of a review in such a prestigious location frames Turow's novel in specific ways for both the literary community and the audience (Binder 1993).

[11] Note that this measure of bestseller status differs from, for example, the *Publisher's Weekly* annual bestseller lists which list books by overall sales volume. Although "number of weeks on the bestseller list" is generally considered less accurate (Reilly 1995), I use this figure because annual sales figures were not available for Canada during the period of my study.

A comparative analysis of Canadian and American best-selling novels

The first and most dramatic finding from the comparison of the American and Canadian bestsellers is the degree to which the two samples are *identical*. That is, the strongest result of the comparison is the extent of overlap between the two countries' longest running annual bestseller lists. If there were no overlap between the bestsellers in the two countries the sample would contain 200 entries. However, the sample actually contains only 135 titles: 39 titles that were exclusively American bestsellers, 37 titles that were exclusively Canadian bestsellers, *and 59 titles that appear in both samples*. In the average year, the American and Canadian bestseller lists were more alike than different. For example, in 1987 both the Canadian and American ten longest-running bestsellers included these seven novels:

Clancy, Tom	*Patriot Games*
King, Stephen	*Misery*
King, Stephen	*The Eyes of the Dragon*
L'Amour, Louis	*The Haunted Mesa*
Sheldon, Sidney	*Windmills of the Gods*
Steel, Danielle	*Fine Things*
Turow, Scott	*Presumed Innocent*

These novels are all American-authored. The exclusively American bestsellers for 1987 included in addition two more American-authored texts, *The Prince of Tides* by Pat Conroy and *Red Storm Rising* by Tom Clancy, and one British-authored text, *Sarum* by Edward Rutherford. The exclusively Canadian bestsellers for 1987 included in addition two British-authored texts, *Destiny* and *Whirlwind*, by Sally Beauman and James Clavell respectively, and the one white Zimbabwean-authored text, *Rage* by Wilbur Smith.

The 135 novels in the best-selling sample are comprised of three groups of texts; exclusively American bestsellers, exclusively Canadian bestsellers, and mutual bestsellers. Four novels made the Canadian top ten list for two years running and two novels made the American list for two years running. These novels are counted twice, thus the following findings are reported based on a total of 141 entries (135 novels plus six repeats). The results reported below describe the 141 entries in four parts: the complete sample of American best-selling entries (N=100), the complete sample of Canadian best-selling entries (N=100), the exclusively American best-selling entries (N=41), and the exclusively Canadian best-selling entries (N=41). Given the extent of the *duplication* in the American and Canadian

Table 6.1   *Nationality of authors and protagonists in the bestsellers (in percentages)*

	Exclusive American (N=41)	Exclusive Canadian (N=41)	Complete American (N=100)	Complete Canadian (N=100)
Authors				
American	81	34	79	60
British	17	32	16	22
Canadian	0	27	1	12
Other European	2	2	2	2
African (white)	0	5	0	2
Australian	0	0	2	2
Protagonists				
American	68	27	64	55
British	10	29	9	17
Canadian	0	20	0	8
Multiple protagonists with multiple identities	10	5	9	7
Other	10	15	12	14
Irrelevant	2	5	6	7

popular-culture novels, the obvious next question is the degree of similarity among the books that are not duplicated.

National identity – authorial

Not surprisingly, the authors of the canonical and prize-winning texts all had national identities corresponding to the country in which they were recognized. This is not true for the popular-culture novels. American authors dominate both the American and Canadian bestseller lists; Canadian authors account for only a small portion of the Canadian bestseller list.

A comparison of the final two columns in table 6.1 shows that the distinction in authorial nationality between the two countries has drastically decreased. Canadian bestsellers are still more likely than American bestsellers to be written by Canadians or Brits and somewhat less likely than American bestsellers to be written by Americans. The complete Canadian sample, however, includes five times as many American-authored texts as Canadian-authored texts (60 percent vs. 12 percent).

National identity – protagonists

The national identities of protagonists in the exclusively American bestsellers are similar to those of the American high-culture texts in that they are most likely to be American. Although American citizenship is far from the assumption it was in the high-culture texts, the nationality of protagonists in the exclusively American bestsellers is still overwhelmingly likely to be American. The exclusively Canadian bestsellers are *not* most likely to have Canadian protagonists, however: only 20 percent of the exclusively Canadian bestsellers have Canadian protagonists. A comparison of the complete best-selling samples, presented in the final two columns, again shows a narrowing of the differences observed in the exclusive samples. However, American bestsellers are still more likely than Canadian bestsellers to feature American protagonists and less likely than Canadian bestsellers to feature British or Canadian protagonists.

In the Canadian prize-winning novels, citizenship often served as an avenue both for exploring issues of personal and national identity development and for situating the self in a meaningful social world. In the American prize-winning novels, citizenship was an assumption about the centrality of American experience and the taken-for-grantedness of American national identity. In both the Canadian and American canonical novels, national identity was an assumption of the text, and was Canadian and American respectively due to the national identity development role of canonical texts. In popular-culture novels, however, the citizenship of protagonists is a less salient characteristic than it is in high-culture novels. In cases where citizenship is salient, rather than serving as a metaphor for self-exploration, citizenship most often serves as an indicator of exoticism or as a shorthand for motivation, e.g., *The Holcroft Covenant* in which the villain's German nationality provides an entire Nazi philosophy and rationale for his rather peculiar aims.

One point of interest in table 6.1 concerns the disparity between author's nationality and protagonist's nationality. The nationalities selected by authors for their protagonists varied widely. Although only 5 percent of the authors have a national identity other than American, Canadian, or British, the nationality of 13 percent of the protagonists comes under the heading of "Other" and includes Sicilian, Egyptian, Japanese–Russian–Basque, Dakotan Indian, Palestinian, Russian, French, Polish, German, Japanese, and Chinese. An additional 6 percent of the protagonists are coded under the "Irrelevant" heading for national identity. This group includes protagonists who have no known national identity either because the novel is set prior to the emergence of nation-states, e.g., Auel's *The*

Mammoth Hunters set in prehistoric times, or because the novel's setting involves fictional national identities, e.g., Herbert's *Heretics of Dune* set in an imaginary planetary system.

The wide range of protagonists' national identity in the best-selling novels, particularly in comparison to the narrow range exhibited by the high-culture novels, is indicative of several functions of popular-culture literature. One of these is the pedagogical function. Many of the texts in the best-selling sample present themselves in an overt fashion as useful aids to learning. Michener's long list of titles, e.g., *Poland*, *Space*, and *The Covenant*, provides perhaps the best example. The wide appeal of Michener's books lies in part in their capacity to provide both feelings of enjoyment or escape *and* an aspect of virtue, since one is learning history and culture as well as engaging in a pleasurable experience (see Radway [1984] for a description of romance readers citing the historical and geographical knowledge they have garnered from romance reading as a justification for it).

A second aspect of the wide range of protagonist national identity has to do with the escape functions of popular-culture literature (Cawelti 1976). Exotic settings and larger-than-life protagonists allow readers to lose themselves in worlds most decidedly unlike their own. Frequently such exotic protagonists and settings provide a degree of sensationalism that helps hold the reader's attention, despite any lapses in technical details such as plot logic or character development. The Russian-by-birth, Japanese-by-childhood-socialization, and Basque-by-choice national identity of Nicholai Hel in *Shibumi*, who has a purchased mistress, an enormous fortune, a peculiar blend of Eastern and Western philosophies, and virtually unbeatable martial skills, is perhaps the best example of this phenomenon.

Gender

The high-culture novels supported previous arguments that female authors and protagonists are more likely in Canadian literature while male authors and protagonists are more likely in American literature. The bestsellers provide a very different picture (see table 6.2). Contrary to the highly skewed gender distribution in the American high-culture texts, the protagonists' gender distribution in exclusively American best-selling texts is *relatively* equal – 56 percent of the texts have male protagonists and 44 percent have female protagonists.[12] The proportion of female protagonists in the

---

[12] This is a simplification of the fact that 46 percent of the novels have male protagonists, 34 percent of the novels have female protagonists, and 20 percent of the novels have both male and female protagonists.

Table 6.2   *Gender of protagonists and authors in the bestsellers (in percentages)*

	Exclusive American (N=41)	Exclusive Canadian (N=41)	Complete American (N=100)	Complete Canadian (N=100)
Protagonists				
Male	46	63	51	58
Female	34	32	33	32
Multiple	20	5	16	10
Authors				
Male	63	78	73	79
Female	37	22	27	21

exclusively American bestsellers is higher than in the prize-winning (44 percent vs. 27 percent) and canonical novels (44 percent vs. 37.5 percent).

Female authors are also more prevalent in the American popular-culture novels. The proportion of women authors in the exclusively American bestsellers (37 percent) is almost twice that of the proportion of women authors in the American prize-winning (20 percent) and canonical (20 percent) novels. Female authors and protagonists remain underrepresentative of the population, however, and particularly underrepresentative of the reading population which is disproportionately female, especially for fiction reading (Zill and Winglee 1990; see Mann [1983] on the British situation).

Unlike the relatively even gender distribution of protagonists in the Canadian high-culture novels, the gender distribution of protagonists in exclusively Canadian bestsellers is heavily in favor of males. The exclusively Canadian bestsellers are twice as likely to have male protagonists as female (65.5 percent vs. 34.5 percent).[13] Authorial gender in the exclusively Canadian bestsellers shows an even greater imbalance in favor of men: 78 percent are written by men and just 22 percent by women.

The best-selling gender comparison is of particular interest since it is in direct opposition to the situation in the high-culture novels. The proportion of female authors is higher in the exclusively American bestsellers (37 percent) than in the exclusively Canadian bestsellers (22 percent). Women writers have the *largest* presence in any of the *American* categories in the

[13] Again, this is a simplification: 63 percent of the novels have male protagonists, 32 percent of the novels have female protagonists, and 5 percent of the novels have both.

bestsellers, where they account for 37 percent of the novels compared to 20 percent in both the canonical and prize-winning samples. Women writers have the *smallest* presence in any of the *Canadian* categories in the bestsellers, accounting for just 22 percent of the novels compared to 50 percent of the canonical novels and 36 percent of the prize-winning novels.

As noted in previous chapters, much has been made of the strong showing of female authors and female protagonists in Canadian literature (e.g., Lipset 1990; Green 1984; Smart 1984). Many reflection theorists describe the central place of female-authored works in Canadian literature as a result of the reconciliatory and non-revolutionary nature of Canadian historical experience – a national-level experience which is seen as similar to, and thus resonant with, personal-level female experience.[14] Furthermore, some theorists argue, the economic, military, and political imbalance in the relationship between Canada and the United States mirrors the imbalance of power between women and men, generating a second layer of resonance between Canadian national-level experience and female experience.

In addition, Tuchman and Fortin (1980, 1984) have argued that male dominance of high-culture novel writing and the concomitant confinement of female authors to popular-culture novel writing is an historical process. They use a comparative analysis of men's and women's entries in the *Dictionary of National Biography* to show that "[A]s the novel gained prestige [in the late nineteenth century], men invaded the emerging profession of novelist and developed the notion of the novel as high culture, thus differentiating it from the novel as popular culture; women remained relegated to the popular novel" (1984: 73–4). Because of the social construction of Victorian gender roles and the values of those controlling literary recognition, women were less likely than men to be perceived as great writers. Novels by "lady writers" were labeled sentimental or worse, and members of the literary establishment considered the majority of women's writing beneath critical notice (see also Tompkins 1985). Tuchman and Fortin argue that women writers have been traditionally more apt to be recognized and rewarded in the world of popular-culture literature than in the world of high-culture literature.

Clearly, a cross-national comparison of gender that considers both America and Canada *and* popular- and high-culture novels calls both sets of arguments into question. Neither an argument about the centrality of women writers to all Canadian literature, nor an argument about the

---

[14] Schodt's (1983) analysis of the apparent disjuncture between the orderliness and docility of Japanese society and the violent action of Japanese *manga*, or lengthy comic books, suggests some possible Canadian parallels.

comparative prevalence of women writers in popular- versus high-culture literature is sustainable once the situation in both Canada and America and in both high-culture and popular-culture novels is considered. Again this distinct difference between popular-culture and high-culture literature supports an argument that there is nothing "natural" about literary distinctiveness, nor is there necessarily a coherent national character that underlies literary difference. Literatures, like other cultural products, are determined by the requirements of their use, mediated through the demands of their constituencies, and shaped by the processes of their production.

Rebellion

Previous researchers have argued that the typical Canadian protagonist is a docile survivor while the typical American protagonist is an aggressive rebel (e.g., Atwood 1972; Lipset 1990). In contrast to these predictions, rebellious protagonists are almost twice as likely in the exclusively Canadian bestsellers as in the exclusively American bestsellers. In fact, rebellious protagonists such as Paul von Lettow in *The Ghosts of Africa,* a German general who refuses to concede Africa to the Allies in World War I, campaigning brilliantly until ordered to surrender, or Joshua Shapiro in *Joshua Then and Now* who invents a fraudulent homosexual correspondence with a fellow author in a creative attempt to scam money from exploitative newspapers and schlock magazines, comprise the majority (56 percent) of protagonists in the exclusively Canadian bestsellers.

Rebellious protagonists appear in only one-quarter (27 percent) of the exclusively American bestsellers, however. Protagonists such as Joe in L'Amour's *The Last of the Breed* may be victorious and independent rebels, but the more typical American protagonist is Anna in Plain's *Evergreen* who suffers for the sake of her marriage and family, or Al in Wambaugh's *The Glitter Dome* who drowns his agony in drink and meaningless sex, experiencing little but cynicism and ironic despair. A comparison of the complete samples shows that this distinction, although muted, remains significant. The complete American bestsellers contain thirty-eight rebellious protagonists while the complete Canadian bestsellers contain fifty rebellious protagonists. The data from the bestsellers, like that from the prize winners and canonical texts, show a clear pattern at variance with previous arguments about the prevalence of passive protagonists in Canadian literature.

Family

The distribution of the conjugal and parental families of the protagonists in the American and Canadian best-selling novels is as shown in table 6.3

Table 6.3   *Familial patterns in the bestsellers (in percentages)*

	Exclusive American (N=33)[a]	Exclusive Canadian (N=40)	Complete American (N=85)	Complete Canadian (N=92)
Conjugal				
Protagonist has/had conjugal family	64	78	64	70
Conjugal family important:	46	58	47	52
postive	6	30	14	24
negative	6	8	7	8
ambivalent	33	20	26	21
Parental				
Protagonist has/had parental family	82	80	78	77
Parental family important:	61	53	51	48
postive	18	18	13	13
negative	9	13	9	11
ambivalent	33	23	28	24
Neither important	27	20	29	26
Both important	33	30	26	25
Either important	82	80	77	79

[a] Texts with multiple protagonists have been dropped from the analysis, resulting in a slightly lower total.

(note that the Ns reflect the subtraction of texts with multiple protagonists in order to produce comparable coding categories).

Conjugal families

Protagonists in the exclusively Canadian bestsellers are more likely both to have conjugal families (78 percent) and to have them be important (58 percent), than are the protagonists in the exclusively American bestsellers (64 percent and 46 percent respectively). Once all six categories of novels are considered, however, the interesting comparison is the relatively high cross-national similarity of conjugal family importance in bestsellers (58 percent Canadian and 46 percent American) and the relatively low cross-national similarity of conjugal family importance in the prize winners (36 percent Canadian and 33 percent American) compared to the significant difference in conjugal family importance between the canonical novels (60 percent Canadian and 30 percent American).

Exclusively Canadian bestsellers are more likely to feature positive important conjugal families (30 percent) than negative (8 percent) or ambivalent (20 percent) ones. Exclusively American bestsellers, however, were more likely to feature ambivalent (33 percent) conjugal families than negative (6 percent) or positive (6 percent) ones. Once again, as in the case of the high-culture samples, the data provide no support for the argument that Canadian literary families are more entrapping or negative than American literary families. Again, the differences in families between the exclusive samples are attenuated in the complete samples. Even in the complete samples, however, Canadian bestsellers remain somewhat more likely than American bestsellers to feature protagonists with conjugal families, with important conjugal families, and with important positive conjugal families.

Parental families

Contrary to the results from *both* the prize-winning and canonical samples, it is the exclusively *American* bestsellers (61 percent) that are more likely than the exclusively Canadian bestsellers (53 percent) to feature protagonists whose parental family is important. The distribution of positive and negative families is roughly equal. No distinctions regarding the presence or importance of parental families are apparent in the comparison of the American and Canadian complete samples.

The comparative presence and importance of both conjugal and parental families in the six categories of literature strongly supports an argument that locates cross-national canonical distinctiveness in self-conscious differentiation, rather than an underlying national character. The canonical novels appear to show clearly that American literature ignores families while Canadian literature is centrally concerned with families: family, of one type or the other, is important in 100 percent of the Canadian canonical novels but in only 40 percent of the American novels. The prize winners and bestsellers, however, equally clearly show little cross-national difference in familial importance, and to the extent there is a difference, more *American* novels have important families: family of either kind is important in 64 percent of the Canadian versus 67 percent of the American prize winners and in 80 percent of the Canadian versus 82 percent of the American bestsellers. The canonical novels represent a deliberate and successful strategy of distinction: the American canonical novels lie at one end of the distribution of family importance (40 percent) while the

Canadian canonical novels lie at the farthest possible other end of the distribution (100 percent). The prize winners and bestsellers occupy *intermediary and similar* positions in the distribution (64 percent, 67 percent, 80 percent, and 82 percent).

Romance

As in the prize-winning novels, although to a much lesser degree, central love relationships remain more likely in the exclusively American bestsellers (49 percent) than in the exclusively Canadian bestsellers (41 percent). In the complete bestsellers this distinction between the Canadian and American texts has all but vanished. Interestingly, but not unexpectedly, the proportion of bestsellers with female protagonists that feature a central love relationship is higher than the proportion of bestsellers with male protagonists that feature a central love relationship for both countries. Remember the contrasting situation in the prize-winning novels. The difference is most apparent in the exclusively American sample in which only 37 percent of the novels with male protagonists feature a central love relationship but an overwhelming 93 percent of those with female protagonists do. The exclusively Canadian numbers are lower than the American, but still twice as many novels feature female protagonists and a central love relationship (62 percent) as feature male protagonists and a central love relationship (31 percent). Genre fiction accounts for a significant proportion of the female stories featuring romance.

Central conflict

There are small distinctions between the exclusively American and exclusively Canadian bestsellers in type of central conflict, two of which are important. These are in the distribution across the categories of interpersonal and familial conflict. Interpersonal conflict accounts for 27 percent of the exclusively Canadian bestsellers but only 10 percent of the exclusively American bestsellers. Familial conflicts comprise 15 percent of the exclusively American bestsellers, but only 2 percent of the exclusively Canadian bestsellers. Success, within self, and the individual vs. group categories comprise only a small number of either group of novels but do show small differences. Only the relative prevalence of interpersonal conflict in the Canadian bestsellers (23 percent) compared to the American bestsellers (16 percent) persists in the comparison of the complete samples (see table 6.4).

Table 6.4   *Type of central conflict in the bestsellers (in percentages)*

	Exclusive American (N=41)	Exclusive Canadian (N=41)	Complete American (N=100)	Complete Canadian (N=100)
Interpersonal	10	27	16	23
Familial	15	2	12	7
Success struggle	12	5	10	7
Within self	17	10	10	7
Individual vs. group	12	20	15	18
No central conflict	7	7	4	4
Institutional	27	29	33	34
Ideological	0	0	0	0

Literary style

Finally, the bestsellers do show some national differences in literary style. Twice as many Canadian texts (10 percent) as American texts (5 percent) incorporate sophisticated or avant-garde stylistic techniques. The overwhelming majority of best-selling novels, however, demonstrate the importance of stylistic convention in popular-culture products. The mass-marketing of popular culture requires that products be standardized and easily labeled. The most extreme form of literary standardization is formulaic fiction, particularly that written in conformity with "spec sheets" that rigidly define both characters and plot (Radway [1984] describes the detailed specs handed out by the publishers of romance lines). Standardized novels can be more efficiently labeled and thus more efficiently advertised and sold.

The processes of standardization and labeling allow publishers to sell texts as "the latest Stephen King thriller" or "a novel by Danielle Steel's heir apparent." It is assumed by publishers, sellers, and buyers alike that a new book by Stephen King will be essentially similar to an old book by Stephen King and that a "Danielle Steel" type of novel will be a consistently reproducible product with given attributes. Thus the classic problem of marketing unique cultural products such as novels – each book is a new and different product and must be made visible and sold in a new way to a new audience each time – becomes less of a hindrance. Standardized texts serve as examples of a conventional genre, and can be sold to a repeat audience as a continuous stream of only marginally differentiated products.

Summary of differences

In sum, the most obvious characteristic of the best-selling comparison is the overlap between the Canadian and American novels. Fifty-nine of the one hundred Canadian and one hundred American best-selling novels are mutual bestsellers, only forty-one novels are solely Canadian or solely American bestsellers.[15] Thus any comparison of the two groups of novels begins with the realization of how close to identical they are. The significant differences between the remaining forty-one Canadian and forty-one American novels are limited, involving the nationality of authors and protagonists, the gender of authors, conjugal family importance, interpersonal conflict, and rebelliousness. Overriding these differences, however, is the dominance of novels written by Americans; 66 percent of the total bestsellers are American-authored.

However, it is not only that the Canadian and American bestsellers are more similar to each other than are the Canadian and American high-culture novels. In addition, the cross-national differences that do exist are often the *opposite* of the differences that exist between the high-culture novels. For example, American and Canadian prize-winning and best-selling novels look very similar in terms of family importance, but American and Canadian canonical novels look very different in terms of family importance; women writers are more prevalent in Canadian high-culture than in Canadian popular-culture novels, but the opposite is true for American women writers. All of this serves to demonstrate that literature, when taken as a whole, is not, at least in any direct and obvious way, a reflection of a coherent, natural, national character.

Economic hegemony and the publishing industry in the United States and Canada

Literary worlds in Canada and the United States do differ, although not by reason of unique national character. Literary worlds differ in terms of their economic and political bases. While high-culture literary worlds are

---

[15] One can argue that mutual bestsellers may not actually be the "same" book in each country. If "the text" is an interaction of readers' horizons of expectations and the capacities of the cultural product itself, readers' horizons may vary systematically enough across nations to produce coherent and consistently different readings in each country. Unfortunately, my research design provides no evidence on this point.

determined by their political affiliations and national goals, popular-culture literary worlds in Canada and the United States are determined by their economic bases. Book publishing is a big business in both the United States and Canada. In 1992, Canadian book sales totaled $1.47 billion (Statistics Canada 1993, Canadian dollars, approximately $1.2 billion American dollars).[16] For the same period, American book sales totaled $15.2 billion (Grannis 1993: 25). Although the book market in both countries is substantial, the Canadian book market is obviously a great deal smaller than the American market. Once the currency difference is considered, the 1992 Canadian book market is approximately 8 percent of the American. Obviously this is largely due to the fact that the United States' population is roughly ten times the size of Canada's population.[17]

The small size of the Canadian market, and the fact that the population is thinly spread over a large area, has had profound consequences for the publishing and selling of books in Canada.[18] Since the field of large-scale production requires "the conquest of the largest possible market" (Bourdieu 1985: 17; see also Peterson 1994), the high per-unit transportation and production costs of Canadian publishers put them at a disadvantage in their own national market. Long print runs in other countries, made possible by large populations and hence large book markets, "make the cost of each book lower than for Canadian publishers, with their smaller markets and shorter print runs . . . [A]n American, British, or French book of fiction might sell in Canada for $19.95 while a Canadian book could be closer to $30" (Statistics Canada 1994: 628, Canadian dollars). As publishing has become increasingly technically complex, resultant economies of scale have meant market size has assumed an ever greater importance for book-selling. Because "mass production . . . requires mass marketing . . . the Canadian market has become an extension of other markets. It is now an extension of the US market" (Hutcheson 1987: 11). Canadian publishers are left at a severe competitive disadvantage (Bergman 1994: 50).

As important as market size is and has been, however, it is not the only consequential difference between Canadian and American publishers. One conclusion to a study of Canadian culture industries more generally described the situation thus: "the structure of the domestic production and

---

[16] The average exchange rate for 1992 was $1.2087 Canadian per American dollar (Europa Publications 1995: 729).

[17] Canada has a population of 27.2 million (Statistics Canada 1994: 115) and the US over 248 million (United States Census Bureau 1993: 8).

[18] Canada's population density is 7.8 people/square mile while in the United States population density is just over 70 people/square mile (Statistics Canada 1994: 110; United States Census Bureau 1993: 8).

distribution industries [in each segment of the culture industry] is organized around the supply of imported content to Canadians" (Hutcheson 1987: 11; Audley 1983). The source of this difference is both historically rooted and exacerbated by modern technologies. Publishers in Canada "came into existence . . . to distribute imported books, not to publish; most original publishing for the Canadian market has grown from that base" (*Publishers Weekly* 1979). Atwood recalls the situation in Canadian publishing in the early 1960s thus: "all the novels and books of poetry by Canadians, published in Canada, in the year 1961, could be and were reviewed in part of one issue of the *University of Toronto Quarterly*. I think there were about five novels and under twenty books of poetry, but that included the mimeo jobs and the flatbed press numbers" (1982: 381).

Although the situation in Canadian publishing has improved since 1961, the distinction in emphasis between both publishing and distributing (American) and primarily distributing (Canadian) remains. The proportion of imported books, largely from the United States, in Canada has remained relatively steady in the past twenty years, hovering around 75–80 percent of all book sales (*Publishers Weekly* 1979; Hutcheson 1987; Bergman 1994). As a comparison, imported books accounted for only 5.9 percent of American book sales in 1992 – and Canadian imports accounted for less than 9 percent of that import total (Grannis 1993: 25).

The overall effect of the small size of the Canadian book market, the historical focus on distributive roles, and an increasingly technological production context has been to establish the economic dominance of the American publishing industry over the Canadian book market. The Canadian book market traditionally absorbs over one-half of all American book exports (Hutcheson 1987: 12). In 1991–92 this represented Canadian importation from the United States of 4.3 million books, worth $702 million, out of the total American world book export of 8.4 million books with a value of $1.6 billion (Grannis 1993: 26, omitting all book shipments under $2,500).[19] In comparison, the next largest importer of American books, the United Kingdom, imported fewer than $229 million dollars worth of books in 1992. Because of this "smothering domination" (Dwyer 1991: 61) of the Canadian market by foreign publishers, the Canadian publishing industry is heavily reliant on the importation, marketing, and distribution of foreign titles for income. The handling of foreign published

[19] US book exports to Canada fell slightly in 1993, to $695.4 million (Milliot 1994a: 10) and indications for the first half of 1994 were soft. In the first six months of 1994, book exports to Canada were off 0.1 percent at $327 million (Milliot 1994b: 10). Prognosticators attributed these drops to the recessionary Canadian economy, however, rather than a strong Canadian publishing industry (Bergman 1994).

books accounted for one-half ($654 million) of the $1.3 billion earned by Canadian publishers in 1990–91 (Statistics Canada 1994: 628, Canadian dollars). When Canadian publishers are primary publishers, the books they issue are generally Canadian-authored. Since Canadian-authored books tend to be Canadian-published, they are therefore often more expensive than foreign-authored and published books (see Griswold [1981] on an analogous situation in the United States in the nineteenth century, although the reasons for the price disparity were somewhat different).[20]

The situation of foreign dominance is not exclusive to the publishing industry. Other Canadian culture industries also experience difficulties competing with American producers (Juneau 1986). Thus, for example, Canadian movies accounted for only 4 percent of Canadian box office receipts in 1992 (Cameron 1993). In 1984 Canada's film and broadcasting exports to the United States totaled $23 million; during the same period Canada's film and broadcasting imports from the United States totaled $136 million – a truly enormous difference when the population gap is taken into account (Hutcheson 1987, Canadian dollars). The picture in Canadian television is similar. Although the Canadian Broadcasting Corporation (CBC) was created to address the issue of American cultural hegemony, 92 percent of the comedies and 85 percent of the dramas currently aired on Canadian television are foreign productions, largely from the United States (Cameron 1993: 4; Ericson, Baranek, and Chan 1987; Enchin 1995). As of 1989, despite government intervention and subsidy, the shortfall between exports and imports in the Canadian culture industries was still $7 billion (Statistics Canada 1994: 627, Canadian dollars).

In the 1970s many Canadian citizens as well as the Canadian government became increasingly alarmed by what was seen as the virtual takeover of Canadian culture by the American culture industry. Although there was historic precedent for Canadian concern regarding American cultural domination, the scale of the threat appeared significantly larger during this period (Smith 1994, especially pp. 98–105). The publishing sector became a prime target for these fears:

the publishing sector, combining the ideals of economic and cultural nationalism, became the most militant and influential base for the movement [to patriate

---

[20] The situation in French language publishing is analogous, although France plays the American role of foreign dominator. Quebec publishers experienced a surge of work during the Vichy regime as French authors sought autonomy, but the postwar period saw production sharply curtailed. Since the end of the 1960s, government subsidies have played an increasing role in keeping Quebec publishing alive as the small market keeps growth limited and the large French publishers have moved into the Canadian market despite Quebec government policies intended to limit foreign ownership and control (Lemire 1988).

Canadian industry]. But because publishing in the US is more a function of the marketplace and less consciously an expression of national goals, American publishers who dealt with Canada were shocked and bewildered at being regarded as agents of American cultural imperialism (*Publisher's Weekly* 1979: 38; see also Bashevkin 1991).

Under an increasingly perceived threat of American cultural homogenization, Canadians sought protection for their culture, and the industries that produce it, from the government. This too had historic precedent. As early as the late nineteenth century, Canadian concern with "America's cultural might" was manifested in demands for the government to ensure the preservation of Canadian cultural life through "copyright, preferential postal rates, and legislated measures to slow the flow of American periodicals into Canada" (Smith 1994: 98; Duncan 1887).

Government intervention

Government subsidy, intervention, and legislation have been the most frequent responses to Canadian worries of American cultural (and financial) hegemony. Legislative action to protect Canadian-owned cultural producers and to curb foreign control of domestic culture markets has been surprisingly common by American standards. Historically, Canadian government action was relatively indirect, involving manipulation of such things as tariffs, postal rates, and copyright. Although Canadian federal moneys were also used more directly even in early periods, for instance, to establish national cultural institutions such as the Dominion Archives in 1872 and the National Gallery in 1880, the role of state power in building a national culture and defending it against the United States was relatively limited until the early twentieth century, and most especially, the post-World War II period. Smith describes the end of the 1930s as a landmark: "By the end of the 1930s the nature of the culture-state situation had changed in important and striking ways. *Earlier honored more in principle than in practice*, state action in the field of culture had now become a fixture of the national life" (1994: 101, emphasis added).

   The postwar era with its rising tide of Canadian nationalism and cultural activists dedicated to the establishment of a truly Canadian cultural life created an even stronger tie between cultural nationalism and state action. In 1974 the Canadian government created FIRA (Foreign Investment Review Agency) as a screening body to advise the Cabinet on possible takeovers of large Canadian firms, including but not limited to firms in the culture industries, by foreign corporations.

   In 1985, then Minister of Communications, Marcel Masse, announced a

"Canadianization of the publishing industry" policy, generally referred to as the Baie Comeau policy, which required foreign companies acquiring ownership of Canadian-based publishers to sell a majority share (51 percent) to a Canadian buyer within two years (Hutcheson 1987; Dwyer 1991).[21] Although critics have charged that loopholes exist, and that the Canadian government has not pursued either of these opportunities to limit foreign control of cultural production vigorously enough, they are indications of the comparative Canadian legislative concern with national ownership of culture producers. Minister Masse drafted other legislative initiatives aimed at curbing foreign control of culture markets in Canada and supporting nationally owned culture producers. Although many of these initiatives have not won Cabinet or Commons approval, the policies are obvious indications of the importance granted by Canada to issues of foreign control of cultural production (Allen 1991).[22] More recently, a revised Copyright Act intended to protect Canadian publishers' income from further foreign "depredations" has been discussed (Bergman 1994: 50–1). Although not submitted as of early 1996, the revised Copyright Act may be submitted by the Industry Minister John Manley once the new Heritage Minister Sheila Copps is acquainted with it (Loring 1996).

In addition to legislative action, the relatively low number of Canadian-authored titles and Canadian-owned firms in book publishing is addressed through the Canada Council and other government arts agencies, both federal and provincial.[23] Government action on behalf of the culture industries, through both legislation and funding, has been substantial. Nonetheless, Hutcheson assessed the state of Canadian culture industries

---

[21] However, in 1986, Masse and the Department of Communications were stymied by free trade forces in the Canadian government and proved unable to prevent the sale of Prentice-Hall despite the Baie Comeau policy (Marsh 1988).

[22] The recent free trade negotiations were also attended by vast amounts of discussion, if in the end little action, about the symbolic importance of the culture industries on the Canadian side and the financial value of the culture industries on the American side (see Smith 1994).

[23] The Canada Council was established in 1957 to support artists and arts organizations in Canada. Originally funded by moneys from two individuals, the Council began receiving parliamentary funds in 1967. In 1992 the Council received $106 million from the Department of Communications and allocated roughly $98 million in artistic grants to approximately 1,200 artists and 300 arts organizations. See footnote 27 of chapter 3. The arts community has responded to reduced government funding with a sense of crisis. Canadian publishers are described as "[R]ed all over" and "fighting for their lives" (Dwyer 1991). The cultural arena more generally is "in crisis" (Dwyer 1992), "increasingly beleaguered" (Allen 1991: 52), and "down the tubes" (Bergman 1994: 52). While government reductions (including a refusal to exempt books from the new federal goods and services tax of 7 percent imposed in 1991) are considered a key aspect of the situation, so are the weak economy, trade sensitivities with the United States, and increasing technological economies of scale that mitigate against the small and highly dispersed Canadian market.

in these terms: "Canadian production holds only a minor share of the market . . . [and] what little there is is a consequence of some form of government support, whether subsidy, regulation, or tax incentive" (1987: 15). Overall, the federal Department of Communications spent $2.9 billion on culture in the 1992–93 fiscal year (Dwyer 1992: 47, Canadian dollars).[24]

Despite the expressions of concern from elites and multiple attempts at action from many levels of the government, Minister of Communications Masse reported to the Cabinet in February of 1986 that the publishing industry remains dominated by foreign producers. At that time twenty-nine subsidiaries of foreign corporations earned 60 percent of publishing revenues in Canada while 173 Canadian-owned companies earned just 40 percent of total publishing revenues (Hutcheson 1987: 18). Three years later, in 1989, the forty-two American- and British-controlled English language branch plants in Canada had actually increased their market share, controlling 62 percent of the $900 million domestic anglophone book market (Dwyer 1991: 61, Canadian dollars). Sales of imported books continue to outnumber sales of Canadian-published books by three to one and the Canadian market still absorbs one-half of American book exports.[25]

Popular taste

Given the consistent inability of Canadian cultural industries to control the popular-culture fields of film and broadcasting, publishing, and television in Canada despite elite outcry and governmental intervention in the form of direct subsidies, regulation, and tax incentives, the question of consumer choice and popular taste inevitably arises. In these popular-culture genres,

---

[24] Despite the traditional strong government support for the arts, many commentators and culture producers feel that the federal government at least is backing off from its commitment to Canadian culture. In addition to cuts to the Canada Council budget, the Mulroney government proposed in 1993 that the Social Science and Humanities Research Council be merged into the Canada Council. Although the measure was defeated, it was seen by many as a move to vitiate federal arts funding. Similarly, the move of federal responsibility for culture from the Department of Communications to a new Heritage Department is also viewed as ominous by many (Crean 1993). The Canadian government is also reviewing ways in which to cut the budget of the Canadian Broadcasting Corporation. However, the CBC is three times as large as American public broadcasting, costing $1.1 billion Canadian annually to fund the CBC's 9,000-employee operation (Clayton 1995: 1).

[25] In 1990–91, 8,126 book titles were published in Canada, a drop of approximately 100 titles from the year before (Grannis 1993: 26). Of these titles, 72 percent were Canadian-authored (Statistics Canada 1994: 656). In comparison, 48,146 titles were published in the United States in the same period, a drop of approximately 5,300 titles from the year before (Grannis 1993:26). The vast majority of Canadian-authored titles are published by Canadian publishers.

art becomes a "commodity" aimed at a "socially heterogeneous market" and oriented "toward a generalization of the social and cultural composition" of the audience (Bourdieu 1985: 28–33). That is, popular-culture products are produced and marketed with an eye toward the broadest, least exclusionary appeal. Popular-culture literature aims *"to be easily read by the widest possible public"* (Bourdieu 1985: 28, italics in original). This is in direct opposition to the strategy of national literatures, which is predicated on exclusion, on distinctiveness, on an idea of differentiation from others. Popular-culture literature embraces the universal, denies difference and cultural distinctiveness, and is marketed as universally appealing.

The dominance of American goods in Canadian popular-culture markets is a result of this appeal to broad-based audiences as well as the economic structure. Available Canadian popular-culture alternatives, be they novels, TV dramas, or movies, are not necessarily preferred by Canadian consumers. Similarly, American popular-culture offerings are not always preferred by Americans.[26] "Canadian-ness" or "American-ness" are qualities less riveting to the average consumer of popular culture than to the elites to whom the legitimation and interpretation of national-level experience fall or to the government whose right and ability to rule are legitimated by the strength of the nation (see Collins [1990] on Canadian television).

Disparate economic power is only one source of the American domination of Canadian culture industries. Popular taste is the other.[27] There is little evidence that Canadian popular taste differs in significant ways from American popular taste. The market, in fact, provides strong evidence that Canadian and American popular taste is extremely similar.[28] Given that

---

[26] Witness, for example, Umberto Eco's dazzling performance at the top of the American best-seller lists (*The Name of the Rose*, 1983). The US is, however, generally considered the world's leading exporter of popular culture (Holmstrom 1991; Nelson 1995). However, see Schmidt (1993) for an argument that American influence is declining.

[27] Of course, for Bourdieu, it is the class position of consumers and their relation to the class position of cultural objects that dictate cultural use and consumption patterns (1984, 1985). However, Bourdieu sees the broadness of popular culture's appeal extending upward, without a concomitant downward appeal of high culture: "consumption in the field of large-scale cultural production is more or less independent of the educational level of consumers . . . [but] works of restricted art owe their specifically cultural rarity to the rarity of the instruments with which they may be deciphered" (1985:23). Peterson (1992) makes a similar, and empirically supported, argument regarding cultural "omnivores," demonstrating that those in upper occupational groups are more apt to engage in a broad range of elite and non-elite cultural activities, while those in lower occupational groups tend to engage only in non-elite activities.

[28] This similarity is not confined to Canadian acceptance and importation of American cultural products. Many Canadian cultural products, e.g., SCTV or the rock artist Bryan Adams, are quite successful in the States. Even Margaret Atwood, long-time icon of contemporary Canadian high culture, is reaching the apex of the American bestseller lists. See Tracy and Redal (1995) on the congruence of TV tastes in the US and English Canada.

American and Canadian popular taste show few distinguishing characteristics, the more powerful American production and distribution system triumphs in the competition for broad markets that drives the field of
large-scale production.[29]

In this chapter I have demonstrated that best-selling novels in the United
States and Canada are not just similar, but often the very same novels.
Almost 60 percent of the top ten bestsellers in the ten-year period over-
lapped. The differences between the remaining forty-one Canadian and
American novels were limited. American best-selling novels are distinguished from Canadian in that they are largely written by Americans
and almost never written by Canadians. Canadian bestsellers are distinguished from American in that they are more likely to be written by
British and Canadian authors and to have rebellious protagonists, but are
less likely to have American protagonists. Although male authors pre-
dominate in both countries, American bestsellers are more likely to have
female authors (over one-third do) than are Canadian bestsellers (fewer
than one-quarter) – a situation in direct contrast to the high-culture
novels.

In explaining the relative lack of distinctions between Canadian and
American popular-culture texts, I raise two issues. The first and most
important is the structure of the popular-literature publishing industry in
the United States and Canada. It is precisely because popular-culture
novels are shaped by similar mass-market strategies and read by similar
audiences that they differ little between the two countries. Popular-culture
literature lacks the nationally symbolic value of high-culture literature.
Popular-culture literature, while free of the symbolic political role constraints imposed on high-culture literature, is nonetheless shaped by its cultural uses and production context. Popular-culture literature is subject to
the mass market constraints generated by the structure and nature of the
publishing industry in the field of large-scale production. Those constraints
minimize national, regional, and subgroup differences through the production of popular-culture novels that are as broadly appealing as possible.
These novels are then packaged and promoted in ways designed to sell as
many copies as possible to the least discriminating, and therefore largest
possible, audience. Production and distribution systems are designed to
lower unit costs as much as possible through economies of scale and other

[29] A variety of production of culture analyses have demonstrated the importance of market
mechanisms and economic determinants in cultural production. See for example, Hirsch
(1972, 1975); Peterson and Berger (1975); DiMaggio (1977); Powell (1985); see Peterson
(1994) for a review of recent work in this vein.

production characteristics. This results in a commodity market driven by economic imperatives.

The second question is that of popular taste. Despite efforts by elites and the government, the average Canadian popular-culture consumer shows no pronounced preference for a "Canadian-identified" product *in popular culture*. The comparatively large number of Canadian "blockade runners" (Escarpit 1971), or high-culture novels that appear on the bestseller lists, by contrast, indicates that highly symbolic cultural products marketed as *distinctively Canadian* may also appeal to a large number of people. Generally, however, since North America forms a convenient pooled market for popular-culture products, the stronger production and distribution system, in this case the American, dominates the field of large-scale production with its emphasis on broadly popular, economically driven cultural products.

7

Literary meaning and cultural use

I began the book by enumerating the inadequacies of reflection theory for an explanation of national literatures. Now, however, I wish to return to the issue of "reflection" more broadly understood. In the simple sense of the term, literary reflection does occur in that characters, settings, and plot devices in fiction tend to resemble "real" people, places, and events.[1] Not surprisingly, there is a connection between literature and society. The problem remains, however, that reflection theory is not *sufficient* to explain which aspects of the social environment are included in literature, which aspects are excluded in literature, and which aspects are ignored.

Ramona's famous question about how Mike went to the bathroom while working all day with his steam shovel is a classic example of this latter insufficiency of reflection theory.[2] Everyone goes to the bathroom, but few authors detail the fact. The "failure" of literature to reflect such aspects of everyday life is obviously driven in part by the requirement for significance in art. But on a larger scale than the absence in most literature of quotidian activities such as eating, urinating, and blowing one's nose, the underlying problem remains. Of course literary depictions draw upon real life. But how do we understand the process by which real life is selectively transformed into literary life? And, more importantly in the case of canonical novels and literary prize-winning novels, how do we understand why it is that this novel or this author is valorized when so many are relegated to obscurity? Why is this "reflection" valued while others are not?

[1] Experienced readers of science fiction and fantasy know how very much even genres such as these "reflect" some recognizable version of our reality.
[2] Ramona, a six-year-old in Beverly Cleary's *Ramona the Pest*, asks, after the teacher reads the perennial children's favorite, *Mike Mulligan and his Steam Shovel*, how Mike was able to go to the bathroom while working all day digging the basement of the town hall. Needless to say the question is not appreciated by the teacher, who feels the topic of bathrooms to be inappropriate – but also seems unclear herself on the workings of literary representation.

The significance of literary difference

The answer lies in the social world. Up to this point, I have emphasized what have traditionally been called structural explanations in my understanding of literary distinctiveness. Nonetheless, the process by which elite interests in the national project in Canada and the United States are transformed into a national canon is not only affected by the political situation, the economy, and the social positions of those who oversee national canon formation. Nor are the specific characteristics of those literary canons constructed out of thin air. The construction of a unique national literature in Canada and the United States was also shaped by the *cultural* environment and the materials contained therein.[3] The socially constructed, readily available cultural materials of a society – the archetypes, the myths, the epigrams and adages, the morals, the means–ends chains, the evaluation criteria, the categorization schemas, all of the materials of shared "tool kits" – are what give specific shape to literary distinctions (Burke 1957; Swidler 1986; Griswold 1992; Lamont 1995). The particular form literary distinctions took in the United States drew upon widely available – if nascent – cultural ideas such as a burgeoning sense of manifest destiny, the litany of dissatisfactions with British rule, and the reformatory narratives of the Puritans, *at the same time* that early canon formation articulated, codified, and legitimated these very ideas as central to the American experience and identity. In Canada, the process was similar but delayed. Canadian literary distinction obviously drew upon a different set of cultural ideas, such as the threatening nature of the physical landscape, the complicated relationship with the French, and the explicit rejection of the American revolutionary spirit.

Novels are selected into the canon based on an understanding of what is culturally meaningful, of what does distinguish one literature from another. This understanding is socially constructed. Only certain differences are powerful, only certain differences are able to carry the weight of significance. And not just any significance – the differences codified in a national literature must be differences that provide a relatively coherent and unified story of the unique nation (Carafiol 1991; Bennett 1991: 134 especially). The preexisting nationalist framework that ordered the relationship between the nation and its literature meant that American and Canadian literary distinctiveness had to make sense within an identifiable narrative of the unique American or Canadian nation and its experience. Griswold

---

[3] See Hays (1994), however, on the false distinction between "cultural" and "structural" arguments.

(1992: 723) describes this process in Nigeria where the "village novel" became the "central myth that arose from specific historical processes," including existing Nigerian and British narratives of Africa and the particularities of the publishing context. This Nigerian "canon" now represents Nigeria and Nigerian identity not only to British outsiders, but to Nigerians themselves. An understanding of the cultural grounding that interacts with political and economic realities, the interests of elites, and historically specific circumstances to create a national canon, makes it possible to address the obvious unresolved issue of the question of the *meaning* of the specific textual differences I found. Why *are* female authors more prevalent in Canadian high-culture literature than in American high-culture literature? Why *do* the protagonists of American canonical novels lack parental families?

Thus the prevalence of women authors and female experience in a literature used to distinguish Canada from the United States is not a reflection of some absolute and timeless truth about the femaleness of Canadian as compared to American life. The prevalence of women authors and female experience in high-culture Canadian literature is a *strategy of distinction* rooted in the shared Western understanding that gender is an important and meaningful distinction, that a literature by and about women is importantly different than a literature largely by and about men. Canonizing novels by women is an *understandable action*, a meaningful choice for distinction given the particular requirements of Canadian nation-building and the shared cultural environment of Canadians, Americans, and the British.

Similarly, American canonical novels feature protagonists without families because the concept of the self as determined by family of origin already existed as a meaningful narrative, and one whose *rejection* was a meaningful way of distinguishing the United States from Britain. Americans – "real" as opposed to literary ones that is – don't generally abandon their parents and create themselves out of thin air. Most Americans send Mother's Day cards, observe their parents' birthdays, visit family for the holidays, and grow up strongly influenced by their parents and their childhood families. Nonetheless, most Americans know that one of the things America stands for is the right to construct yourself anew. The choice of self-determination is always viable. In England, so the American story goes, you are who you are born, but in America you are who you make yourself. American canonical novels do not necessarily reflect some deep and enduring truth about American *life* or a preexisting psychological propensity inherent among Americans, but an important, and perhaps enduring, truth about how Americans distinguish themselves and their country from other peoples and other nations.

Thus larger, socially available meaning systems privilege the importance and symbolic weight of some distinctions over others. No one would have cared if Fiedler (1966) had argued that classic American novels were all about men escaping into the woods with dark-*haired* rather than dark-*skinned* companions. Historical contingencies and environmental conditions create a situation in which some distinctions are important and some distinctions have been or can be integrated within the "unique nation" framework more easily than others (Griswold 1981; 1992). The cultural milieu determines not only which distinctions are important (skin color but not hair color) but also which distinctions are appropriate and culturally resonant. Gender may be an important and meaningful category to Americans, but American distinction from Britain could not easily be achieved through tropes of femininity because the available images and narratives of the intrepid and rugged pioneer were rooted in a comparison to the pampered and effete aristocrat who symbolized a vitiated and hierarchical Britain. The American story was not well served by the symbolic meanings of the female. Similarly, although the geographic and climatic conditions experienced by the vast majority of Canadians – 80 percent of whom live within 100 miles of the American border – do not differ appreciably from those experienced by most midwestern Americans, the image of a malevolent natural world requiring firmly rooted communal solidarity to withstand, is a compelling one that powerfully symbolizes Canadian national life in a manner meaningful to Canadians and outsiders alike.

National literatures work by demonstrating what is important and special about "us," by distinguishing between "us" and "them" through the specification of boundaries marking both who and what are within the nation and who and what are outside the nation. The boundary specification and maintenance work of national literatures is accomplished by delineating the difference between one nation and other relevant nations. In her work on national boundaries, Lamont uses the concept of the "historic cultural repertoire" of a nation to demonstrate that "patterns of . . . specific criteria of definition and evaluation of others" differ for Americans and for the French (1995: 365, 350–1). The concept of national cultural repertoires provides a way to discuss systematic and nationally distinctive patterns without becoming mired in the problems of specifying the mechanics of reflection.

National repertoires and patterns of action

Through the concept of national cultural repertoires, we can begin to specify the relationship between a national society or environment, the behavior of its members, and the characteristics of its cultural works, without relying on either the simple reflection metaphor or the notion of inherent national character. The concept of a national cultural repertoire draws upon theoretical conceptualizations of culture's effect on behavior as occurring through the provision of tools, schemas, or capacities, rather than the provision of a unitary system of values (Swidler 1986; Schudson 1989; Sewell 1992; see Corse and Robinson [1994] for a review). Swidler (1986) conceives of culture as affecting behavior by providing a tool kit from which people construct strategies of action, i.e., habitual and persisting ways of organizing their behavior. Central to Swidler's (1986) formulation is the notion of people as active, even "skilled," users of culture who have an abundance of materials in their tool kits that represent a greater range of possible strategies than they deploy at any one time. Cultural repertoires may even contain contradictory materials. Thus, at least some of the time, people actively select the cultural materials they will use and will even create new cultural materials (Sewell 1992).

The connection of the two ideas of active users and national cultural repertoires is crucial. The tension between the agency of actors, on the one hand, and the bounded possibilities of the cultural repertoire, on the other, structures the entire process. The construction of distinct national literatures is a reciprocal process in which materials such as symbols and narratives become available in the cultural environment through importation or innovation. Some of these cultural materials are especially responsive to incorporation within the nationalist framework and are therefore used as symbolic markers of national distinctiveness. National cultural repertoires both *provide* potential materials for distinguishing the nation and *are shaped by* new, or newly interpreted, materials made available in codified national discourses. The development of national canons is an ongoing process. Elites draw on national cultural repertoires to develop an image of the nation as distinct. National populations, in turn, draw on literature for the cultural materials that help them construct unique identities. But this is not a one-sided process. The initial repertoire drawn on to imagine the nation is modified and reconstructed through the interactions of elites, the everyday experiences of national populations, and the continued codification of national identity. Legitimated texts are themselves reinterpreted and revised as needed in the ongoing process of constructing the meaning of the nation (e.g., Tompkins 1985). Legitimated forms of culture such as the canon and the cultural repertoires of social actors are mutually constitutive.

The need for a distinctive national literature draws *selectively* on the *multiplicity* of possible materials contained in a national cultural repertoire.

For example, while the American cultural repertoire contains images and narratives of American individualism and self-determination, which are mobilized in the construction of a national literature and national identity distinctive from the British, other, even antithetical ideas, images, narratives, and behaviors are *also* available in the American cultural repertoire. That is, Americans may have a story about individualism and the irrelevance of parental families, but that story may frequently be ignored or contradicted both by other stories and by the actual behaviors of many Americans. After all, the American story may be *Huck Finn*, but it is also the Norman Rockwell magazine cover of small town, red-cheeked, extended families gathered around the Thanksgiving turkey, the Waltons television series, and the observations of Varenne (1977) and Tocqueville [1835] (1966).

It is not that American individualism is true or not true, an accurate or inaccurate reflection, but that individualism is one idea, one category, one symbol of American identity, contained in the American cultural repertoire. Individualism may be mobilized in certain situations and ignored in others. In the situation of national canon formation, individualism becomes a powerful tool for distinguishing America from England. In other situations, individualism may be less relevant. The comparison between the bestsellers and the high-culture novels provides ample evidence of this multiplicity, and of the flexibility and breadth of national cultural repertoires. The bestsellers undermine or destabilize almost all of the defining characteristics of the canonical novels. Individualism may mark the American canon in which only one protagonist in ten has an important parental family while eight of ten Canadian canonical novels have important parental families, but the bestsellers are indistinguishable from each other – just over one-half of the American bestsellers and just under one-half of the Canadian bestsellers have important parental families. Similarly, the Canadian affinity for femaleness may mark the Canadian canon, with female authors achieving parity with male authors while the American women are outnumbered by four to one, but the bestsellers reverse the situation – neither American nor Canadian bestsellers achieve gender parity and, in fact, the proportion of women writers is higher for American bestsellers than for Canadian bestsellers.

Remember, however, that national repertoires are not infinitely open or flexible. Individualism, for example, is a highly salient concept to most Americans, particularly in thinking about their American-ness. Similarly, communal or social definitions of the self are highly salient to most Canadians, even when they are admiring the "get up and go" quality of American life. The construction of national identity through codified discourses such as literature makes certain images and lines of action readily available and easily mobilized while making others less easily imagined, less possible (Corse and Dougherty 1996).

Acknowledging both the agency of social actors and the parameters that structure the possibilities within which people imagine action, allows us to consider both the systematic variations in national culture and the complexity of the link between culture, nation, and individual action. Thus one arrives at a model of cross-national variation in behavior which is rooted in specifiable, shared patterns, but acknowledges the agency of individuals, and is free from a reliance on the dubious link between behavior and a notion of a unitary, shared, and absolute set of values.[4]

Literary elites and the national project

A second important issue for an understanding of nationalism and literature is the structure of the relationship between the literary elite and the national project. As I discussed in chapter 2, members of the American literary world were historically deeply and consciously committed to the national project. Canadian members of the literary world, as I described in chapter 3, were historically disinterested in or even hostile to the national project, except as that project was defined either by the subnation of Quebec or by the supranation of the British Commonwealth.

The contemporary situation, however, is significantly different. In brief, the members of the literary elite in the United States are generally disengaged from, and even disdainful of, traditional notions of literary nationalism. In Canada, the story is more complicated. The Canadian literary elite is clearly divided on the issue. One contingent is outspokenly and self-consciously committed to the national project while a second group sounds the internationalist refrain.

Interestingly, the situation in the general population seems largely a reverse of that pertaining to the literary elite. While the general population in America seems comfortable with the traditional pairing of nation and literature, and distinctly suspicious of the more radical ideas destabilizing literary nationalism, the general population in Canada seems less supportive of the idea of cultural nationalism than does the majority of the literary elite.

American interest in literary nationalism among the literary elite is largely confined to critics whose location within the academy is American

---

[4] See, for example, Pfeffer (1982), Scheier and Carver (1977), and Fiske and Taylor (1984) on the weak connection between behavior and values.

literary scholarship or American studies (e.g., Spengemann 1989; Carafiol 1991; Vandersee 1994). On the other hand, the overwhelming interest of departments of English literature in European theories of post-structuralism and postmodernism and the concomitant interest with fragmentation, marginalization, and the periphery, certainly orients a primary interest *away* from national integration and themes of unity. Radical dislocations of the author and the meaning of texts make the imposition of a coherent and unified narrative of nation and literature difficult, to say the least (Lacan 1977; Derrida 1980; Foucault 1980; see also Lamont and Wuthnow 1990). Even within the traditional scholarship in American literature, critics are attempting to undermine the tradition of "two centuries during which a belief in an idealized national identity sustained popular and scholarly discourse about American writing" and to destabilize the "characteristic . . . narrative coherence" that has structured and unified the story equating America and its literature (Carafiol 1991: 3, 5). Within the currently dominant perspectives in literary theory, the historical construction of the narrative of nationalism and literature no longer makes sense.

The internationalization of literary standards and the literary world provides a further countervailing force against the national project. Pan-national organizations such as PEN, the Nobel Prize for Literature apparatus, and the increasing cosmopolitanism of writers, literary critics, and the publishing world have led to the globalization of high culture within a new transnational social world (Buell 1994). Academic institutions sponsor visits by an increasingly international group of writers and scholars, literature begins to be taught and understood within pan-national groupings such as "European feminism" and "Post-colonial literatures of the Caribbean," and the traditional story of an exceptional American literature is seen as outmoded and only appropriate for, if anything, plebeian introductory classes.

In addition to the dissension and disunity regarding the project of American literature among literary critics and the increasing internationalization of the literary world, it is clear that broad public support for federal arts funding is also lacking in America. The National Endowment for the Arts (NEA) and the National Endowment for the Humanities (NEH) have sustained deep cuts and public broadcasting is seriously threatened. Indeed, it has been noted that the "entire budget of the National Endowment for the Arts is less than the Defense Department's allocation for military bands" (Bogart 1995: 304, quoted in Schudson 1995: 811). Nonetheless, despite the attacks on literary nationalism and cohesive narrative within the academy, and despite the increasing disinterest of the federal government in supporting a national culture, the traditional story of the nation and its reflection in literature is still the dominant interpretive framework in secondary schools and among the general population.

Although many of the same forces for internationalization and the deconstruction of the national canon can be seen in Canada, the situation is nonetheless very different. The recent free trade negotiations made clear the complicated relationship between cultural producers and the national project in Canada. There is a conflict between those who believe in an explicit equation of nation and culture backed by the power and financial support of the state, and those who believe in a highly internationalized vision of Canada. Although one group of writers and other artists formed an anti-free trade group which was active in the attempt to undermine or at least contain the sweeping changes envisioned by NAFTA, a second group coalesced about John Metcalf, known for his frequent attacks on Canadian arts subsidies as indicative of Canadian provincialism and inability to compete at world class standards, to promote free trade (for a discussion of the varying positions of these groups and their assumptions about art, the nation, and the political process see Davey [1993: 10–24]). The two groups' statements, one supporting the idea of free trade, the other decrying it, were published in the *Globe and Mail* on the same day. Such a juxtaposition demonstrates the contested nature of cultural authority most powerfully. Although the Canadian literary and cultural elite are relatively more invested in the national project than is the case in the United States, the national canon is under attack in both countries, and from the very people charged with sustaining it.

Despite this open contestation, and the concomitant ambivalent position of Canadian literary elites, the general tone of the free trade negotiations pertaining to cultural production demonstrated the continued Canadian commitment to culture at a national level. Throughout the negotiations, the Canadian concern with protecting national cultural production was evident, as was the concomitant American disinterest in and even hostility toward this stance. The American difficulty in comprehending the Canadian position of governmental protection of culture is infamous. For example, the US ambassador to Canada, Thomas Niles, made the following judgment in 1985: "We think that these questions [on cultural subsidy and legislation] should be resolved on a *commercial* basis and that governments shouldn't get mixed up in them" (quoted in Smith 1994: 89, emphasis added). Similarly, US trade representative Clayton Yeutter's (purposively one hopes) disingenuous 1987 statement that, "I'm prepared to have American culture on the table and have it damaged by Canadian influences after the free trade agreement. I hope Canada's prepared to run the risk too" (quoted in Smith 1994: 89) indicates the divergence between

American and Canadian conceptions of the relationship between culture and the nation at the governmental level (see also Trueheart [1996], especially compared to, for example, Fagan [1996]).

The increasingly contested nature of the power to grant canonization is clearly one part of the destabilization of the traditional conflation of the nation and its literature. Although change is an essential part of canon formation in both Canada and the United States, and the authority to control that change has always been contested, the current environment is one in which the arena of competition for that control is rife with contenders. A new and wide assortment of previously excluded groups is challenging not just the content of the canon, but the very parameters within which canon formation occurs (von Hallberg 1984; *New York Times Book Review* 1988; Lecker 1990, 1991, 1995; Lauter 1991; Davey 1993; Corse and Griffin 1996). Not only has the canon debate been opened up to previously excluded groups within the academy, it is no longer even the sole preserve of academics (DiMaggio 1991).[5] The contested nature of cultural authority is more clearly visible than perhaps ever before.

The context of high-culture production

The complex relationship among literary producers, the government, and the traditional role of literature in the service of the nation in Canada and the United States has consequences for the production context of high-culture literature. The commitment of at least a significant proportion of cultural producers to the national project in Canada has been fostered by a very different relationship between the government and the literary world than that of the United States. As I have noted in chapters 5 and 6, the Canadian government, at both the federal and provincial levels, provides significant amounts of funding for cultural producers in Canada. The effect of this historic largesse has been to encourage many in the literary world to conceive of their work within specifically national terms. The Canadian government funds writer-in-residence programs, poetry and fiction readings across Canada, a national book fair, and a variety of literary magazines and presses. Such programs make it difficult to ignore the nationalist context of cultural production in Canada.[6]

---

[5] See, however, Rogers for a dissenting position: "*canonical novels that get recognized as such* reflect the cultural authority high-status men carved out for themselves . . . the literary place 'minority' writers occupy remains wobbly" (1991: 64, 66, italics in original). Note that she assumes there are somehow *unrecognized* yet *canonical* novels.

[6] Of course the high level of provincial funding for culture also exaggerates regional tensions and identities.

In the literary world, one important result of the depth of government commitment to culture has been the proliferation of smaller publishing houses. Numerous small presses that concentrate on the publication and promotion of works by Canadian authors, particularly those who might be ignored by the larger, often foreign-owned publishers, were able to begin operations with government subsidies in the 1960s and 1970s. These presses, exemplified by names such as Anansi and NeWest, have created a pool of high-culture Canadian texts that may never have existed in the American context. Although the size of the population in the United States generates a larger market than is available in Canada, the significantly lower level of government support results in a disproportionate reliance on the market in America.

Finally, the context of high-culture production affects the interpretation of the increasing commercialization of the publishing industry. In the United States, the rapid changes in and commercialization of the publishing industry are rarely understood as *national* issues, but the process is almost always understood as a national issue in Canada. In the United States there is a great deal of consternation in the literary world over the increasing difficulties involved in publishing contemporary high-culture literature. Authors bemoan the conglomerization of publishing houses, the advent of the MBAs, and the collapse of the gentleman publishers whose interest in literature was not confined to profit; critics decry the publishers' abandonment of a commitment to first novels, the fostering of new high-culture talent, and the high-culture fiction trade more generally; and publishers lament the disinterest of the younger generation in reading and the pernicious rise of electronic media (Yardley 1989; Zill and Winglee 1990; Robinson 1993; Maughan and Bing 1994; Max 1994; Proulx 1994; Abel 1995). The same story is heard in Canada, but there the debate is cast in *national* terms. Increasing commercialization and the decline of an educated reading public is in America a sign of the times; in Canada, however, it is largely understood within terms of the Americanization of the publishing industry.

Despite these controversies, despite the myriad difficulties of high literary culture, the powerful and important cultural work of equating the nation and its culture continues to be done. The historical weight of canon formation, and the still solid framework of literature and nation in the minds of the general population, mean that – at this point at least – attacks on the canon and the fretting over the decline of high-culture literature actually help maintain the canon and reinforce the idea of its importance rather than the reverse.

The high culture/popular culture distinction

A final issue I wish to raise is the increasingly problematic nature of the high culture/popular culture divide. Although I have used Bourdieu's distinction between the field of restricted production and the field of large-scale production as a central analytic dimension to distinguish between what I have called "high" and "popular" culture, it is crucially important to understand that the distinction is not absolute. Although the symbolic value of canonical and literary prize-winning novels is of great importance, such novels are still produced within the market economy. Although the breadth of Canadian government support buffers some production, as mentioned already, the recent level of support may no longer be sustainable (see footnotes 23 and 24 in chapter 6).

Market forces and economic value are influential factors that shape the production, consumption, and evaluation of high-culture works as well as popular-culture works (see, for example, Powell 1985; Tompkins 1985; Griswold 1992). The power of economic considerations in contemporary high-culture publishing was made clear in a recent *New York Times* article investigating the economic benefits of literary prizes: "People in publishing say that the rule of thumb is that a National Book Award, [or] a Pulitzer Prize . . . will double and sometimes triple sales of a book" (Fein 1992: D8). Carl Lennertz, vice president of marketing at Knopf, explicitly equated the prize status and commercial benefit: "Awards are like confirmations . . . People who read books feel that they have to buy the books that win the awards" (Fein 1992: D8).[7] In addition, there is increasing evidence that the symbolic value of high-culture literature is of decreasing "worth" to publishers (e.g., Max 1994).

In readdressing the distinction between high culture and popular culture, it is not only important to recognize the economic value of high culture, but the importance of the symbolic value of popular culture must also be acknowledged. The filling of Canadian airwaves with American sitcoms is hardly a high-culture issue, yet a great deal of Canadian attention has been focused on an attempt to control the dominance of American television programming and to provide a range of Canadian alternatives (Collins 1990; Enchin 1995). Similarly, chapter 6 makes very clear the extent of Canadian concern with American encroachment in popular-culture literature. Few would argue that the prominence of Judith Krantz or Tom Clancy on the *Maclean's* bestsellers list is an issue of high culture. Nonetheless, the

---

[7] However, see Reid (1992) for a less optimistic view on the power of literary prizes to affect sales.

issue of American domination of popular culture is of grave concern to Canadians (e.g. Flaherty and Manning 1993) – and to a number of other importers of American popular culture (e.g., Holmstrom 1991; Nelson 1995). Much of the legislation, government subsidy, and other "Canadianization" measures have been expended in the popular-culture realm. Therefore, a full understanding of the contexts shaping high-culture and popular-culture literature must take account of both economic and symbolic value, of both market forces and political processes.

Finally, as I discussed in chapters 1 and 6, a number of theorists believe the relevance of the divide between high and popular culture is decreasing because of the declining correlation between people's class positions and their patterns of cultural consumption (Gans 1985; DiMaggio 1987; Blau 1988; Levine 1988; Crane 1992; Peterson 1992; see also Gartman 1991). Even Bourdieu (1984) has noted the tendency of higher status persons to consume more culture of all types (Gartman 1991: 430). Peterson (1992) has described this pattern empirically for musical taste. He has dubbed the phenomenon of higher status individuals engaging in both traditional high-culture activities and a wide range of popular-culture activities the cultural "omnivore."

Thus it is important to understand that the analytic distinction between high and popular culture, although necessary for an understanding of the diverse constraints and influences on types of literature, is not sufficient for a complete description of the conditions within which cultural works are produced, consumed, and evaluated. Nonetheless, it is a mistake to consider high culture and popular culture as synonymous. Increasingly populist notions are entering Canadian and particularly American cultural repertoires, and although these will no doubt interact with other forces shaping nations, national cultures, and national identities, the realm of high culture, if not its form in literature, may well endure.

Conclusion

This has been a book about books. This has been a book about the role literature plays in the making of the nation and the sustenance of a peculiar ideal of national cultural distinctiveness.

My central argument is that high-culture and popular-culture literature have different primary uses and are, therefore, shaped by different requirements and production contexts. Canonical literature is primarily influenced by its use as an adjunct to the unique nation. The construction of the nation as a cultural entity is a complex but specifiable process. Literature plays a not insignificant role in that process. The requirements of the nation-building process shape the form and content of national literatures. Because of the overriding need for national differentiation, canonical literature is required above all else to be unlike the literature of other countries. Historical contingencies such as the timing of the national project, the attributes of relevant "other" nations, and the cultural materials available for constructing the narrative of the unique nation shape the specific forms of literary distinctiveness in each country. Contemporary high-culture literature continues to address issues of national experience and identity, but it does so by responding to an established, *internal* literary tradition rather than by reacting against an *external* "other."

In contrast, popular-culture literature can be primarily understood as a mass-market commodity. Popular-culture literature is shaped by the requirements of mass-market techniques, such as advertising and standardization, and by its orientation toward the largest possible audience. Popular-culture literature is not used to construct or distinguish the nation. Because popular-culture literature is produced and distributed within the mass-market economy, and because it serves no competing purpose for the nation-state, it is the profit demands of business enterprise and the broadest popular taste which *primarily* influence popular-culture texts.

Unlike previous researchers, my model of national literatures situates canon formation within broad and concrete social processes. Canon formation cannot be understood as a purely literary process. And canon formation cannot be understood as following naturally from some inherent national identity. The process of nation-building and the political construction of a unique national identity drives canon formation toward a particular goal. Inherent textual attributes cannot explain the canonization of one set of texts over another. The requirements of the national project and the oppositional definition of high culture vis-à-vis popular culture are the parameters that structure the canon formation process. Thus, we can look to the specific, concrete events and persons that shaped the national canon and therefore participated in the creation of national identity. In this account, I have considered popular historical accounts of the explicit concern for a nationally distinctive literature in Canada and the United States, the concrete relations of cultural elites, the particularities of the canon formation process and the historical circumstances of its development, and the actual content of canonical, literary prize-winning, and best-selling texts.

Although a number of questions regarding future research directions can be drawn from this work, I will remark only upon the two categories of questions of greatest interest to me. The first type of questions are those regarding ordinary readers and high-culture literature. Long (1986, 1987) has provocatively suggested that while the ordinary readers she has studied accept academic and critical cultural authority in their *choice* of books, their interpretations of the texts are much *less* responsive to the dicta of experts. Despite the rigid framework within which the majority of readers encounter the classic works of their country, the possibility for resistance and for improvisation remain. Given the multivocality of many high-culture works, the potential for more expansive readings seems clear. The question, then, is whether ordinary readers of high-culture literature actually use these works as courses in American and Canadian literature suggest they should. Do ordinary readers actually "read" the nation in canonical texts?

This leads us to the question of the extent to which ordinary readers have internalized the nationalist interpretive framework, and how and when they apply it. In chapter 6, I noted that popular taste differs little between Canadians and Americans and suggested that national concerns are of little interest to large parts of the general population. Weber made this point himself: "An unbroken scale of quite varied and highly changeable attitudes toward the idea of the 'nation' is to be found among social strata within single groups to whom language usage ascribes the quality of 'nations.' The scale extends from emphatic affirmation to emphatic negation and finally complete indifference" (1978: 924). Although there are many reasons to believe that the canon has influenced and continues to influence the ways that general populations experience the nation, it remains to be studied how various strata see the nation differently through literary texts, and which, if any, strata are indifferent to it.

A second type of question I find of great interest is the issue of how generalizable the relationship between nationalism and literature is. That is, under what conditions and types of nation-building does national canon formation work as I propose? Griswold (1992) suggests that my model is appropriate in at least some third world contexts. She is explicit about how clearly Nigerian literary elites understand their role as constructors of the nation:

It is, in Chinua Achebe's words, "morning yet on creation day," and the African writer is the cultural creator in this new dawn . . . Writers have defined Nigeria to itself and others. The theme of the Association of Nigerian Authors' 1991 annual meeting was "Literature and Nation Building"; the underlying assumption that writers should be deeply involved in the construction of Nigeria was never questioned (1992: 713).

Such a statement seems perfectly congruent with the sentiments of Huxley, Whitman, and Atwood. It is, however, unclear whether the various trajectories and conditions of nation formation may involve more or less similar relationships between literature and the national project (see, for example, Tiryakian and Nevitte 1985; Smith 1986).

If my analysis of the place of national literatures in the making of the nation is correct, the answers to these questions will lead us to broader conclusions about the development, maintenance, and sustainability of national cultures and national distinctiveness in an increasingly "post-national" world.

Appendix A: The canonical novels

United States

Chopin, Kate	*The Awakening*
Dreiser, Theodore	*Sister Carrie*
Faulkner, William	*Light in August*
Fitzgerald, F. Scott	*The Great Gatsby*
Hawthorne, Nathaniel	*The Scarlet Letter*
Hemingway, Ernest	*The Sun Also Rises*
James, Henry	*Portrait of A Lady*
Melville, Herman	*Moby Dick*
Stowe, Harriet Beecher	*Uncle Tom's Cabin*
Twain, Mark	*The Adventures of Huckleberry Finn*

Canada

Atwood, Margaret	*Lady Oracle*
Buckler, Ernest	*The Mountain and the Valley*
Davies, Robertson K.	*Fifth Business*
Duncan, Sara J.	*The Imperialist*
Grove, Frederick Philip	*Fruits of the Earth*
Laurence, Margaret	*The Diviners*
Laurence, Margaret	*The Stone Angel*
MacLennan, Hugh	*Two Solitudes*
Munro, Alice	*Lives of Girls and Women*
Ross, Sinclair	*As for Me and My House*

Appendix B: The literary prize winners (1978–1987)

United States

1978	Settle, Mary Lee	*Blood Tie*
1979	O'Brien, Tim	*Going After Cacciato*
1980	Mailer, Norman	*The Executioner's Song*
1980	Styron, William	*Sophie's Choice*
1981	Morris, Wright	*Plains Song*
1981	Toole, John Kennedy	*A Confederacy of Dunces*
1982*	Updike, John	*Rabbit Is Rich*
1983*	Walker, Alice	*The Color Purple*
1984	Kennedy, William	*Ironweed*
1985	DeLillo, Don	*White Noise*
1985	Lurie, Alison	*Foreign Affairs*
1986	Doctorow, E. L.	*World's Fair*
1986	McMurty, Larry	*Lonesome Dove*
1987	Heinemann, Larry	*Paco's Story*
1987	Taylor, Peter	*A Summons to Memphis*

* Won both Pulitzer and National Book Award that year.
In 1978, 1979, and 1984 one of the prize winners was a collection of short stories.

Canada

1978	Rule, Jane	*The Young in One Another's Arms*
1979	Engel, Marian	*The Glassy Sea*
1979	Hodgins, Jack	*The Resurrection of Joseph Bourne*
1980	Bowering, George	*Burning Water*
1981	MacLennan, Hugh	*Voices in Time*
1982	Kogawa, Joy	*Obasan*
1983	Kinsella, W. P.	*Shoeless Joe*
1983	Rooke, Leon	*Shakespeare's Dog*

1984	Robertson, Heather	*Willie: A Romance*
1984	Skvorecky, Josef	*The Engineer of Human Souls*
1985	Atwood, Margaret	*The Handmaid's Tale*
1985	Findley, Timothy	*Not Wanted On The Voyage*
1986	Davies, Robertson K.	*What's Bred in the Bone*
1987	Kelly, M. T.	*A Dream Like Mine*

In 1978, 1981, 1982, and 1986 the GGA was for a collection of short stories. In 1980 and 1987 no novel was considered to merit the CAA award.

Appendix C: The bestsellers (1978–1987)

(AB=American bestseller; CB=Canadian bestseller; *=also a prize winner)

AB78 CB78	Krantz, Judith	*Scruples*
AB78 CB78	Ludlum, Robert	*The Holcroft Covenant*
AB78 CB78	McCullough, Colleen	*The Thorn Birds*
AB78 CB78	Sheldon, Sidney	*Bloodline*
AB78 CB78	Tolkien, J. R. R.	*The Simarillion*
AB78	Bach, Richard	*Illusions*
AB78	Follett, Ken	*Eye of the Needle*
AB78	French, Marilyn	*The Women's Room*
AB78	Plain, Belva	*Evergreen*
CB78	Deighton, Len	*SS-GB*
CB78	Greene, Graham	*The Human Factor*
CB78	Templeton, Charles	*The Third Temptation*
CB78	Vidal, Gore	*Kalki*
AB78 CB78 AB79 CB79	Michener, James	*Chesapeake*
AB79 CB79	Hailey, Arthur	*Overload*
AB79 CB79	Heller, Joseph	*Good As Gold*
AB79 CB79	Ludlum, Robert	*The Matarese Circle*
AB79 CB79	Stewart, Mary	*The Last Enchantment*
AB79 CB79	Trevanian	*Shibumi*
AB79 CB79	Wouk, Herman	*War and Remembrance*
AB79	Hackett, Gen. Sir John *et al.*	*The Third World War*
AB79	Hill, Ruth Beebe	*Hanta Yo*
AB79*	Styron, William	*Sophie's Choice*
CB79	Benchley, Peter	*The Island*
CB79	La Marsh, Judy	*A Very Political Lady*
CB79	Wallace, Irving	*The Pigeon Project*
AB80 CB80	Forsyth, Frederick	*The Devil's Alternative*

AB80 CB80	Krantz, Judith	*Princess Daisy*
AB80 CB80	le Carré, John	*Smiley's People*
AB80 CB80	Ludlum, Robert	*The Bourne Identity*
AB80 CB80	Plain, Belva	*Random Winds*
AB80	Archer, Jeffrey	*Kane and Abel*
AB80	de Borchgrave, Arnaud and R. Moss	*The Spike*
AB80	Freeman, Cynthia	*Portraits*
AB80	Van Lustbader, Eric	*The Ninja*
CB80	Atwood, Margaret	*Life Before Man*
CB80	French, Marilyn	*The Bleeding Heart*
CB80	Higgins, Jack	*Solo*
CB80	Richler, Mordecai	*Joshua Then and Now*
AB80 CB80 CB81	Sheldon, Sidney	*Rage of Angels*
AB81 CB81	Herbert, Frank	*God Emperor of Dune*
AB81 CB81	Michener, James	*The Covenant*
AB81 CB81	Robbins, Harold	*Goodbye, Janette*
AB81 CB81	Smith, Martin Cruz	*Gorky Park*
AB81	Caldwell, Taylor	*Answer As A Man*
AB81	Greeley, Andrew M.	*The Cardinal Sins*
AB81	Sanders, Lawrence	*The Third Deadly Sin*
AB81	Thomas, D. M.	*The White Hotel*
AB81	Wambaugh, Joseph	*The Glitter Dome*
CB81	Deighton, Len	*XPD*
CB81	Follett, Ken	*The Key to Rebecca*
CB81	King, Stephen	*Firestarter*
CB81	Stevenson, William	*The Ghosts of Africa*
AB81 CB81 CB82	Clavell, James	*Noble House*
AB82 CB82	Archer, Jeffrey	*The Prodigal Daughter*
AB82 CB82	Donaldson, Stephen R.	*The One Tree*
AB82 CB82	Follett, Ken	*The Man From St. Petersburg*
AB82 CB82	Irving, John	*The Hotel New Hampshire*
AB82 CB82	Ludlum, Robert	*The Parsifal Mosaic*
AB82 CB82	McCullough, Colleen	*An Indecent Obsession*
AB82	Greeley, Andrew M.	*Thy Brother's Wife*
AB82	Jakes, John	*North and South*
AB82	Lord, Bette Bao	*Spring Moon*
AB82	Tyler, Anne	*Dinner at the Homesick Restaurant*
CB82	Atwood, Margaret	*Bodily Harm*
CB82	Davies, Robertson K.	*The Rebel Angels*
CB82	Mitchell, W. O.	*How I Spent My Summer Holidays*

AB83 CB83	Donaldson, Stephen R.	*White Gold Wielder*
AB83 CB83	King, Stephen	*Christine*
AB83 CB83	le Carré, John	*The Little Drummer Girl*
AB83 CB83	Michener, James	*Space: A Novel*
AB83 CB83	Sheldon, Sidney	*Master of the Game*
AB83	Auel, Jean M.	*The Valley of the Horses*
AB83	Collins, Jackie	*Hollywood Wives*
AB83	Ephron, Nora	*Heartburn*
AB83	L'Amour, Louis	*The Lonesome Gods*
CB83	Bradford, Barbara Taylor	*Voices of the Heart*
CB83	Clarke, Arthur C.	*2010: Odyssey Two*
CB83	Mailer, Norman	*Ancient Evenings*
CB83	Straub, Peter	*Floating Dragon*
AB83 CB83		
CB84	Eco, Umberto	*The Name of the Rose*
AB84 CB84	Herbert, Frank	*Heretics of Dune*
AB84 CB84	King, Stephen	*Pet Sematary*
AB84 CB84	Ludlum, Robert	*The Aquitaine Progression*
AB84 CB84	Michener, James	*Poland*
AB84 CB84	Steel, Danielle	*Full Circle*
AB84 CB84	Uris, Leon	*The Haj*
AB84	Blume, Judy	*Smart Women*
AB84	Chastain, Thomas and	
	B. Adler	*Who Killed the Robins Family?*
AB84	Santmyer, Helen Hooven	*" . . . And Ladies of the Club"*
AB84	Vidal, Gore	*Lincoln*
CB84	Archer, Jeffrey	*First Among Equals*
CB84	Stewart, Mary	*The Wicked Day*
AB85 CB84	Puzo, Mario	*The Sicilian*
AB85 CB85	Irving, John	*The Cider House Rules*
AB85 CB85	King, Stephen	
	(as R. Bachman)	*Thinner*
AB85 CB85	Sheldon, Sidney	*If Tomorrow Comes*
AB85 CB85	Steel, Danielle	*Family Album*
AB85 CB85	Wouk, Herman	*Inside, Outside*
AB85	Adams, Douglas	*So Long, and Thanks for all the Fish*
AB85	Bradford, Barbara Taylor	*Hold the Dream*
AB85	Clancy, Tom	*The Hunt for Red October*
AB85*	McMurty, Larry	*Lonesome Dove*
CB85	Collins, Jackie	*Lucky*
CB85	Hailey, Arthur	*Strong Medicine*
CB85	Herbert, Frank	*Chapterhouse: Dune*

CB85	King, Stephen and	
	Peter Straub	*The Talisman*
CB85	L'Amour, Louis	*Jubal Sackett*
AB86 CB86	Auel, Jean M.	*The Mammoth Hunters*
AB86 CB86	Follett, Ken	*Lie Down With Lions*
AB86 CB86	Krantz, Judith	*I'll Take Manhattan*
AB86 CB86	Ludlum, Robert	*The Bourne Supremacy*
AB86	Keillor, Garrison	*Lake Wobegon Days*
AB86	Koen, Karleen	*Through a Glass Darkly*
AB86	L'Amour, Louis	*Last of the Breed*
AB86	Michener, James	*Texas*
AB86	Steel, Danielle	*Wanderlust*
CB86	Archer, Jeffrey	*A Matter of Honour*
CB86 *	Atwood, Margaret	*The Handmaid's Tale*
CB86 *	Davies, Robertson K.	*What's Bred in the Bone*
CB86	le Carré, John	*A Perfect Spy*
CB86	Smith, Wilbur	*The Power of the Sword*
AB86 AB87		
CB86	Clancy, Tom	*Red Storm Rising*
AB87 CB87	Clancy, Tom	*Patriot Games*
AB87 CB87	King, Stephen	*Misery*
AB87 CB87	King, Stephen	*The Eyes of the Dragon*
AB87 CB87	L'Amour, Louis	*The Haunted Mesa*
AB87 CB87	Sheldon, Sidney	*Windmills of the Gods*
AB87 CB87	Steel, Danielle	*Fine Things*
AB87 CB87	Turow, Scott	*Presumed Innocent*
AB87	Conroy, Pat	*The Prince of Tides*
AB87	Rutherford, Edward	*Sarum*
CB87	Beauman, Sally	*Destiny*
CB87	Clavell, James	*Whirlwind*
CB87	Smith, Wilbur	*Rage*

Appendix D: Coding sheet

Genre _____

Author _____Title _____

Gender _____Nationality_____

Publisher _____Publication date _____Page length _____

Year _____ Country _____Type _____

I. Plot summary

   (a) Summarize central conflict:

   (b) Describe characters and story:

Main plot is:

1) story of individual(s)

2) story of group; focus on relationships among several people

3) story of situation

II. Characteristics

A. Setting

   1. city

   2. town

   3. rural

   4. wilderness

   5. other_____

B. Location

   1. US

   2. Canada

   3. Europe

   4. Asia

   5. other_____

C. Period
1. current at publication
2. post-WWII
3. WWI–WWII
4. 1900–WWI
5. pre-1900
6. future
7. other _____

D. Protagonist (describe demographically, socially, psychologically)
1. male
2. female
3. religious membership
   a. Catholic b. Protestant c. Jewish d. unknown e. other:
   important/not important
4. nationality
   a. US b. Canadian c. Western European d. Eastern European
   e. Asian f. Latin American g. Soviet h. African i. other:
   important/not important
5. social status
   a. upper class/jet set b. upper-middle class/professional c. middle class
   d. working class/blue collar e. lower class/agrarian poor f. criminal
   g. capitalist
   important/not important   income/education levels:
6. social mobility
   a. low to high b. high to low c. other:
   important/not important
7. marital history
   a. single b. married c. divorced d. widowed
   e. progression of states _____
   important/not important
8. work history
   a. leisure b. capitalist/entrepreneur c. professional d. clerical
   e. laborer f. none g. progression _____
   h. other _____
   important/not
9. parental status
   a. no children b. one child c. 2–3 d. 4–5 e. 5+ children
   important/not important
10. parents mentioned   important/not
11. siblings mentioned   important/not
12. heterosexual relationship mentioned   important/not
13. sexual history mentioned   important/not
14. strong same sex friendship(s) mentioned   important/not
15. homosexual relationship mentioned   important/not

16. financially successful
17. defiant or rebellious to authority
18a. familial relationship (spousal)
   a. no mention b. family left before story begun c. positive family presence
   d. negative family e. ambivalent family presence f. family left during novel
   g. family reunited during novel h. other: _____
   important/not
18b. familial relationship (parental)
   a. no mention b. family left before story begun c. positive family presence
   d. negative family e. ambivalent family presence f. family left during novel
   g. family reunited during novel h. other: _____
   important/not
19. ethnic identity
   a. British b. French c. Hispanic d. Slavic e. Russian f. Black African
   g. Italian h. Scandinavia i. German j. Native American k. Indian
   l. Arab m. Chinese n. Japanese o. unknown p. other: _____
   important/not
20. protagonist dead at end of story
21. other important things about protagonist:

III. Plot attributes	Absent	Some	Central
"mere" survival			
difficult physical setting			
familial conflict			
familial escape			
monetary success			
moral/ethical success			
romantic/sexual success			
conflict between:			
protagonist/government			
protagonist/due authority (other)			
interpersonal conflict			
institutional conflict			
focus on			
art/culture/education			
scholarly/intellectual activity			
patriotism as good			
patriotism as bad/naive			
international conflict			
regional conflict			
racial conflict			
tone of pessimism/defeat			
tone of fulfillment/victory			
explicit sex			

III. Plot attributes   Absent   Some   Central
explicit violence against women
explicit political persuasion
minorities
Can you make a thematic summary or moral
from this book?
  If yes, what is it?

IV. Literary characteristics
1. style (realism, postmodernism, etc.):
2. centrality of character development or plot/action
3. coherent linear plot or fragmented presentation
4. stream of consciousness writing
5. main story coherent/logical or ambiguous/incomprehensible
6. time realistic or shifting/ambiguous
7. narrative stance: person, voice, definite, or ambiguous
8. self-consciously "literary"?
9. other stylistic aspects:

Appendix E: Generic categories

Adventure/thriller
Allegorical adventure
Coming-of-age narrative
Docu-history (fictional narratives presented as accurate history)
Espionage narrative
Experimental novel
Fable (focus on moment of epiphany about learning, faith, or belief)
Fairy tale
Family drama (focus on functioning of family unit)
Family saga (inter-generational family story, less psychological than above)
Fantasy
Farce
Horror
Human condition (author's view of h.c., often features multiple protagonists)
Humor
Immigrant experience
Legend (re-told account of classic stories, e.g., Arthurian legend)
Life story (differs from S-K/PG because lacks self-awareness of protagonist)
Minority experience
Modern relationship
Morality tale
Mystery
Police story
Postmodern life (incorporates literary style)
Psychological thriller
Romance
Science fiction
Sensationalism (explicit or exploitive sex, crime, consumerism, scandal)
Self-knowledge/personal growth (story of growing self-understanding)
Slice of life (description of lesser known culture or subculture, e.g., energy industry)

Spiritual exploration
Tragedy
War experience (describes effects, good or bad, of war on people involved)
War scenario (posits war scenarios, often focusing on weapons systems and deployment)
Western
Woman's success story (e.g., the first woman president's story)

References

Abel, Richard 1995, "The Best-Seller Fishpond Invaded, Or, the Storming of the Best-Seller Lists by Leviathan," *Publishing Research Quarterly* 11(2): 103–11.

Ahmad, Aijaz 1992, *In Theory: Classes, Nations, Literatures*, London: Verso.

Albrecht, Milton C. 1954, "The Relationship of Literature and Society," *American Journal of Sociology* 59: 425–36.

Allen, Glen 1991, "Culture's New Pilot: Perrin Beatty Takes on the Arts Portfolio," *Maclean's* May 6: 52.

Anderson, Benedict 1991, *Imagined Communities*, revised edn, London: Verso.

Anheier, Helmut K., Gerhards, Jurgen, and Romo, Frank P. 1995, "Forms of Capital and Social Structure in Cultural Fields," *American Journal of Sociology* 100: 859–903.

Arnold, Matthew 1949, *The Portable Matthew Arnold*, edited by Lionel Trilling, New York: Viking.

Atwood, Margaret 1972, *Survival: A Thematic Guide to Canadian Literature*, Boston: Beacon Press.

  1982, *Second Words: Selected Critical Prose*, Boston: Beacon Press.

  1995, "How Many Canadas?" *New York Times*, November 5, Section 4: 15.

Audley, Paul 1983, *Canada's Cultural Industries*, Toronto: Lorimer.

Baker, Carlos 1957, "Forty Years of Pulitzer Prizes," *Princeton University Library Chronicle* 28(2): 55–70.

Baker, Houston A. Jr. and Redmond, Patricia (eds.) 1989, *Afro-American Literary Study in the 1990s*, University of Chicago Press.

Barlow, Maude and Campbell, Bruce 1993, *Take Back the Nation 2: Meeting the Threat of NAFTA*, revised edn, Toronto: Key Porter Books.

Bashevkin, Sylvia B. 1988, "Does Public Opinion Matter? The Adoption of Federal Royal Commission and Task Force Recommendations on the National Question, 1951–87," *Canadian Public Administration* 31: 396–400.

1991, *True Patriot Love: The Politics of Canadian Nationalism*, Toronto: Oxford University Press.

Bates, J. Douglas 1991, *The Pulitzer Prize*, New York: Carol Publishing Group.

Baxandall, Michael 1985, *Patterns of Intention: On the Historical Explanation of Pictures*, New Haven: Yale University Press.

1988, *Painting and Experience in Fifteenth Century Italy*, 2nd edn, New York: Oxford University Press.

Bayard, Caroline 1991, "Critical Instincts in Quebec: From the Quiet Revolution to the Postmodern Age, 1960–1990," in Lecker (ed.), pp. 124–30.

Baym, Nina 1985, "Melodramas of Beset Manhood," in Showalter (ed.), pp. 63–80.

Behiels, Michael D. 1985, *Prelude to Quebec's Quiet Revolution: Liberalism versus Neo-nationalism, 1945–1960,* Montreal: McGill–Queen's University Press.

Bellah, Robert N., Madsen, Richard, Sullivan, William M., Swidler, Ann, and Tipton, Steven M. 1985, *Habits of the Heart: Individualism and Commitment in American Life*, Berkeley: University of California Press.

Bennett, Donna 1991, "Conflicted Vision: A Consideration of Canon and Genre in English–Canadian Literature," in Lecker (ed.), pp. 131–49.

Berezin, Mabel 1994a, "Cultural Form and Political Meaning: State-subsidized Theater, Ideology, and the Language of Style in Fascist Italy," *American Journal of Sociology* 99: 1237–86.

1994b, "Fissured Terrain: Methodological Approaches and Research Styles in Culture and Politics," in Crane, Diana (ed.), *Sociology of Culture: Emerging Theoretical Perspectives*, London: Basil Blackwell, pp. 91–116.

Berger, Carl 1970, *The Sense of Power: Studies in the Ideas of Canadian Imperialism 1867–1914,* University of Toronto Press.

Bergman, Brian 1994, "Publish and Perish: Despite a Healthy Literary Culture, Canada's Book Industry Struggles," *Maclean's*, October 17: 50–2.

Berton, Pierre 1980, *The Invasion of Canada*, Boston: Little Brown.

1988, "War of 1812," *The Canadian Encyclopedia*, vol. IV, 2nd edn, Edmonton: Hurtig Publishers.

Binder, Amy 1993, "Constructing Racial Rhetoric: Media Depictions of Harm in Heavy Metal and Rap Music," *American Sociological Review* 58: 753–67.

Birch, Anthony H. 1989, *Nationalism and National Integration*, London: Unwin Hyman.

Blau, Judith R. 1988, "Study of the Arts: A Reappraisal," *Annual Review of Sociology* 14: 269–92.

Blau, P. M., Blau, J. R., Quets, G. A., and Tada, T. 1986, "Social Inequality and Arts Institutions," *Sociological Forum* 1: 561–85.

Bogart, Leo 1995, *Commercial Culture: The Media System and the Public Interest*, New York: Oxford University Press.

Boivin, Aurelien 1975, *Le conte littéraire québécois au XIXe siècle*, Montreal: Fides.

Bourdieu, Pierre 1980, "The Production of Belief: Contribution to an Economy of Symbolic Goods," translated by Richard Nice, *Media, Culture, and Society* 2: 261–93.

   1984, *Distinction: A Social Critique of the Judgement of Taste*, translated by Richard Nice, Cambridge, MA: Harvard University Press.

   1985, "The Market of Symbolic Goods," translated by Rupert Swyer, *Poetics* 14: 13–44.

   1993, *The Field of Cultural Production: Essays on Art and Literature*, New York: Columbia University Press.

Bradley, Sculley, Beatty, Richmond Croom, Long, E. Hudson, and Gross, Seymour (eds.) 1978, Norton Critical Edition of *The Scarlet Letter*, Nathaniel Hawthorne, New York: Norton.

Breton, Raymond 1988, "From Ethnic to Civic Nationalism: English Canada and Quebec," *Ethnic and Racial Studies* 11:85–102.

Brooks, Cleanth 1975, *The Well Wrought Urn: Studies in the Structure of Poetry*, New York: Harvest-Harcourt.

Brown, Russell M. 1980, "A Search for America: Some Canadian Literary Responses," *Journal of American Culture* 2: 670–81.

Brubaker, Rogers 1992, *Citizenship and Nationhood in France and Germany*, Cambridge, MA: Harvard University Press.

   1993, "National Minorities, New Nation States and External National Homelands in Europe: Past and Present," The Historical Formation of Nation and Citizen Session, American Sociological Association Meetings, Miami.

Brunet, Michel 1969, *Les Canadiens après la Conquête, 1759–1775*, Montreal: Fides.

Buell, Frederick 1994, *National Culture and the New Global System*, Baltimore: Johns Hopkins University Press.

Burke, Kenneth 1957, "Literature as Equipment for Living," in *The*

Philosophy of Literary Form: Studies in Symbolic Action, New York: Random House, pp. 293–304.

Bynack, V. P. 1984, "Noah Webster's Linguistic Thought and the Idea of an American National Culture," *Journal of the History of Ideas* 45: 99–114.

Cagnon, Maurice 1986, *The French Novel of Quebec*, Boston: Twayne Publishers.

Calhoun, Craig 1991, "Indirect Relationships and Imagined Communities," in Bourdieu, Pierre and Coleman, James S. (eds.), *Social Theory for a Changing Society*, Boulder, CO: Westview Press, pp. 95–121.

Calverton, Victor Francis 1929, *Anthology of American Negro Literature*, New York: The Modern Library.

Cameron, Duncan 1993, "Protecting Culture," *The Canadian Forum*, September: 4–5.

Canada Council 1991, *The Canada Council 34th Annual Report*, 1990–91 Supplement, Ottawa.

Candido, Antonio 1995, *On Literature and Society*, translated, edited, and introduced by Howard S. Becker, New Jersey: Princeton University Press.

Carafiol, Peter 1991, *The American Ideal: Literary History as a Worldly Activity*, New York: Oxford University Press.

Cawelti, John 1976, *Adventure, Mystery and Romance*, University of Chicago Press.

Chandler, James 1984, "The Pope Controversy: Romantic Poetics and the English Canon," in von Hallberg (ed.), pp. 197–226.

Channing, William Ellery [1823] 1841, *Works*, vol. I, Boston: James Monroe.

Chicago Times–Herald 1899, "Books of the Day," June 1: 9.

Chodorow, Nancy 1978, *The Reproduction of Mothering*, Berkeley: University of California Press.

Chronicle of Higher Education 1982, "Footnotes," September 29.

Clark, The Right Honourable Joe 1994, *A Nation Too Good To Lose: Renewing the Purpose of Canada*, Toronto: Key Porter Books.

Clark, Priscilla 1982, "Literature and Sociology," in Barricelli, Jean-Pierre and Gibaldi, Joseph (eds.), *Interrelations of Literature*, New York: Modern Language Association of America, pp. 107–22.

  1983, "Literature and Society: A Comparatist Perspective," *Yearbook of Comparative and General Literature* 32: 85–92.

Clark, T. J. 1982, "On the Social History of Art," in Frascina, F. and Harrison, C. (eds.), *Modern Art and Modernism*, London: Harper & Row.

Clarkson, Stephen and McCall, Christina 1990, *Trudeau and Our Times*, vol. I, Toronto: McClelland and Stewart.

Clayton, Mark 1995, "Mirroring the US, Canada's Budget for Public TV Destined for Cutbacks," *Christian Science Monitor*, June 21: 13: 1.

Cochran, Susan D. and Peplau, L. Anne 1985, "Value Orientations in Heterosexual Relationships," *Psychology of Women Quarterly* 9: 477–88.

Colby, Anne and Damon, William 1987, "Listening to a Different Voice: A Review of Gilligan's *In a Different Voice*," in Walsh, M. R. (ed.), *The Psychology of Women: Ongoing Debates*, New Haven: Yale University Press.

Collins, Richard 1990, *Culture, Communication and National Identity: The Case of Canadian Television*, University of Toronto Press.

Cook, Ramsay 1971, *The Maple Leaf Forever: Essays on Nationalism and Politics in Canada*, Toronto: Macmillan of Canada.

   1986, *Canada, Quebec, and the Uses of Nationalism*, Toronto: McClelland and Stewart.

Corse, Sarah M. 1995, "Nations and Novels: Cultural Politics and Literary Use," *Social Forces* 73: 1279–1308.

Corse, Sarah M. and Deborah Dougherty 1996, "Innovation and Organizational Rationality: Bringing Culture Back In," unpublished manuscript, Department of Sociology, University of Virginia.

Corse, Sarah M. and Griffin, Monica 1996, "Reception, Evaluation, and African–American Literary History: Re-constructing the Canon," *Sociological Forum*.

Corse, Sarah M. and Robinson, Marian A. 1994, "Cross-Cultural Measurement and New Conceptions of Culture: Measuring Cultural Capacities in Japanese and American Preschools," *Poetics: Journal of Empirical Research on Literature, the Media and the Arts* 22: 313–25.

Corse, Sarah M. and Westervelt, Saundra Davis 1995, "Self, Gender, and Narrative Reinterpretation: *The Awakening* of a Feminist Novel," unpublished manuscript, Department of Sociology, University of Virginia.

Coser, Lewis, Kadushin, Charles and Powell, Walter W. 1982, *Books: The Culture and Commerce of Publishing*, New York: Basic.

Cotnam, Jacques 1983, "Novels in French: Beginnings to 1900," in Toye, William (ed.), *The Oxford Companion to Canadian Literature*, Toronto: Oxford University Press, pp. 594–5.

Crane, Diana 1992, "High Culture versus Popular Culture Revisited: A Reconceptualization of Recorded Cultures," in Lamont and Fournier (eds.), pp. 58–74.

Crean, Susan 1993, "Culture in the Crunch," *The Canadian Forum* July/August: 12–17.

Daniels, Bruce 1988, "'We Are Not Tenants and They Are Not Landlords': Canadian Popular and Political Perceptions of the United States," *Journal of Popular Culture* 22 (Winter): 85–100.

Davey, Frank 1990, "Critical Response I: Canadian Canons," *Critical Inquiry* 16: 672–81.

1993, *Post-National Arguments: The Politics of the Anglophone–Canadian Novel since 1967,* University of Toronto Press.

de Nooy, W. 1988, "Gentlemen of the Jury . . . The Features of Experts Awarding Literary Prizes," *Poetics: Journal of Empirical Research on Literature, the Media and the Arts* 17: 531–45.

DeNora, Tia 1991, "Musical Patronage and Social Change in Beethoven's Vienna," *American Journal of Sociology* 97: 310–46.

Derrida, Jacques 1980, *Writing and Difference,* University of Chicago Press.

Desan, Philippe, Ferguson, Priscilla Parkhurst and Griswold, Wendy (eds.) 1989, *Literature and Social Practice,* University of Chicago Press.

DeVault, Marjorie 1990, "Novel Readings: The Social Organization of Interpretation," *American Journal of Sociology* 95: 887–921.

DiMaggio, Paul 1977, "Market Structures, the Creative Process, and Popular Culture: Toward an Organizational Reinterpretation of Mass-Culture Theory," *Journal of Popular Culture* 11(Fall): 436–52.

1982, "Cultural Entrepreneurship in Nineteenth-Century Boston," Parts I and II, *Media, Culture and Society* 4: 33–50, 303–20.

1987, "Classification in Art," *American Sociological Review* 52: 440–55.

1991, "Social Structure, Institutions, and Cultural Goods," in Bourdieu, Pierre and Coleman, James S. (eds.), *Social Theory for a Changing Society,* Boulder, CO: Westview Press, pp. 135–55.

Dionne, René 1988, "Literature in French," *The Canadian Encyclopedia,* vol. II, 2nd edn, Edmonton: Hurtig Publishers.

Dominguez, Virginia R. 1992, "Invoking Culture: The Messy Side of 'Cultural Politics,'" *South Atlantic Quarterly* 91: 19–42.

Doran, Charles F. and Sigler, John H. (eds.) 1985, *Canada and the United States: Enduring Friendship, Persistent Stress,* Englewood Cliffs, NJ: Prentice-Hall.

Dufault, Roseanna Lewis 1991, *Metaphors of Identity: The Treatment of Childhood in Selected Québécois Novels,* Cranbury, NJ: Associated University Presses.

Duncan, Sara Jeanette 1887, "American Influence on Canadian Thought," *The Week* 4 (July 7): 518.

Dwyer, Victor 1991, "Red all Over: Canada's Publishing Industry is in Trouble," *Maclean's* April 22: 60–2.

1992, "Culture in Crisis," *Maclean's* July 20: 46–50.

Earle, Robert L. and Wirth, John D. 1995, *Identities in North America*, Stanford University Press.

Edwards, Mary Jane 1983, "Novels in English: Beginnings to 1900," in Toye, William (ed.), *The Oxford Companion to Canadian Literature*, Toronto: Oxford University Press, pp. 565–9.

Ekos Research Associates Inc 1992, *Reading in Canada, 1991*, Ottawa: Department of Communications.

Enchin, Harvey 1995, "Canadians Tuning Out Specialty TV," *Globe and Mail*, July 6: A1–2.

English, James F. 1993, "An Economy of Prestige: Literary Prizes and the Circulation of Cultural Value," unpublished manuscript, Department of English, University of Pennsylvania.

Ericson, Richard, Baranek, Patricia M. and Chan, Janet B. L. 1987, *Visualizing Deviance: A Study of News Organization*, University of Toronto Press.

Escarpit, Robert 1971, *The Sociology of Literature*, London: Frank Cass.

Ethier-Blais, Jean 1973, *Signets*, vol. III, Montreal: Le Cercle du Livre de France.

Europa Publications Ltd. 1995, *Europa World Year Book*, vol. I, 36th edn, London: Europa Publications Ltd.

Fagan, Drew 1996, "Will that be Culture – or Cash?" *Globe and Mail*, January 29: B1–2.

Farnsworth, Clyde H. 1995a, "Quebec Vote Bares Latent Ethnic Anger," *New York Times*, international section, November 5: 10.

1995b, "For Quebec, the Neverendum," *New York Times*, Section 4, November 5: 3.

Fein, Esther B. 1992, "Even in Book Awards, to Victors Go the Spoils," *New York Times*, March 16: D8.

Fiedler, Leslie [1960] 1966, *Love and Death in the American Novel*, revised edn, New York: Dell Publishing.

Fish, Stanley 1980, *Is There a Text in This Class?* Cambridge, MA: Harvard University Press.

Fiske, Susan T. and Taylor, Shelley E. 1984, *Social Cognition*, New York: Random House.

Fitzgerald, F. Scott [1925] 1953, *The Great Gatsby*, New York: Charles Scribner's Sons.

Flaherty, David H. and Manning, Frank E. 1993, *The Beaver Bites Back: American Popular Culture in Canada*, Montreal: McGill–Queen's University Press.

Fogel, Stanley 1984, *A Tale of Two Countries: Contemporary Fiction in Canada and the United States*, Toronto: ECW Press.

Foucault, Michel 1980, *Power-Knowledge*, New York: Pantheon.

Fournier, Louis 1984, *FLQ: The Anatomy of an Underground Movement*, translated by Edward Baxter, Toronto: NC Press.

Fraser, Graham 1989, "Metcalf's Criticism and the Canadian Canon," *The American Review of Canadian Studies* 19(Winter): 381–96.

Frye, Northrop 1971, *The Bush Garden: Essays on the Canadian Imagination*, Toronto: House of Anansi Press.

Gans, Herbert 1974, *Popular Culture and High Culture*, New York: Basic.
  1985, "American Popular Culture and High Culture in a Changing Class Structure," *Prospects: An Annual of American Cultural Studies* 10: 17–37.

Gartman, David 1991, "Culture as Class Symbolization or Mass Reification? A Critique of Bourdieu's Distinction," *American Journal of Sociology* 97: 421–47.

Gates, Henry Louis Jr. 1989, "Canon-Formation, Literary History, and The Afro-American Tradition," in Baker and Redmond (eds.), pp. 14–39.

Geertz, Clifford 1973, "Thick Description: Toward an Interpretive Theory of Culture," in *The Interpretation of Cultures*, New York: Basic, pp. 3–30.

Gellner, Ernest 1983, *Nations and Nationalism*, Oxford: Blackwell.
  1994, *Encounters with Nationalism*, Oxford: Blackwell.

Gerson, Carole 1991, "The Canon between the Wars," in Lecker (ed.), pp. 46–56.

Giddens, Anthony 1984, *The Constitution of Society: Outline of a Theory of Structuration*, Los Angeles: University of California Press.

Gilligan, Carol 1982, *In a Different Voice*, Cambridge, MA: Harvard University Press.

Gilligan, Carol, Ward, Janie Victoria and Taylor, Jill McLean (eds.) 1988, *Mapping the Moral Domain*, Cambridge, MA: Harvard University Press.

Godard, Barbara 1990, "Critical Discourse in/on Quebec," in Davidson, Arnold E. (ed.), *Studies on Canadian Literature*, New York: Modern Languages Association, pp. 271–95.

Golding, Alan C. 1984, "A History of American Poetry Anthologies," in von Hallberg, Robert (ed.), *Canons*, University of Chicago Press, pp. 279–308.

Goldmann, Lucien 1964, *The Hidden God*, London: Routledge and Kegan Paul.
  1970, "The Sociology of Literature: Status and Problems of Method," in

Albrecht, Milton, Barnett, James H. and Griff, Mason, *The Sociology of Literature*, New York: Praeger Publishers.

Gougeon, Gilles 1994, *A History of Quebec Nationalism: Conversations with Seven Leading Quebec Historians*, translated by Louisa Blair, Robert Chodos, and Jane Ubertino, Toronto: James Lorimer.

Grannis, Chandler B. 1993, "US Book Import–Export Data for 1992," *Publishers Weekly* November 22: 24–6.

Green, Mary Jean 1984, "Writing in a Motherland," unpublished manuscript, Department of French and Italian, Dartmouth College.

    1986, "Tradition as Mother: Women's Fiction and the Canadian Past," unpublished manuscript, Department of French and Italian, Dartmouth College.

Greenfeld, Liah 1992, *Nationalism: Five Roads to Modernity*, Cambridge, MA: Harvard University Press.

Griswold, Wendy 1981, "American Character and the American Novel: An Expansion of Reflection Theory in the Sociology of Literature," *American Journal of Sociology* 86: 740–65.

    1986, *Renaissance Revivals: City Comedy and Revenge Tragedy in the London Theatre 1576–1980*, University of Chicago Press.

    1987a, "A Methodological Framework for the Sociology of Culture," *Sociological Methodology* 17: 1–35.

    1987b, "The Fabrication of Meaning," *American Journal of Sociology* 92: 1077–1117.

    1991, "Comment," in Bourdieu, Pierre and Coleman, James S. (eds.), *Social Theory for a Changing Society*, Boulder, CO: Westview Press, pp. 156–9.

    1992, "The Writing on the Mud Wall: Nigerian Novels and the Imaginary Village," *American Sociological Review* 57: 709–24.

    1994, *Cultures and Societies in a Changing World*, Thousand Oaks, CA: Pine Forge Press.

Grove, Frederick P. [1933] 1965, *Fruits of the Earth*, Toronto: McClelland and Stewart.

Guillory, John 1993, *Cultural Capital: The Problem of Literary Canon Formation*, University of Chicago Press.

Hadaway, C. Kirk, Marler, Penny Long and Chaves, Mark 1993, "What the Polls Don't Show: A Closer Look at US Church Attendance," *American Sociological Review* 58: 741–52.

Handler, Richard 1988, *Nationalism and the Politics of Culture in Quebec*, Madison, WI: University of Wisconsin Press.

Hart, James D. (ed.) 1983, "National Book Awards," in *The Oxford Companion to American Literature*, New York: Oxford University Press, p. 524.

Hayne, David M. 1988, "Literature in French: Scholarship and Teaching," *The Canadian Encyclopedia*, vol. II, 2nd edn, Edmonton: Hurtig Publishers.

Hays, Sharon 1994, "Structure and Agency and the Sticky Problem of Culture," *Sociological Theory* 12: 57–72.

Hedley, R. Alan 1994, "Identity: Sense of Self and Nation," *Canadian Review of Sociology and Anthropology* 31(2): 200–14.

Henry, Kathryn 1990, "Between Cultures: Third Wave Russian Prose," unpublished dissertation, Department of Slavic Languages and Literature, Stanford University.

Hirsch, Paul M. 1972, "Processing Fads and Fashions," *American Journal of Sociology* 77: 639–59.

1975, "Organizational Effectiveness and the Institutional Environment," *Administrative Science Quarterly* 20: 327–44.

Hobsbawm, Eric 1992, *Nations and Nationalism since 1780: Programme, Myth, Reality*, 2nd edn, Cambridge University Press.

Hobsbawm, Eric and Ranger, Terence (eds.) 1983, *The Invention of Tradition*, Cambridge University Press.

Hofstede, Geert 1991, *Cultures and Organizations: Software of the Mind*, New York: McGraw–Hill.

Holmstrom, David 1991, "USA: Big Seller Everywhere: In the World Marketplace US Dominates Mass Culture," *Christian Science Monitor*, May 9: 9–14.

Holub, Robert C. 1984, *Reception Theory: A Critical Introduction*, New York: Methuen.

Howes, David 1988, "We, The Other People: Two Views on Identity," *The Canadian Forum* 775(January): 11–14.

Hubbell, Jay B. 1972, *Who Are the Major American Writers? A Study of the Changing Literary Canon*, Durham, NC: Duke University Press.

Hutcheon, Linda 1988, *The Canadian Postmodern: A Study of Contemporary English-Canadian Fiction*, Oxford University Press.

Hutcheson, John 1987, "The Thief of Arts," *The Canadian Forum* 66 (February): 9–18.

Huxley, Aldous 1959, *Texts and Pretexts*, London: Chatto & Windus.

Iannone, Carol 1991, "Literature by Quota," *Commentary* March: 50–3.

Ibsch, Elrud, Schram, Dick and Steen, Gerard (eds.) 1995, *Empirical Studies of Literature: Proceedings of the Second IGEL-Conference, Amsterdam 1989,* Amsterdam: Rodopi.

Innis, Harold 1956, *Essays in Canadian Economic History*, University of Toronto Press.

Jauss, Hans Robert 1982, *Towards an Aesthetic of Reception*, translated by Timothy Bahti, Minneapolis: University of Minnesota Press.

Jenson, Jane 1993, "Naming Nations: Making Nationalist Claims in Canadian Public Discourse," *Canadian Review of Sociology and Anthropology* 30(3): 337–58.

1995, "Identity Work is Hard Work: Majority and Minority Identities in Contemporary Canada," American Sociological Meetings, Washington DC.

Johnson, James Weldon 1922, *The Book of American Negro Poetry, Chosen and Edited with an Essay on the Negro's Creative Genius*, New York: Harcourt Brace.

Johnson, William 1994, *A Canadian Myth: Quebec, Between Canada and the Illusion of Utopia*, Montreal: Robert Davies Publishing.

Juneau, Pierre 1986, "The Impact of Cultural Industries on Canadian Identity," address by the President of the Canadian Broadcasting Corporation to the 28th Annual Canadian–American Seminar, Ontario.

Kammen, Michael 1993, "The Problem of American Exceptionalism: A Reconsideration," *American Quarterly* 45: 1–43.

Keith, W. J. 1985, *Canadian Literature in English*, London: Longman.

1986, "The Quest for the (Instant) Canadian Classic," in Metcalf, John (ed.), *The Bumper Book*, Toronto: ECW Press, pp. 155–65.

Kenner, Hugh 1984, "The Making of the Modernist Canon," in von Hallberg (ed.), pp. 363–75.

Kent, Thomas 1986, *Interpretation and Genre: The Role of Generic Perception in the Study of Narrative Texts*, Lewisburg: Bucknell University Press, London: Associated University Presses.

Kertzer, David 1988, *Ritual, Politics, and Power*, New Haven: Yale University Press.

King, Stephen 1985, *The Bachman Books: Four Early Novels*, New York: New American Library.

King, Stephen [1987] 1988, *Misery*, New York: Penguin Books.

Kolakowski, Leszek 1990, *Modernity on Endless Trial*, University of Chicago Press.

Kollar, Nathan 1989, "Controversial Issues in North American Fundamentalism," unpublished manuscript, St. John Fisher College, Rochester, NY.

Kroetsch, Robert 1989, "Disunity or Unity: A Canadian Strategy," in *The Lovely Treachery of Words: Essays Selected and New*, Toronto: Oxford University Press.

Lacan, Jacques 1977, *Ecrits: A Selection*, New York: Norton.

Laferrière, Michel 1988, "Cultural Dualism," *The Canadian Encyclopedia*, vol. I, 2nd edn, Edmonton: Hurtig Publishers.

Lahaise, Robert 1971, *Histoire de l'Amérique du Nord britannique, 1760–1867*, Montreal: HMH.

Lamont, Michèle 1992, *Money, Morals, and Manners: The Culture of the French and the American Upper-Middle Class*, University of Chicago Press.

1995, "National Identity and National Boundary Patterns in France and the United States," *French Historical Studies* 19: 349–65.

Lamont, Michèle and Fournier, Marcel (eds.) 1992, *Cultivating Differences: Symbolic Boundaries and the Making of Inequality*, University of Chicago Press.

Lamont, Michèle and Wuthnow, Robert 1990, "Betwixt and Between," in Ritzer, George (ed.), *Frontiers of Social Theory*, New York: Columbia University Press, pp. 287–315.

Lang, Gladys Engel and Lang, Kurt 1988, "Recognition and Renown: The Survival of Artistic Reputation," *American Journal of Sociology* 94: 79–109.

Lauter, Paul 1981, "A Small Survey of Introductory Courses in American Literature," *Women's Studies Quarterly* 9: 12.

1991, *Canons and Contexts*, University of Chicago Press.

Lease, Benjamin 1981, *Anglo-American Encounters: England and the Rise of American Literature*, Cambridge University Press.

Leavis, F. R. 1948, *The Great Tradition*, New York: G. W. Stewart.

1969, *English Literature in Our Time*, London: Chatto & Windus.

Lecker, Robert 1990, "The Canonization of Canadian Literature: An Inquiry Into Value," *Critical Inquiry* 16: 656–71.

1993, "A Country without a Canon?: Canadian Literature and the Esthetics of Idealism," *Mosaic* 26: 1–19.

1995, *Making it Real: The Canonization of English-Canadian Literature*, Concord, Ont.: Anansi.

Lecker, Robert (ed.) 1991, "Introduction," in *Canadian Canons: Essays in Literary Value*, University of Toronto Press, pp. 3–16.

Lemire, Maurice 1970, *Les Grandes thèmes nationalistes du roman historique canadien–français*, Quebec: Les Presses de l'Université Laval.

1988, "Book Publishing, French Language," *The Canadian Encyclopedia*, vol. I, 2nd edn, Edmonton: Hurtig Publishers.

Levine, Lawrence W. 1988, *Highbrow/Lowbrow: The Emergence of Cultural Hierarchy in America*, Cambridge, MA: Harvard University Press.

Liebes, Tamar and Katz, Elihu 1990, *The Export of Meaning*, New York: Oxford University Press.

Linteau, Paul-André, Durocher, René, and Robert, Jean-Claude 1983, *Quebec: A History, 1867–1929*, translated by Robert Chodos, Toronto: James Lorimer.

Lipset, Seymour Martin 1963, *The First New Nation: The United States in Historical and Comparative Perspective*, New York: Basic Books.

1985, "Canada and the United States: The Cultural Dimension," in Doran and Sigler (eds.), pp. 109–60.

1986, "Historical Traditions and National Characteristics," *Canadian Journal of Sociology* 11: 113–55.

1988, *Revolution and Counterrevolution: Change and Persistence in Social Structures*, 3rd edn, New Brunswick, NJ: Transaction Books.

1990, *Continental Divide: The Values and Institutions of the United States and Canada*, New York: Routledge.

1996, *American Exceptionalism*, New York: W. W. Norton.

Lloyd, David 1987, *Nationalism and Minor Literature: James Clarence Mangan and the Emergence of Irish Cultural Nationalism*, Berkeley: University of California Press.

Long, Elizabeth 1986, "Women, Reading, and Cultural Authority," *American Quarterly* 38(4): 591–612.

1987, "Reading Groups and the Postmodern Crisis of Cultural Authority," *Cultural Studies* 1(2): 306–27.

Loring, John 1996, "The (Copy) Right Stuff," *Globe and Mail*, February 10: C1–2.

Lucas, Alec 1971, "Curriculum Crisis," *Canadian Dimension* 8(4–5): 58–60.

MacLennan, Hugh 1949, "The Psychology of Canadian Nationalism," *Foreign Affairs* 27(April): 413–25.

MacLulich, T. D. 1987, "Thematic Criticism, Literary Nationalism, and the Critic's New Clothes," *Essays on Canadian Writing* 35(Winter): 17–36.

Mann, Peter H. 1982, *From Author to Reader: A Social Study of Books*, London: Routledge & Kegan Paul.

1983, "The Novel in British Society," *Poetics* 12: 435–48.

Marsh, James 1988, "Cultural Policy," *The Canadian Encyclopedia*, vol. I, 2nd edn, Edmonton: Hurtig Publishers.

Marx, Leo 1964, *The Machine in the Garden*, New York: Oxford University Press.

Maughan, Shannon and Bing, Jonathan 1994, "Tuning in to Twentysomething," *Publishers Weekly* 241: 48–52.

Mauss, Marcel 1969, "La nation" and "La nation et l'internationalisme," in Karady, Victor (ed.), *Oeuvres*, vol. III, Paris: Editions de Minuit, pp. 573–639.

Max, D. T. 1994, "The End of the Book?" *The Atlantic Monthly* 274(September): 61, 62, 64, 67, 68, 70, 71.

McCarthy, Dermot 1991, "Early Canadian Literary Histories and the Function of a Canon," in Lecker (ed.), pp. 30–45.

McCrone, David 1992, *Understanding Scotland: The Sociology of a Stateless Nation*, London: Routledge.

McGregor, Gaile 1985, *The Wacousta Syndrome: Explorations in the Canadian Langscape*, University of Toronto Press.

Meyer, John W. and Hannan, Michael T. (eds.) 1979, *National Development and the World System: Educational, Economic, and Political Change, 1950–1970*, University of Chicago Press.

Meyer, John W., Ramirez, Francisco O. and Soysal, Yasemin Nuhoglu 1992, "World Expansion of Mass Education, 1870–1980," *Sociology of Education* 65: 128–49.

Milliot, Jim 1994a, "US Book Exports Inch Up By Less Than 2% in 1993," *Publishers Weekly* March 14: 10.

1994b, "Exports Growth Still Sluggish," *Publishers Weekly* September 5: 10.

Modleski, Tanya 1982, *Loving With A Vengeance: Mass Produced Fantasies for Women*, New York: Methuen.

Monet, Jacques 1981, *Le première révolution tranquille*, Montreal: Fides.

National Endowment for the Arts, Research Division 1992, "Survey of Public Participation in the Arts – Questionnaire," Washington, DC.

Neil, J. Meredith 1975, *Toward a National Taste: America's Quest for Aesthetic Independence*, Honolulu: University Press of Hawaii.

Nelson, Mark M. 1995, "War's End: Europe: Peacetime Invasion," *Wall Street Journal*, April 24: 11: 1.

Nevitte, Neil and Gibbins, Roger 1990, *New Elites in Old States: Ideologies in the Anglo-American Democracies*, Toronto: Oxford University Press.

New, W. H. 1989, *A History of Canadian Literature*, New York: New Amsterdam Books.

New York Times 1995, "Decline Found in Reading Proficiency of High School Seniors," April 28: A18.

New York Times Book Review 1988, "Black Writers in Praise of Toni Morrison," January 24: 93: 36.

Noble, Trevor 1976, "Sociology and Literature," *British Journal of Sociology* 27: 211–24.

O'Connor, John 1983, "Translations: French to English," in Toye, William (ed.), *The Oxford Companion to Canadian Literature*, Toronto: Oxford University Press, pp. 795–8.

Ohmann, Richard 1984, "The Shaping of a Canon, US Fiction 1960–75," in von Hallberg (ed.), pp. 377–401.

1987, *Politics of Letters*, Middletown, CT: Wesleyan University Press.

Orton, Fred and Pollock, Griselda 1980, "Les Données Bretonnantes: La Prairie de Représentation," *Art History* 3: 314–44.

Ouellet, Fernand 1980, *Economic and Social History of Quebec 1760–1850*, Toronto: Macmillan.

Pache, Walter 1985, "The Fiction Makes Us Real: Aspects of Postmodernism in Canada," in Kroetsch, Robert and Nischik, Reingard M. (eds.), *Gaining Ground: European Critics on Canadian Literature*, Western Canadian Literary Documents 6, Edmonton: NeWest, pp. 64–78.

Parker, Roszika and Pollock, Griselda 1981, *Old Mistresses: Women, Art, and Ideology*, New York: Pantheon.

Parker, Theodore 1907, *Social Classes in a Republic*, edited by Samuel A. Eliot, Boston: American Unitary Association.

Parsons, Talcott 1949, "The Social Structure of the Family," in Ruth Nanda Anshen (ed.), *The Family: Its Function and Destiny*, New York: Harper & Row, pp. 173–201.

Parsons, Talcott and Bales, Robert (eds.) 1955, *Family, Socialization and Inter-action Process*, Glencoe, IL: Free Press.

Percy, Walker 1986, "The Diagnostic Novel: On the Uses of Modern Fiction," *Harper's Magazine* 272(June): 39–45.

Perkins, H. Wesley 1984, "Research Note: Religious Content in American, British, and Canadian Popular Publications from 1937 to 1979," *Sociological Analysis* 45: 159–65.

Peterson, Richard A. 1979, "Revitalizing the Culture Concept," *Annual Review of Sociology* 5: 137–66.

  1992, "Understanding Audience Segmentation: From Elite and Mass to Omnivore and Univore," *Poetics: Journal of Empirical Research on Literature, the Media and the Arts* 21: 243–58.

  1994, "Culture Studies Through the Production Perspective: Progress and Prospects," in Crane, Diana (ed.), *Sociology of Culture: Emerging Theoretical Perspectives*, London: Basil Blackwell, pp. 163–89.

Peterson, Richard A. and Berger, David G. 1975, "Cycles in Symbol Production: The Case of Popular Music," *American Sociological Review* 40: 158–73.

Pfeffer, Jeffrey 1982, *Organizations and Organization Theory*, Boston: Pitman Publishing.

Poggi, Gianfranco 1978, *The Development of the Modern State*, Stanford University Press.

Powell, Walter W. 1985, *Getting Into Print*, University of Chicago Press.

Press, Andrea L. 1991, *Women Watching Television*, Philadelphia: University of Pennsylvania Press.

  1994, "The Sociology of Cultural Reception: Notes Toward an Emerging Paradigm," in Crane, Diana (ed.), *Sociology of Culture: Emerging Theoretical Perspectives*, London: Basil Blackwell, pp. 221–45.

Proulx, E. Annie 1994, "Books on Top," *New York Times*, May 26: A23.

Publishers Weekly 1979, "Politics and Nationalism Influence Book Trade in Northernmost American," August 12: 320.

1988, "NBA Names Judges for 1988, Increases Fiction Jury to Five," March 5: 38–69.

Radway, Janice 1984, *Reading the Romance*, Chapel Hill: University of North Carolina Press.

1989, "The Book-of-the-Month Club and the General Reader: On the Uses of 'Serious' Fiction," in Desan, Philippe, Ferguson, Priscilla Parkhurst and Griswold, Wendy (eds.), pp. 154–76.

Reid, Calvin 1992, "Book Awards: Prestigious, But Do They Sell Books? *Publishers Weekly* March 23: 11.

Reilly, Patrick M. 1995, "How a Book Makes the Bestseller Lists, And How the Bestseller Lists Make a Book," *Wall Street Journal*, September 7: B1.

Ricard, François 1989, "Marcel Rioux entre la culture et les cultures," *Liberté* 31(April): 3–13.

Robinson, John P. 1993, *Arts Participation in America, 1982–1992*, Research Division Report 27, National Endowment for the Arts, prepared by Jack Faucett Associates, Washington, DC.

Rocher, François, (ed.) 1992, *Bilan québécois du fédéralisme canadien*, Montreal: VLB Editeur.

Rogers, Mary F. 1991, *Novel, Novelists, and Readers: Toward a Phenomenological Sociology of Literature*, Albany: State University of New York Press.

Rosmarin, Adena 1985, *The Power of Genre*, Minneapolis: University of Minnesota Press.

Ross, Malcolm 1982, "The Ballot," in Steele, Charles R. (ed.), pp. 136–41.

Ruland, Richard, (ed.) 1972, *The Native Muse: Theories of American Literature*, vol. I, New York: E. P. Dutton.

Scheier, M. F. and Carver, C. S. 1977, "Self-focused Attention and the Experience of Emotion: Attraction, Repulsion, Elation, and Depression," *Journal of Personality and Social Psychology*, 35: 625–36.

Schmidt, William E. 1993, "In Europe, America's Grip on Pop Culture is Fading," *New York Times*, March 28: 3: 1.

Schodt, Frederick 1983, *Manga! Manga!: The World of Japanese Comics*, Tokyo: Kodansha International.

Schroeder, Ralph 1992, *Max Weber and the Sociology of Culture*, London: Sage.

Schudson, Michael 1989, "How Culture Works," *Theory and Society* 18: 153–80.

1994, "Culture and the Integration of National Societies," in Crane,

Diana (ed.), *Sociology of Culture: Emerging Theoretical Perspectives*, London: Basil Blackwell, pp. 21–43.

1995, "Review of *Commercial Culture: The Media System and the Public Interest*, by Leo Bogart," *Contemporary Sociology* 24: 810–11.

Schuster, J. Mark Davidson 1985, *Supporting the Arts: An International Comparative Study*, report of a study funded by the Policy and Planning Division, National Endowment for the Arts.

Séguin, Maurice 1968, *L'idée d'indépendance au Québec*, Trois-Rivières: Boréal Express.

Sewell, William Jr. 1992, "A Theory of Structure: Duality, Agency, and Transformation," *American Journal of Sociology* 98: 1–29.

Shavit, Zohar 1989, "Canonicity and Literary Institutions," in Ibsch, Elrud, Schram, Dick and Steen, Gerard (eds.), pp. 231–8.

Shaw, David 1984, *Press Watch*, New York: Macmillan Publishing.

Shively, JoEllen 1992, "Perceptions of Western Films Among American Indians and Anglos," *American Sociological Review* 57: 725–34.

Shouldice, Larry 1979, *Contemporary Quebec Criticism*, University of Toronto Press.

Showalter, Elaine (ed.) 1985, *The New Feminist Criticism*, New York: Pantheon.

Shrum, Wesley 1991, "Critics and Publics: Cultural Mediation in Highbrow and Popular Performing Arts," *American Journal of Sociology* 97: 347–75.

Simon, Sherry 1991, "Culture and Its Values: Critical Revisionism in Quebec in the 1980s," in Lecker (ed.), pp. 167–79.

Smart, Patricia 1984, "Our Two Cultures," *Canadian Forum* 64 (December): 15.

Smith, Allan 1994, *Canada – An American Nation? Essays on Continentalism, Identity, and the Canadian Frame of Mind*, Montreal: McGill–Queen's University Press.

Smith, Anthony D. 1986, "State-Making and Nation-Building," in Hall, John A. (ed.), *States in History*, Oxford: Basil Blackwell, pp. 228–63.

Smith, Barbara Herrnstein 1983, "Contingencies of Value," *Critical Inquiry* 10: 1–35.

Soysal, Yasemin N. 1994, *The Limits of Citizenship: Migrants and Postnational Membership in Europe*, University of Chicago Press.

Spencer, Benjamin 1957, *The Quest for Nationality*, Syracuse University Press.

Spengemann, William C. 1989, *A Mirror for Americanists: Reflections on the Idea of American Literature*, Hanover, NH: University Press of New England.

Stanley, George F. G. 1983, *The War of 1812,* Toronto: Macmillan.

1988, "Riel, Louis," *The Canadian Encyclopedia*, vol. III, 2nd edn, Edmonton: Hurtig Publishers.

Statistics Canada 1989, *Canada: A Portrait*, 52nd edn, Ottawa: Statistics Canada, Communications Division.

1993, *Book Publishing: 1991–1992 Culture Statistics*, Ottawa: Statistics Canada, Education, Culture and Tourism Division.

1994, *Canada Year Book*, Ottawa: Statistics Canada.

Steele, Charles R. (ed.), 1982, *Taking Stock: The Calgary Conference on the Canadian Novel*, Downsview, Ont.: ECW Press.

Stinchcombe, Arthur L. 1965, "Social Structure and Organizations," in March, James G. (ed.) *Handbook of Organizations*, Chicago: Rand McNally, pp. 142–93.

Stouck, David 1988, *Major Canadian Authors*, 2nd edn, Lincoln, NE: University of Nebraska Press.

Stuckey, W. J. 1981, *The Pulitzer Prize Novels: A Critical Backward Look*, 2nd edn, Norman, OK: University of Oklahoma Press.

Surette, Leon 1991, "Creating the Canadian Canon," in Lecker (ed.), pp. 17–29.

Sutherland, Ronald 1977, *The New Hero: Essays in Comparative Quebec/Canadian Literature*, Toronto: Macmillan of Canada.

Swidler, Ann 1986, "Culture in Action: Symbols and Strategies," *American Sociological Review* 51: 273–86.

Tavris, Carol 1992, *The Mismeasure of Woman*, New York: Simon and Schuster.

Thomas, George M., Meyer, John W., Ramirez, Francisco O. and Boli, John (eds.) 1987, *Institutional Structure: Constituting State, Society, and the Individual*, Newbury Park, CA: Sage.

Tiryakian, Edward A. and Nevitte, Neil 1985, "Nationalism and Modernity," in Tiryakian, Edward A. and Ragowski, Ronald (eds.), *New Nationalisms of the Developed West*, Boston: Allen & Unwin, pp. 57–86.

Tocqueville, Alexis de [1835] 1966, *Democracy in America*, edited by J. P. Mayer and Max Lerner, translated by George Lawrence, New York: Harper & Row.

Tompkins, Jane 1985, *Sensational Designs: The Cultural Work of American Fiction 1790–1860,* New York: Oxford University Press.

Towers, Robert 1987, "Grace Street Blues: *Presumed Innocent* by Scott Turow," *New York Review of Books*, November 19: 21–2.

Tracy, Michael and Redal, Wendy W. 1995, "The New Parochialism: The Triumph of the Populist in the Flow of International Television," *Canadian Journal of Communication* 20: 343–65.

Trofimenkoff, Susan Mann 1982, *The Dream of a Nation: A Social and Intellectual History of Quebec*, Toronto: Macmillan.

Trudeau, Pierre Elliott [1968] 1980, *Federalism and the French Canadians*, Toronto: Macmillan.

Trueheart, Charles 1996, "Canada Turns Down Borders Book Chain Expansion," *Washington Post*, February 10: A18.

Tuchman, Gaye and Fortin, Nina 1980, "Edging Women Out: Some Suggestions about the Structure of Opportunities and the Victorian Novel," *Signs: Journal of Women in Culture and Society* 6: 308–25.

  1984, "Fame and Misfortune: Edging Women Out of the Great Literary Tradition," *American Journal of Sociology* 90: 72–96.

Turbide, Diane 1994, "The Arts: Minister in the Hot Seat," *Maclean's* May 9: 54–5.

United States Census Bureau 1993, *Statistical Abstract of the United States* 113th edn, Washington, DC: US Department of Commerce.

van Rees, C. J. 1989, "The Institutional Foundation of a Critic's Connoisseurship," *Poetics: Journal of Empirical Research on Literature, the Media and the Arts* 18: 179–98.

Vandersee, Charles 1994, "American Parapedagogy for 2000 and Beyond," *American Literary History* 6: 409–33.

Varenne, Hervé 1977, *Americans Together*, New York: Teachers College Press.

Vincent, Tom 1983, "Poetry in English, To 1900," in Toye, William (ed.), *The Oxford Companion to Canadian Literature*, Toronto: Oxford University Press, pp. 652–6.

von Hallberg, Robert, (ed.) 1984, *Canons*, University of Chicago Press.

Warwick, Jack 1983, "Writing in New France," in Toye, William (ed.), *The Oxford Companion to Canadian Literature*, Toronto: Oxford University Press, pp. 552–8.

Watt, Ian 1957, *The Rise of the Novel*, Berkeley: University of California Press.

Weber, Max 1978, "The Nation," in Roth, Guenther and Wittich, Claus (eds.), *Economy and Society*, vol. II, Berkeley: University of California Press, pp. 921–26.

Weir, Lorraine 1991, "Normalizing the Subject: Linda Hutcheon and the English–Canadian Postmodern," in Lecker (ed.), pp. 180–95.

Whitman, Walt 1982, *Complete Poetry and Collected Prose*, New York: Viking Press.

Williams, Raymond 1977, *Marxism and Literature*, Oxford University Press.

  1978, "Base and Superstructure in Marxist Cultural Theory," *New Left Review* 82: 3–16.

Wolfenstein, Martha and Leites, Nathan 1950, *Movies: A Psychological Study*, Glencoe, IL: Free Press.

Wolff, Janet 1981, *The Social Production of Art*, New York University Press.

1992, "Excess and Inhibition: Interdisciplinarity in the Study of Art," in Grossberg, Lawrence, Nelson, Cary and Treichler, Paula A. (eds.), *Cultural Studies*, New York: Routledge, pp. 706–16.

World Currency Year Book 1989, Brooklyn, NY: International Currency Analysis Inc.

Wright, Will 1975, *Sixguns and Society*, Berkeley: University of California Press.

Yardley, Jonathan 1989, "Readership Down," *Washington Post*, August 28: B2.

1993, "A Novel Explanation," *Washington Post*, March 15: D2.

Zerubavel, Eviatar 1992, *Terra Cognita: The Mental Discovery of America*, New Brunswick, NJ: Rutgers University Press.

Ziff, Larzer 1981, *Literary Democracy: The Declaration of Cultural Independence in America*, New York: Viking.

Zill, Nicholas and Winglee, Marianne 1990, *Who Reads Literature?* Report 22, Research Division of the National Endowment for the Arts, Cabin John, MD: Seven Locks Press.

Index